JACQUELINE MARTIN

LOOKING AT The English LEGAL SYSTEM

Hodder & Stoughton

A MEMBER OF THE HODDER HEADLINE GROUP

Orders: please contact Bookpoint Ltd, 130 Milton Park, Abingdon, Oxon OX14 4SB. Telephone: (44) 01235 827720. Fax: (44) 01235 400454. Lines are open from 9.00–6.00, Monday to Saturday, with a 24 hour message answering service. You can also order through our website www.hodderheadline.co.uk

British Library Cataloguing in Publication Data
A catalogue record for this title is available from the British Library

ISBN 0 340 81104 8

First Published 2003
Impression number 10 9 8 7 6 5 4 3 2 1
Year 2007 2006 2005 2004 2003

Typeset by Phoenix Photosetting, Chatham, Kent
Printed in Great Britain for Hodder & Stoughton Educational, a division of Hodder Headline Plc, 338 Euston Road, London NW1 3BH by J.W. Arrowsmiths Ltd, Bristol.

CONTENTS

Acknowledgements vii

Introduction viii

CHAPTER 1 Rule of Law 1

Exercise 1 Differences between civil and criminal law 1
Exercise 2 Law and morality – the right to life 1
Exercise 3 Law and morality – euthanasia 2
Exercise 4 Operating on conjoined twins 3
Exercise 5 Law and morality – rights of pregnant women 4
Exercise 6 Law and justice – the Diane Blood case 5
Exercise 7 Law and justice – use of cannabis 6

CHAPTER 2 Judicial Precedent 7

Exercise 1 House of Lords' own past decisions 7
Exercise 2 Modern law-making in the House of Lords 8
Exercise 3 The effect of decisions of the House of Lords on the Court of Appeal 8
Exercise 4 The Court of Appeal and the decision in *Young v Bristol Aeroplane Co.* 9
Exercise 5 The Court of Appeal and its own past decisions 10
Exercise 6 *Davis v Johnson* in the House of Lords 10
Exercise 7 Judicial precedent and changing social values 11
Exercise 8 The problems of overruling a past decision 11

CHAPTER 3 Legislation 15

Exercise 1 Acts of Parliament 15
Exercise 2 Delegated legislation 16
Exercise 3 The literal rule 17
Exercise 4 The use of *Hansard* in statutory interpretation 17
Exercise 5 The problems of using *Hansard* 18
Exercise 6 The mischief rule and aids to interpretation 19
Exercise 7 The purposive approach 20

CHAPTER 4 European Law 23

Exercise 1 The effect of EU law 23
Exercise 2 Preliminary rulings from the European Court of Justice 24
Exercise 3 The European Court of Justice 24
Exercise 4 Applying European law in the English legal system 25
Exercise 5 Restrictions on exports of calves 26
Exercise 6 Discrimination because of sexual orientation 27
Exercise 7 The Working Time Directive 27
Exercise 8 Applying the Working Time Directive 28

CHAPTER 5 Law Reform 31

Exercise 1 Different influences on law reform 31
Exercise 2 The Law Commission 32
Exercise 3 The effectiveness of the Law Commission 33
Exercise 4 The views of the Chairman of the Law Commission 33
Exercise 5 The problems of unreformed law 34

OVERVIEW I A Review of Chapters 1–5 37

Exercise 1 Law and morality, the role of judges and the role of Parliament 37
Exercise 2 Binding precedent and the role of judges 37
Exercise 3 Precedent, judicial law-making and the role of Parliament 39
Exercise 4 Parliamentary law-making and statutory interpretation 39
Exercise 5 Acts of Parliament, statutory interpretation and European law 40

CHAPTER 6 Civil Courts 41

Exercise 1 The Woolf reforms 41
Exercise 2 The impact of the Woolf reforms on pre-action behaviour 42
Exercise 3 The fast track 42
Exercise 4 Cases in the Queen's Bench Division 43
Exercise 5 Delays in the courts 44
Exercise 6 Enforcement of court judgments 44
Exercise 7 Which court? 45

CHAPTER 7 Alternative Methods of Dispute Resolution 47

Exercise 1 Alternative Dispute Resolution 47
Exercise 2 Mediation 48
Exercise 3 ADR and the Civil Procedure Rules 49
Exercise 4 Arbitration 50
Exercise 5 Online Dispute Resolution 51
Exercise 6 Tribunals and the use of legal representation 51

CHAPTER 8 Police Powers 53

Exercise 1 Recording crime 53
Exercise 2 Stop and search powers 54
Exercise 3 Powers of arrest – arrestable offences 55
Exercise 4 Powers of arrest – general arrest conditions 56
Exercise 5 Detention at the police station 57
Exercise 6 The right to silence 57

CHAPTER 9 Pre-trial matters in criminal cases 59

Exercise 1 When and who makes the decision about granting bail 59
Exercise 2 Grounds for and the consequences of the decision on granting bail 60
Exercise 3 Making decisions on granting bail 60
Exercise 4 Disclosure of evidence 61
Exercise 5 The role of the Director of Public Prosecutions and the Crown Prosecution Service 62
Exercise 6 Private prosecutions 63

CHAPTER 10 Criminal Courts 65

Exercise 1 Should more cases be dealt with in the Magistrates' Court? 65
Exercise 2 Magistrates' Court or Crown Court? 66
Exercise 3 Disposal of cases at the Crown Court 67
Exercise 4 Appealing from the Magistrates' Court 67
Exercise 5 Should the prosecution have more rights of appeal? 67
Exercise 6 Further rights of appeal after an acquittal 68
Exercise 7 Youth Courts 68
Exercise 8 The role of the Criminal Cases Review Commission 69
Exercise 9 The way the Criminal Cases Review Commission works 70
Exercise 10 Evaluation of the Criminal Cases Review Commission 71

CHAPTER 11 Sentencing 73

Exercise 1 Aims of sentencing 73

Exercise 2 Guidelines on sentencing burglars 74
Exercise 3 Sentences for phone muggers 75
Exercise 4 Referral orders for young offenders 75
Exercise 5 Sentencing of young offenders 76
Exercise 6 Proposed changes in sentencing 77
Exercise 7 Drug testing in the criminal justice system 78

OVERVIEW II A Review of Chapters 6–11 79

Exercise 1 Litigation, ADR or negotiation 79
Exercise 2 Problems in the criminal justice system 80
Exercise 3 The Youth Court 80
Exercise 4 Statistics on race and the criminal justice system 81
Exercise 5 Women and the criminal justice system 81

CHAPTER 12 The Legal Profession 83

Exercise 1 Solicitors' training 83
Exercise 2 The role of solicitors 84
Exercise 3 Problems for would-be barristers 84
Exercise 4 Queen's Counsel 85
Exercise 5 Statistics on women in the legal profession 86
Exercise 6 Women in the legal profession – a glass ceiling? 87
Exercise 7 Legal Services Ombudsman 88

CHAPTER 13 The judiciary 91

Exercise 1 Advertising for judges 91
Exercise 2 Appointment of judges 92
Exercise 3 Women and ethnic minorities in the judiciary 92
Exercise 4 Appointment of judges in Canada 93
Exercise 5 Training judges 94
Exercise 6 The role of judges 94
Exercise 7 Disciplining judges 95
Exercise 8 Judicial independence 95
Exercise 9 The Lord Chancellor 96

CHAPTER 14 Lay People in the Legal System 99

Exercise 1 Appointment of lay magistrates (1) 99
Exercise 2 Appointment of lay magistrates (2) 99
Exercise 3 The view of a lay magistrate 100
Exercise 4 Qualifications for jury service 101
Exercise 5 Using juries to try criminal cases 102
Exercise 6 Trial by judge alone 103
Exercise 7 Juries in civil cases 103
Exercise 8 Refusal of a jury in a personal injury case 104

CHAPTER 15 Funding of Cases 105

Exercise 1 Citizens Advice Bureaux 105
Exercise 2 The Community Legal Service 106
Exercise 3 Access to justice 107
Exercise 4 Conditional fees or contingency fees? 107
Exercise 5 Conditional fees 108
Exercise 6 The Criminal Defence Service 108
Exercise 7 Public Defenders 109

CHAPTER 16 The Concept of Liability 111

Exercise 1 Criminal liability for omissions 111

Exercise 2 Continuing acts 112
Exercise 3 Strict liability 112
Exercise 4 Different types of assault 113
Exercise 5 The duty of care 113
Exercise 6 Fair, just and reasonable? 114
Exercise 7 The standard of care 114

Revision 117

The Key Skill of Communication 129

ACKNOWLEDGEMENTS

The author and publisher would like to thank the following for permission to reproduce copyright material:

Bob Woffinden, p. 71.
Crown copyright material is reproduced with the permission of the Controller of Her Majesty's Stationery Office: pp. 43, 48, 51, 94, 99.
Fontana Press, p. 95.
Home Office Research Studies, pp. 54, 57, 58, 59, 60, 61, 73, 75, 78, 81, 82.
Justice of the Peace, pp. 40.
Mr Justice Carnwath, for permission to use extract, p. 33.
Neil Addison, pp. 93, 95.
New Law Journal, pp. 47, 84, 86, 87, 92, 93, 102, 107, 108.
Paula Davies, p. 100.
Scott Ingram, p. 66.
Christopher Sharp, p. 4.
Bryan Clark, p. 51.
Evening Standard, p. 75.
Sir Iain Glidewell, p. 62.
Text from The Judicial Functions of the House of Lords (JUSTICE's written evidence to the Royal Commission on the Reform of the House of Lords), published by JUSTICE, May 1999: pp. 95, 96.
The Guardian, p. 5.
The Independent, p. 3.
The Law Society, pp. 61 (extract from article by Michael Matthews), 83, 84.
The Legal Executive Journal, pp. 49, 50, 63, 69, 70.
The Lord Chancellor, for permission to use the extract on pp. 24–25.
The Lord Chancellor's Department, London, for permission to use the extract on p. 51.
The Times, pp. 4, 6, 28, 74, 76.

Every effort has been made to trace copyright holders but this has not been possible in all cases; any omissions brought to our attention will be corrected in future printings.

INTRODUCTION

Aims

This book provides a variety of exercises based on source material on key topics in the English legal system for students to work through. This has three aims. First, it is intended that the study of original source material and doing exercises on it will help students to gain a clearer understanding of the topics they are studying. Second, some examinations require students to answer questions based on source material and this book gives students the practice they need. Third, the introduction to a wide variety of source material will benefit those going on to study law at a higher level, where research into source material is necessary.

Source material

The types of source material used in this book include extracts from statutes, government White Papers, case judgments, research findings, annual reports of official bodies such as the Law Commission and the Law Society, statistics, articles from legal journals and newspaper articles. In this second edition, out-of-date source material has been replaced, especially in the topics of the courts, sentencing and funding.

The order of topics is aimed at modular AS Units for Law and is appropriate for the specifications of all examination boards. Chapters 1–5 cover sources of law, which is a Unit for all boards. Chapters 6–11 cover the machinery of justice and Chapters 12–15 legal personnel and funding, again suitable for all boards. Finally, Chapter 16 contains some substantive law on the concept of liability, in order to provide material for AQA Unit 3.

How to use this book

Each chapter concentrates on one area of the English legal system and there are also overview chapters in which links between topics are explored. Key points are briefly outlined in the introduction to each chapter, but it is recommended that, before attempting any exercise, students read up on that topic in mainstream textbooks. In this way the maximum benefit will be gained from the exercise.

Revision with a difference

Success in law examinations is achieved only with sound knowledge and understanding of the topics involved. Students need to learn and remember a considerable amount of information if they wish to achieve the higher grades. Learning and revising can be a chore, so in the final part of this book there are revision exercises, including some with a fun element, such as crosswords and acrostics. Enjoy revising with these.

Answers

As there have been many requests for answers, these are being provided in a teachers book, *Looking at the English Legal System Teachers' Resource* along with other material useful for teaching the English Legal System.

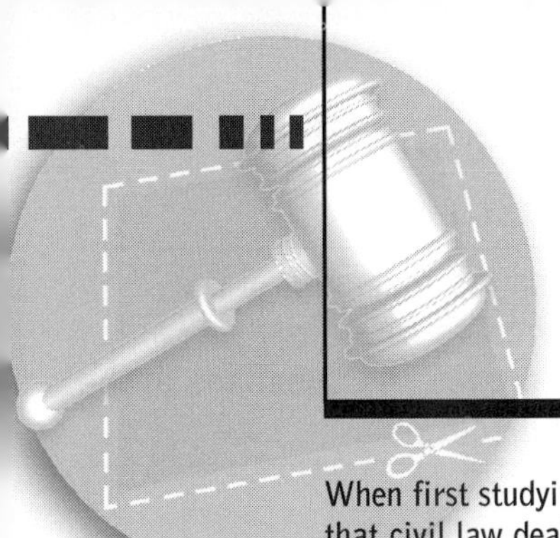

CHAPTER 1

RULE OF LAW

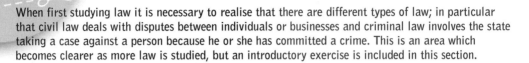

When first studying law it is necessary to realise that there are different types of law; in particular that civil law deals with disputes between individuals or businesses and criminal law involves the state taking a case against a person because he or she has committed a crime. This is an area which becomes clearer as more law is studied, but an introductory exercise is included in this section.

There are also broad issues regarding over which areas of life the law should rule. Should the law impose moral values on people? Does the law always provide justice? There are exercises in this section which focus on particular problems that have come before the courts in the past few years.

This section contains exercises on the following:

- key differences between civil and criminal cases
- a newspaper article on the right to life of a disabled child
- extracts from *Airedale NHS Trust v Bland* and the problems of euthanasia
- an extract from an article about a decision to separate conjoined twins even though one of them would die
- extracts from *R v Collins and others, ex parte S* on the right of a pregnant woman to refuse medical treatment
- extracts from two newspaper articles on the right to use sperm taken from a dying husband
- an article on the acquittal of a man for supplying cannabis.

EXERCISE 1 Differences between civil and criminal law

Decide whether the following words are used in civil cases or criminal cases:

- bail
- claimant
- damages
- fine
- guilty
- liable
- prosecution
- sue.

One of these courts hears civil cases and one criminal cases. Which is which?

- County Court
- Crown Court.

Decide which of the following situations are a breach of civil law and which are a breach of criminal law:

- A enters a supermarket and shoplifts two bottles of wine
- B fails to pay the monthly instalments due on the hire purchase of his car
- C drives at 50 m.p.h. in an area where the speed limit is 30 m.p.h.
- D and E want to bring their marriage to an end, but they cannot agree on how to divide their property between them
- F has been left with serious disabilities after an operation. F claims that the disabilities were caused by the surgeon's negligence.

EXERCISE 2 Law and morality – the right to life

Read the following extract from a newspaper article and answer the questions at the end.

'The mother of a severely handicapped child launched a legal challenge yesterday to what she claimed was a decision by doctors to deny the boy potentially life-saving drugs and "allow nature to take its course".

Carol Glass told a judge in the High Court in London that Portsmouth Hospitals NHS Trust had unlawfully acted against her wishes by giving her 12-year-old son, David, only the painkiller, diamorphine, which could hasten his death.

She said that the drug would adversely affect his respiratory system, but the trust said that it was necessary to balance the child's distress against that risk . . .

Last October, David became seriously ill and was taken to hospital. A consultant paediatrician treating the child described in an affidavit read to the court how the atmosphere was "extremely fraught" as the boy, he asserted, lay dying.

The doctor said that in normal circumstances hospital staff would have recommended the family to hold their child and calm him while he was allowed to die peacefully.

But female members of the family started "blowing raspberries in his ears, banging his chest and rubbing his arms and legs very vigorously despite being asked not to".

The paediatrician said: "In my view this was extremely cruel. [The child] should have been allowed to pass away peacefully and with dignity." '

'Mother fights to prolong son's life', Kate Watson-Smyth, *The Independent*, 22 April 1999

Questions

1. Should parents have the right to demand treatment for a child? Give reasons for your answer.
2. Do you agree with the doctor when he said that David 'should have been allowed to pass away peacefully and with dignity'?
3. The child in this case was very severely handicapped. Do you think any difference should be made between the treatment of a handicapped child and that of a normal child?

EXERCISE 3 Law and morality – euthanasia

Read this extract from the judgment of the House of Lords in *Airedale NHS Trust* v *Bland* [1993] AC 789 and answer the questions at the end or use them for discussion.

Facts

Anthony Bland was a young man who had been so severely injured in the Hillsborough disaster that, although his brain stem was alive, he was unaware of anything and was being kept alive by artificial feeding and ventilation, being said to be in a persistent vegetative state (P.V.S.). His parents wanted him to be allowed to die.

Judgment

LORD BROWNE-WILKINSON

'My Lords, in this case the courts are asked to give the answer to two questions: whether the Airedale NHS Trust and the physicians attending Anthony Bland may:

> "(1) lawfully discontinue all life-sustaining treatment and medical support measures designed to keep [Mr Bland] alive in his existing persistent vegetative state including the termination of ventilation, nutrition and hydration by artificial means; and (2) lawfully discontinue and thereafter need not furnish medical treatment to [Mr Bland] except for the sole purpose of enabling [Mr Bland] to end his life and die peacefully with the greatest dignity and the least of pain, suffering and distress."

Those are questions of law. But behind the questions of law lie moral, ethical, medical and practical issues of fundamental importance to society. As Hoffmann LJ in the Court of Appeal emphasised, the law regulating the termination of artificial life support being given to patients must, to be acceptable, reflect a moral attitude which society accepts. This has led judges into the consideration of the ethical and other non-legal problems raised by the ability to sustain life artificially which new medical technology has recently made possible. But in my judgment in giving the legal answer to these questions judges are faced with a dilemma. The ability to sustain life artificially is of relatively recent origin. Existing law may not provide an acceptable answer to the new legal questions which it raises ...

Until recently there was no doubt what was life and what was death. A man was dead if he stopped breathing and his heart stopped beating. There was no artificial means of sustaining these indications of life for more than a short while. Death in the traditional sense was beyond human control. Apart from cases of unlawful homicide, death occurred automatically in the course of nature when the natural functions of the body failed to sustain the lungs and the heart.

Recent developments in medial science have fundamentally affected these previous certainties . . .

To my mind, these technical developments have raised a wholly new series of ethical and social problems. What is meant now by "life" in the moral precept which requires respect for the sanctity of human life? If the quality of life of a person such as Anthony Bland is non-existent since he is unaware of anything that happens to him, has he a right to be sustained in that state of living death and are his family and medical attendants under a duty to maintain it? If Anthony Bland has no such right and others no such duty, should society draw a distinction (which some would see as artificial) between adopting a course of action designed to produce certain death, on the one hand through the lack of food, and on the other from a fatal injection, the former being permissible and the latter (euthanasia) prohibited? If the withdrawal of life support is legitimate in the case of Anthony Bland whose P.V.S. is very severe, what of others in this country also in P.V.S. (whom we are told number between 1,000 and 1,500) and others suffering from medical conditions having similar impact . . . Who is to decide, and according to what criteria, who is to live and who is to die? What rights have the relatives of the patient in taking that decision? . . .

On the moral issues raised by this case, society is not all of one mind. Although it is probably true that the majority would favour the withdrawal of life support in the present case, there is undoubtedly a substantial body of opinion that is strongly opposed. The evidence shows that the Roman Catholic church and orthodox Jews are opposed. Within the medical profession itself, there are those . . . who draw a distinction between withholding treatment on the one hand and withholding food and care on the other, the latter not being acceptable. The present case is an extreme one, since Anthony Bland can appreciate nothing whether he is alive or dead: but I have no doubt that less extreme cases will come before the courts on which public opinion may be more sharply divided.'

Questions

1. Doctors can now keep people alive by putting them on life-support machines. Why can this cause 'ethical and social' problems?
2. Where a person is not capable of consenting to or refusing treatment, discuss whether relatives should be allowed to make the decision on discontinuing treatment.
3. If relatives should not make such decisions, then who should do so?
4. Do you agree that Anthony Bland should have been allowed to die by his physicians withdrawing food and care?
5. Do you think that in such a case euthanasia should be allowed so that Anthony Bland could have been given a fatal injection?

EXERCISE 4 Operating on conjoined twins

This exercise is based on an article about the decision to separate conjoined twins. Read it and then do the work at the end.

'The twins, who were born in Manchester on August 8 [2000], have been identified as Jodie and Mary to preserve anonymity. They share some common organs in the area where they are joined (at the pelvis) but most importantly a common aorta. Mary, in addition to having only a primitive brain, has no functioning heart or lungs and is wholly dependent on her sister for her supply of oxygenated blood. She is (in the words of Ward LJ) sucking the lifeblood from her sister, and both will probably die within six months if no surgery is performed. Jodie, if separated, will probably be able to live a comparatively normal life. Mary is incapable of an independent existence without the "life-support machine" that is her sister.

...

In being asked to rule on the twins' upbringing (which is defined in s105 of the Children Act 1989 so as to include care) the court is bound by the overriding welfare principle in s1 of that Act that "the child's welfare shall be the court's paramount consideration." In this case the court had to consider the welfare of each twin. As Ward LJ put it, the cruel reality is that surgery will save Jodie but kill Mary. It is in the best interests of Jodie that separation takes place: it is the best interests of Mary that it does not.

...

The approach that Ward and Brooke LJJ followed was not to value the potential of one life against another (Ward LJ stresses that the value of each life in the eyes of God and in the eyes of the law is equal) but to look at the actual condition of the children as they are and assess their legitimate expectations when determining whether it is worthwhile treating them.

...

The conclusion was that it was not worthwhile treating Mary, who was fated for or "designated" for an early death, but it was worthwhile treating Jodie, and thus Ward LJ concluded that it was in the best interests of the twins to give the chance of life to the child whose actual bodily condition is capable of accepting the chance to her advantage "even if that has to be at the cost of the sacrifice of a life which is so unnaturally supported".'

'The Manchester conjoined twins case', Christopher Sharp QC, *New Law Journal*, 6 October 2000

Questions

1. The parents of the twins had refused consent to the operation as it would kill one of the twins. Do you think that in such a case the parents should make the final decision?
2. Is it right that the courts have to make decisions about life or death?
3. If both twins had had an equal chance of survival, do you think that an operation to separate should be carried out even though only one of them could survive after the operation?

RESEARCH

Search newspapers on the Internet and/or CD-ROMs to find out what happened to the twins in this case.

EXERCISE 5 Law and morality – rights of pregnant women

Read the following extract from the judgment in *R v Collins, ex parte S, The Times*, 8 May 1998 and then discuss or research the points suggested below.

'On 25th April 1996, S, a single woman, sought to register as a new patient at a NHS practice in London. She was approximately 36 weeks pregnant but had not sought ante-natal care. She was diagnosed with pre-eclampsia and advised that she needed urgent attention, bedrest and admission to hospital for an induced delivery. Without that treatment the health and life of both herself and the unborn child were in real danger. She fully understood the risks but rejected the advice. She wanted her baby to be born naturally.

She was seen by Louise Collins, a social worker approved under the Mental Health Act 1983, and two doctors. They repeated the advice and she refused to accept it.

An application was made under s.2 of the 1983 Act by Ms Collins for her admission to Springfield Hospital for assessment. The doctors signed the necessary written recommendation and S was admitted to hospital against her will. Later that day she was transferred to St George's Hospital, again against her will. In view of her continuing adamant refusal to consent to treatment an application was made ex parte on behalf of the hospital authority to Mrs Justice Hogg who effectively dispensed with S's consent to treatment.

Appropriate medical procedures were carried out and S was delivered of a baby girl by Caesarean section. On April 30 she was returned to Springfield Hospital and on May 2 her detention under section 2 of the Act was terminated. During the period when she was a patient no specific treatment for mental disorder or mental illness was prescribed. ...

Even when his or her life depended on receiving medical treatment, an adult of sound mind was entitled to refuse it. That reflected the autonomy of the individual and the right of self-determination. ...

Although human, and protected by the law in a number of different ways ... an unborn child was not a separate person from its mother. Its needs did not prevail over her rights. She was entitled not to be forced to submit to an invasion of her body against her will, whether her own life or that of her unborn child depended upon it. Her right was not reduced or diminished merely because her decision to exercise it might appear morally repugnant.

The declaration granted in this case involved the removal of the baby from within the body of her mother under physical compulsion. Unless lawfully justified, that constituted an infringement of the mother's autonomy. Of themselves the perceived needs of the foetus did not provide the necessary justification. The 1983 Act could not be deployed to achieve the detention of an individual against her will merely because her thinking process was unusual, even bizarre and irrational, and contrary to the view of the overwhelming majority of the community at large.'

DISCUSS

1. Should the needs of an unborn child be given priority over the wishes of the mother?
2. Should an adult be forced to submit to medical treatment, even if that treatment is need to save the adult's life?

RESEARCH

The judgment states that an unborn child is 'protected by the law in a number of different ways'. Try to discover what rights an unborn child has.

EXERCISE 6 Law and justice – the Diane Blood case

Read the following extracts from two articles in *The Guardian* newspaper and answer the questions below.

'She was known only by her initials, until yesterday. Diane Blood waived her right to anonymity to appeal for funds to continue her fight for the right to conceive. Her desire to have a baby by her dead husband, first revealed in the *Guardian*, remained overwhelming.

The High Court yesterday dismissed her challenge to the Human Fertilisation and Embryology Authority, which refused to allow her to be artificially inseminated with her husband's sperm. It was taken from him when he was in a coma with bacterial meningitis, and so he had not given the required written consent. She will take her case to the Court of Appeal.

Mrs Blood was "as determined as anyone could be" to continue. After losing the case, she struggled through a press conference to explain. "I think that I have the most right of anybody to my husband's sperm and I desperately wanted his baby. We planned a baby before he died. I just want that back. I don't see why my whole life as I planned it should have ended. I just feel the whole system is unjust to put me through this, the costs and everything. It seems like people are trying to put a price on justice. For me justice has no price."

The High Court was told the couple had talked about a magazine article about a widow wanting to be inseminated with her dead husband's sperm. Mrs Blood said: "We agreed that if we were ever in that position, that's what we'd like to do."

Mrs Blood, whose legal battle has so far cost her £50,000 and a second mortgage on the bungalow she shared with her husband in Worksop, Nottingham, could have a child by a stranger, if there was written permission. But not by the man she loved.'

From 'Widow will fight on to have baby by husband', Clare Dyer, *The Guardian*, 18 October 1996

'Diane Blood, the widow who has battled for nearly two years to have her dead husband's baby, could be artificially inseminated with his sperm in a Belgian clinic next month after winning a landmark court victory yesterday.

The Human Fertilisation and Embryology Authority had banned her from using sperm taken from her husband, Stephen, in March 1995 when he lay dying in a coma because he had not given written consent.

The HFEA could still maintain its ban when it reconsiders her case at the end of this month. But yesterday's Court of Appeal judgment, delivered on what would have been Stephen Blood's 32nd birthday, makes a go-ahead virtually certain. . . .

European Community law, which gives the citizens of EC countries the right to have medical treatment in other member states, came to Mrs Blood's rescue after she was turned down last October by the High Court's family division. She will have to pay for treatment in Belgium.

The Human Fertilisation and Embryology Act bans treatment in Britain after a sperm donor's death without his consent. But three judges, led by the Master of the Rolls, Lord Woolf, ruled yesterday that the authority's refusal to exercise its discretion to allow the sperm to be taken abroad was flawed, because it failed to take full account of rights under EC law. Lord Woolf added: "It is regrettable if the agonising situation of Mrs Blood will be prolonged by this judgment.

"Unfortunately her case raises problems for which there are no clear precedents and in relation to which the law is only clarified by the passage through the courts." '

From 'Widow wins legal fight to have dead man's baby', Clare Dyer, *The Guardian*, 7 February 1997

Questions

1. Do you think it right that written consent of the donor must be given before sperm can be used?
2. Did this rule produce 'justice' in the case of Diane Blood?
3. Should this rule be removed where the parties are husband and wife?
4. Why did the Court of Appeal say the refusal to allow the sperm to be taken abroad was 'flawed'?

EXERCISE 7 Law and justice – use of cannabis

The following newspaper article raises the problem of whether the use of cannabis should be legalised in certain circumstances. Read the article and use it as a basis for discussion.

'A campaigner for the legalisation of cannabis to ease the pain of the seriously ill was cleared yesterday of supplying the drug.

Colin Davies, 42, of Brinnington, Stockport, vowed to continue growing, using and supplying cannabis after he was acquitted by a jury at Manchester Crown Court.

It was the second time in 13 months that Mr Davies, a father of two, had mounted a successful defence. At the first trial he was cleared of possessing the drug.

Yesterday's verdict, greeted by cheers from the public gallery, was hailed by campaigners as a turning point in the fight to legalise the use of cannabis as a painkiller. It was the first prosecution in a British court for the supply of the drug for medical reasons.

Mr Davies, wearing a yellow badge with the words, "No victim – no crime", called for a moratorium on prosecutions and urged the Government to take public soundings on a change in the law.

He said: "This verdict represents a victory for compassion over bureaucracy. People should be allowed to use cannabis as a safe and effective form of pain relief."

Mr Davies, a former joiner, broke his back in a 60ft fall from a bridge five years ago. He walks with a limp and is in constant pain.

He says that conventional treatments prescribed by doctors prompted spasms and sickness, so he turned to cannabis in desperation and began cultivating the plants in his flat.

After he was acquitted on the first charge of possession and cultivation last year he openly set up the Medical Marijuana Co-operative, which claims to have 100 members. It offered to supply cannabis on a non-profit-making basis to people with multiple sclerosis, cancer, paraplegia and other serious illnesses.'

From 'Jury clears "medicinal" cannabis grower', Russell Jenkins, *The Times*, 23 July 1999

DISCUSS

1. The possession and supply of cannabis is illegal. Do you think that the decision of the jury in this case was 'justice' or should the law be strictly enforced?
2. Should the use of cannabis be legalised?

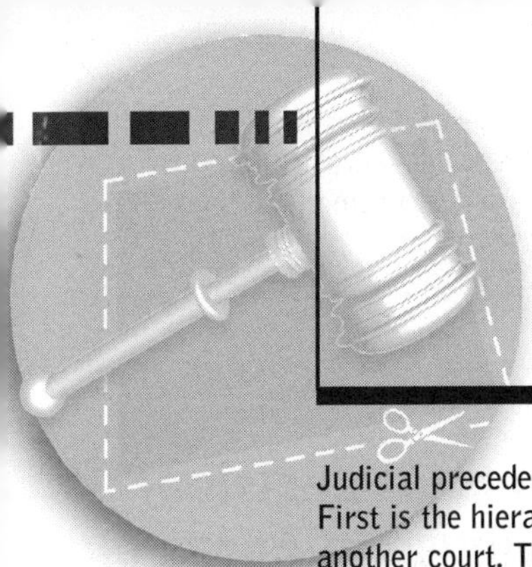

CHAPTER 2

JUDICIAL PRECEDENT

Judicial precedent is a very important topic in sources of law. There are three main areas to consider. First is the hierarchy of the courts. This lays down rules about which court has to follow a decision of another court. The main points are:

- the position of the House of Lords about its own past decisions and
- the position of the Court of Appeal both as to House of Lords' decisions and as to its own past decisions.

Second is what can be called the mechanics of precedent. This covers the concepts of *ratio decidendi, obiter dicta,* overruling and distinguishing. Finally, there is the major role that precedent has in creating law today.

As judicial precedent is all about how cases decided by the courts make law, the exercises in this section are all based on real cases. The exercises are on:

- decisions of the House of Lords
- the House of Lords' Practice Statement
- the effect of decisions of the House of Lords on the Court of Appeal
- the Court of Appeal and its own past decisions
- judicial precedent and changing social values
- the problems of overruling a past decision.

EXERCISE 1 House of Lords' own past decisions

The following is an extract from the judgment in *London Street Tramways v London County Council* [1898] AC 375. This was a decision of the House of Lords during which the Law Lords considered whether the House should follow its own past decisions.

Judgment

EARL OF HALSBURY, LORD CHANCELLOR

'My Lords, for my own part I am prepared to say that I adhere in terms to what has been said . . . that a decision of this House once given upon a point of law is conclusive upon this House afterwards, and that it is impossible to raise that question again . . . That is a principle which has been, I believe, without any real decision to the contrary, established now for some centuries, and I am therefore of the opinion that in this case it is not competent for us to rehear and for counsel to re-argue a question which has been recently decided . . .

My Lords it is totally impossible, as it appears to me, to disregard the whole of current authority upon this subject, and to suppose that what some people call an "extraordinary case", an "unusual case", a case somewhat different from the common, in the opinion of each litigant in turn, is sufficient to justify the rehearing and re-arguing before the final court of appeal of a question which has already been decided. Of course I do not deny that cases of individual hardship may arise, and there may be a current of opinion in the profession that such and such a judgment was erroneous; but what is that occasional interference with what is perhaps abstract justice as compared with the inconvenience – the disastrous inconvenience – of having each question subject to being re-argued and the dealings of mankind rendered doubtful by reason of different decisions, so that in truth and in fact there would be no real final court of appeal? My Lords, [in the public interest] there should be *finis litium* [a final decision] at some time, and that there could be no *finis litium* if it were possible to suggest that in each case that it might be re-argued, because it is "not an ordinary case" whatever that may mean.'

Questions

1. What did the House of Lords decide about whether they should follow a previous decision of their own?
2. What reasons did the Law Lords give for making this decision?
3. Read the next source and compare the arguments in that with this judgment.

EXERCISE 2 Modern law-making in the House of Lords

In 1966 the Lord Chancellor issued a Practice Statement announcing a change to the rule in *London Street Tramways* v *London County Council.* The Practice Statement said:

'Their Lordships regard the use of precedent as an indispensable foundation upon which to decide what is the law and its application to individual cases. It provides at least some degree of certainty upon which individuals can rely in the conduct of their affairs, as well as a basis for orderly development of legal rules.

Their Lordships nevertheless recognise that the rigid adherence to precedent may lead to injustice in a particular case and also unduly restrict the proper development of the law. They, therefore, propose to modify their present practice and while treating former decisions of this House as normally binding, to depart from a previous decision when it appears right to do so.

In this connection they will bear in mind the danger of disturbing retrospectively the basis on which contracts, settlement of property and fiscal arrangements have been entered into and also the especial need for certainty as to the criminal law.

This announcement is not intended to affect the use of precedent elsewhere than in this House.'

Questions

1. To which court does this Practice Statement apply?
2. Why is following previous precedents considered an 'indispensable foundation'?
3. What reasons are given for modifying the rule about following former decisions?
4. When will their Lordships depart from a previous decision?
5. What special factors will they bear in mind when considering whether to depart from a previous decision?

EXERCISE 3 The effect of decisions of the House of Lords on the Court of Appeal

The following is an extract from the judgment of the House of Lords in *Broome v Cassell & Co Ltd* [1972] AC 1027. Read it and answer the questions below.

Judgment

LORD HAILSHAM

'From the point of view of the litigants it is obvious, I would have thought, that, on the view taken by the Court of Appeal, the course taken was unnecessary. Private litigants have been put to immense expense, of which most must be borne by the loser, discussing broad issues of law unnecessary for the disposal of their dispute. If the Court of Appeal felt, as they were well entitled to do, that in the light of the Australian and other Commonwealth decisions *Rookes* v *Barnard* ought to be looked at again by the House of Lords, either generally or under the practice declaration of 1966 they were perfectly at liberty to say so. More, they could have suggested that so soon as a case at first instance arose in which the ratio decidendi of *Rookes* v *Barnard* was unavoidably involved, the parties concerned might wish to make use of the so-called "leap-frogging" procedure now available to them under the Administration of Justice Act 1969, and thus avoid one stage in our three tier system of appeals. But to impose on these litigants, to whom the question was, on the court's view, unnecessary, the inevitable burden of further costs after all they had been through up to date was not, in my view, defensible.

Moreover, it is necessary to say something of the direction to judges of first instance to ignore *Rookes* v *Barnard* as "unworkable". As will be seen when I come to examine *Rookes* v *Barnard* in the latter part of this opinion, I am driven to the conclusion that when the Court of Appeal described the decision in *Rookes* v *Barnard* as decided "per incuriam" or "unworkable" they really only meant that they did not agree with it. But, in my view, even if this were not so, it is not open to the Court of Appeal to give gratuitous advice to judges of first instance to ignore decisions of the House of Lords in this way and, if it were open to the Court of Appeal to do so, it would be highly undesirable. The course taken would have put judges of first instance in an embarrassing position, as driving them to take sides in an unedifying dispute between the Court of Appeal or three members of it (for there is no guarantee that other Lords Justices would have followed them and no particular reason why they should) and the House of Lords. But much worse than this, litigants would not have known where they stood. None could have reached finality short of the House of Lords and, in the meantime, the task of their professional advisers of advising them either as to their rights, or as to the probable cost of obtaining or defending them, would have been, quite literally, impossible. Whatever the merits, chaos would have reigned until the dispute was settled, and, in legal matters, some degree of certainty is at least as valuable a part of justice as perfection.

The fact is, and I hope it will never be necessary to say so again, that, in the hierarchical system of the courts which exists in this country, it is necessary for each lower tier, including the Court of Appeal, to accept loyally the decisions of the higher tiers. Where decisions manifestly conflict, the decision in *Young v Bristol Aeroplane Co Ltd* offers guidance to each tier in matters affecting its own decisions. It does not entitle it to question considered decisions in the upper tiers with the same freedom. Even this House, since it has taken freedom to review its own decisions, will do so cautiously.'

Questions

1. What are the stages in the 'three tier system of appeals'? (first paragraph)
2. What is the 'leap-frogging' procedure? (first paragraph)
3. What is meant by 'judges of first instance'? (second paragraph)
4. Lord Hailsham states that 'it is necessary for each lower tier, including the Court of Appeal, to accept loyally the decisions of the higher tiers'. (last paragraph) What reasons does he give in the first two paragraphs for coming to this conclusion?
5. The extract finishes by saying that 'Even this House, since it has taken freedom to review its own decisions, will do so cautiously'.
   (a) What has given the House of Lords this 'freedom'?
   (b) Why is the House of Lords cautious in reviewing its own decisions?

EXERCISE 4 The Court of Appeal and the decision in *Young v Bristol Aeroplane Co.*

The Court of Appeal is normally bound by its own previous decisions, but there are some exceptions, as explained in by the Court of Appeal in *Young v Bristol Aeroplane Co. Ltd* [1944] KB 718. Read the following extract from the judgment in that case and answer the questions below.

Judgment

MR = master of the Rolls [head of court of appeals – civil division]

LORD GREENE MR

'In considering the question of whether or not the court is bound by its previous decisions ... it is necessary to distinguish four classes of case.

The first is that with which we are now concerned, namely, cases where this court finds itself confronted with one or more decisions of its own ... which cover the question before it, and there is no conflicting decision of this court ... The second is where there is such a conflicting decision. The third is where this court comes to the conclusion that a previous decision, although not expressly overruled, cannot stand with a subsequent decision of the House of Lords. The fourth (a special case) is where this court comes to the conclusion that a previous decision was given *per incuriam*.

In the second and third classes of case it is beyond question that the previous decision is open to examination. In the second class, the court is unquestionably entitled to choose between the two conflicting decisions. In the third class of case the court is merely giving effect to what it considers to have been a decision of the House of Lords by which it is bound. The fourth class requires more detailed examination and we will refer to it again later in this judgment ...

On a careful examination of the whole matter we have come to the clear conclusion that this court is bound to follow previous decisions of its own. ... The only exceptions to this rule (two of them apparent only) are those already mentioned which for convenience we here summarise:

(i) The court is entitled and bound to decide which of two conflicting decisions of its own it will follow.
(ii) The court is bound to refuse to follow a decision of its own which, though not expressly overruled, cannot in its opinion stand with a decision of the House of Lords.

(iii) The court is not bound to follow a decision of its own if it is satisfied that the decision was given *per incuriam*.'

Questions

1. The Court of Appeal has to follow decisions made by higher courts. Which courts are these?
2. What is the normal rule about the Court of Appeal following its own previous decisions?
3. Explain in your own words the three exceptions to the rule that the Court of Appeal must follow its own previous decision.
4. What are the advantages of the Court of Appeal normally following its own past decisions?

EXERCISE 5 The Court of Appeal and its own past decisions

The question as to whether the Court of Appeal was bound by its own past decisions was considered again in *Davis v Johnson* [1979] AC 264. Read this extract from the Court of Appeal judgment in the case and answer the questions.

Judgment

LORD DENNING

'On principle, it seems to me that, while this court should regard itself as normally bound by a previous decision of the court, nevertheless it should be at liberty to depart from it, if it is convinced that the previous decision was wrong. What is the argument to the contrary?

It is said that, if an error has been made, this court has no option but to continue the error and leave it to be corrected by the House of Lords.

The answer is this: the House of Lords may never have an opportunity to correct the error; and thus it may be perpetuated indefinitely, perhaps for ever. That often happened in the old days when there was no legal aid. A poor person had to accept the decision of this court because he had not the means to take it to the House of Lords . . .

Apart from monetary considerations, there have been many incidents where cases have been settled pending an appeal to the House of Lords; or, for one reason or another, not taken there, especially with claims against insurance companies or big employers. When such a body has obtained a decision of this court in its favour, it will buy off an appeal to the House of Lords by paying ample compensation to the appellant. By so doing, it will have a legal precedent on its side which it can use with effect in later cases . . . By such means an erroneous decision on a point of law can again be perpetuated for ever. Even if all those objections are put on one side and there is an appeal to the House of Lords, it usually takes twelve months or more for the House to reach its decision. What then is the position of the lower courts meanwhile? They are in a dilemma. Either they have to apply the erroneous decision of the Court of Appeal, or they have to adjourn all fresh cases to await the decision of the House of Lords. That has often happened. So justice is delayed, and often denied, by the lapse of time before the error is corrected . . .

To my mind, this court should apply similar guidelines to those adopted by the House of Lords in 1966. Whenever it appears to this court that a previous decision was wrong, we should be at liberty to depart from it if we think it right to do so. Normally, in nearly every case of course, we should adhere to it. But in an exceptional case we are at liberty to depart from it.'

Questions

1. Why did Lord Denning say that the Court of Appeal should be at liberty to depart from a previous decision if it is convinced that the previous decision was wrong?
2. What reasons does Lord Denning give for an appeal not going to the House of Lords?
3. What were the guidelines adopted by the House of Lords in 1966?
4. Discuss whether the Court of Appeal should have more freedom to depart from its own decisions.

EXERCISE 6 *Davis v Johnson* in the House of Lords

The case of *Davis v Johnson* was appealed to the House of Lords and this is what the House of Lords said about Lord Denning's wish to have more freedom for the Court of Appeal.

Judgment

LORD DIPLOCK

'In an appellate court of last resort a balance must be struck between the need on the one side for legal certainty resulting from the binding effect of previous decisions and on the other side the avoidance of undue restriction on the proper development of the law.

In the case of an intermediate appellate court, however, the second [point] can be taken care of by appeal to a superior appellate court . . .

In my opinion, this House should take this occasion to re-affirm expressly, unequivocally and unanimously that the rule laid down in the *Bristol Aeroplane* case as to *stare decisis* is still binding on the Court of Appeal.'

Questions

1. What is an 'appellate court of last resort'? Which court is this normally in the English legal system?
2. What is meant by an 'intermediate appellate court'? Give an example of such a court.
3. Explain the words '*stare decisis*'.
4. Lord Diplock says that there is a need for balance between certainty and allowing the law to develop. How does the House of Lords achieve this balance?
5. For what reason does Lord Diplock say that the Court of Appeal does not need to be able to develop the law?
6. What is the rule in the *Bristol Aeroplane* case which the House of Lords said still applies to the Court of Appeal?

EXERCISE 7 Judicial precedent and changing social values

This exercise is based on the case of *R v R* [1992] 1 AC 599. Read the material and answer the questions at the end.

Facts

The defendant's wife had left him, informed him of her intention to petition for divorce, and returned to live with her parents. While she was staying at her parents' house, the defendant forced his way in to the house and attempted to have sexual intercourse with his wife. He also assaulted her. He was charged with attempted rape and assault occasioning actual bodily harm and found guilty on both charges. He appealed against his conviction for attempted rape.

Law

Changing social values was an important aspect in this case. Hale's *History of the Pleas of the Crown* written in 1736 stated the law as it was then:

'But the husband cannot be guilty of a rape committed by himself upon his lawful wife, for by their mutual matrimonial consent and contract the wife hath given up herself in this kind unto her husband which she cannot retract.'

The wording of s1(1) of the Sexual Offences Act 1976 was also important in the case. This subsection says:

'For the purposes of section 1 of the Sexual Offences Act 1956 a man commits rape if (a) he has unlawful sexual intercourse with a woman who at the time of the intercourse does not consent to it; and (b) at the time he knows that she does not consent to the intercourse or he is reckless as to whether she consents to it . . .'

House of Lords' judgment

'For over 150 years after the publication of Hale's work there appears to have been no reported case in which judicial consideration was given to his proposition . . . It may be taken that the proposition was generally regarded as an accurate statement of the common law of England. The common law is, however, capable of evolving in the light of changing social, economic and cultural developments. Hale's proposition reflected the state of affairs in these respects at the time it was enunciated. Since then the status of women, and particularly of married women, has changed out of all recognition . . . Apart from property matters and the availability of matrimonial remedies, one of the most important changes is that marriage is in modern times regarded as a partnership of equals, and no longer one in which the wife must be the subservient chattel of the husband. Hale's proposition involves that by marriage a wife gives her irrevocable consent to sexual intercourse with her husband under all circumstances . . . *In modern times any reasonable person must regard that conception as quite unacceptable* . . .

On grounds of principle there is no good reason why the whole proposition should not be held inapplicable in modern times.

The only question is whether s1(1) of the 1976 Act presents an insuperable obstacle to that sensible course. The argument is that "unlawful" in the subsection means outside the bond of marriage. That is not the most natural meaning of the word, which normally describes something which is contrary to some law or enactment or is done without lawful justification or excuse. Certainly in modern times sexual intercourse outside marriage would not ordinarily be described as unlawful . . .

The fact is that it is clearly unlawful to have sexual intercourse with any woman without her consent, and that the use of the word in the subsection adds nothing. I am therefore of the opinion that s1(1) of the 1976 Act presents no obstacle to this House declaring that in modern times the supposed marital exception in rape forms no part of the law of England.'

Questions

1. What was the old law on rape of a woman by her husband?
2. Why did Lord Keith state that this rule was quite unacceptable? (See words in italics.)
3. How does this case illustrate that judges can change law to meet changes in society?
4. Give examples of other cases in which the law has changed or developed to meet changing social views.

DISCUSS

Should judges have the power to change the law in this way?

EXERCISE 8 The problems of overruling a past decision

A major problem is that when the House of Lords overrules a past decision, the law is supposed to have always been that of the new law. This is known as retrospective overruling. The case of *Kleinwort Ltd v Lincoln Council* [1998] 3 WLR 1095 illustrates what problems this can cause.

This is a longer extract than the ones in the previous exercises. It is also more challenging in the concepts it deals with.

Read the extracts from the judgment in this case and then answer the questions below.

Judgment

LORD BROWNE-WILKINSON

'There are two questions to be considered. First, when the common law is changed by later judicial decision, have all payments made on the basis of the previous law been made under a mistake of law? Second, in what circumstances can it be said that there was earlier law which was changed by judicial decision? Does there have to be a clear judicial decision overruled by a later judicial decision of a higher court or is it enough that, at the date of payment, there was a generally accepted view of the law which view was upset by the later decision?

Where the law is established by judicial decision subsequently overruled

I will take the case where the law has been established by a single decision of the Court of Appeal made in 1930. In 1990 the payer makes a payment which would only have been due to the payee if the Court of Appeal decision was good law. In 1997 this House overruled the Court of Appeal decision. Is the plaintiff entitled to recover the payment made in 1990 on the ground of mistake of law?

There is, as I understand it, no dispute that in order to recover the plaintiff has to have been labouring under the mistake at the date of payment and to have made the payment because of that mistake. Certainly that position has been accepted by the bank [Kleinworts] in their written reply and by my noble and learned friend, Lord Goff of Chieveley. The question is whether the subsequent overruling of the 1930 Court of Appeal decision requires the court to hold that at the date of payment (1990) the law (contrary to what the plaintiff had been advised) was not the law established by the Court of Appeal decision in 1930.

The theoretical position has been that judges do not make or change the law: they discover and declare the law which is throughout the same. According to this theory, when an earlier decision is overruled the law is not changed: its true nature is disclosed, having existed in that form all along. This theoretical position is, as Lord Reid said in the article "The Judge as the Law Maker", a fairy tale in which no one any longer believes. In truth, judges make and change the law. The whole of common law is judge made and only by judicial change in the law is the common law kept relevant in a changing world. But while the underlying myth has been rejected its progeny – the retrospective effect of a change made by judicial decision – remains. As Lord Goff in his speech demonstrates, in the absence of some form of prospective overruling, a judgment overruling an earlier decision is bound to operate to some extent retrospectively: once the higher court in the particular case has stated the changed law, the law as so stated applies not only to that case but also to all cases subsequently coming before the courts for a decision, even though the events in question in such cases occurred before the Court of Appeal decision was overruled.

Therefore the precise question is whether the fact that the later overruling decision operates retrospectively so far as the substantive law is concerned also requires it to be assumed (contrary to the facts) that *at the date of each payment* the plaintiff made a mistake as to what the law then was. In my judgment it does not. The main effect of your Lordships' decision in the present case is to abolish the rule that money paid under a mistake of law cannot be recovered which rule was based on the artificial assumption that a man is presumed to know the law. It would be unfortunate to introduce into the amended law a new artificiality viz, that a man is making a mistake at the date of payment when he acts on the basis of the law as it is then established. He was not mistaken at the date of payment. He paid on the basis that the then binding Court of Appeal decision stated the law, which it did: the fact that the law was later retrospectively changed cannot alter retrospectively the state of the payer's mind at the time of payment. As Deane J said . . .

> "A parliament may legislate that, for the purpose of the law which it controls, past facts or past laws are to be deemed and treated as having been different to what they were. It cannot, however objectively, expunge the past or 'alter the facts of history'."

If that be true of statutory legislation, the same must . . . be true of judicial decision. In my judgment, therefore, if a man has made a payment on an understanding of the law which was correct as the law stood at the date of such payment he has not made that payment under a mistake of law if the law is subsequently changed.'

LORD GOFF

'. . . we all know that in reality the law is the subject of development by the judges – normally, of course, by appellate judges. We describe as leading cases the decisions which mark the principal stages in the development, and we have no difficulty in identifying the judges who are primarily responsible. It is universally recognised that judicial development of the common law is inevitable. If it had never taken place, the common law would be the same now as it was in the reign of King Henry II; it is because of it that the common law is a living system of law, reacting to new events and new ideas, and so capable of providing the citizens of this country with a system of practical justice relevant to the times in which they live. The recognition that this is what actually happens requires, however, that we should look at the declaratory theory of judicial decision with open eyes and reinterpret it in the light of the way in which all judges . . . actually decide cases today.

When a judge decides a case which comes before him, he does so on the basis of what he understands the law to be. This he discovers from the applicable statutes, if any, and from precedents drawn from reports of previous judicial decisions. Nowadays, he derives much assistance from academic writings in interpreting statutes and, more especially, the effect of reported cases; and he has regard, where appropriate, to decisions of judges in other jurisdictions. In the course of deciding the case before him he may, on occasion, develop the common law in the perceived interests of justice, though as a general rule he does this "only interstitially" . . . This means not only that he must act within the confines of the doctrine of precedent, but that the change so made must be seen as a development, usually a very modest development, of existing principle and so can take its place as a congruent part of the common law as a whole . . .

Occasionally, a judicial development of the law will be of a more radical nature, constituting a departure, even a major departure, from what has previously been considered to be established principle . . .

Bearing these matters in mind, the law which the judge then states to be applicable to the case before him is the law which, as so developed, is perceived by him as applying not only to the case before him, but to all other comparable cases, as a congruent part of the body of the law. Moreover, when he states the applicable principles of law, the judge is declaring these as constituting the law relevant to his decision. Subject to consideration by appellate tribunals, and (within limits) by judges of equal jurisdiction, what he states to be the law will, generally speaking, be applicable not only to the case before him but, as part of the common law, to other comparable cases which come before the courts, whenever the events which are the subject of those cases in fact occur.

It is in this context that we have to reinterpret the declaratory theory of judicial decision. We can see that, in fact, it does not presume the existence of an ideal system of the common law, which the judges from time to time reveal in their decisions. The historical theory of judicial decision, though it may in the past have served its purpose, was indeed a fiction. But it does mean that, when the judges state what the law is, their decisions do, in the sense I have described, have a retrospective effect. That is, I believe, inevitable. It is inevitable in relation to the particular case before the court, in which the events must have occurred some time, perhaps some years, before the judge's decision is made. But it is also inevitable in relation to other cases in which the law as so stated will in future fail to be applied. I must confess that I cannot imagine how a common law system, or indeed any legal system, can operate otherwise if the law is to be applied equally to all and yet be capable of organic change. This I understand to be the conclusion reached in *Cross and Harris on Precedent in English Law* from which I have derived much assistance, when they ask the question: "what can our judges do but make new law and how can they prevent it from having retrospective effect?" '

Questions

1. What was the key point in this case?
2. Explain the difference between retrospective overruling and prospective overruling.
3. What used to be considered the theoretical position of judges in declaring the law? (Lord Browne-Wilkinson's speech)
4. Why is this said to be no longer true?
5. Do you agree with the decision that the law in this case was changed retrospectively? Give reasons for your answer.

ACTIVITY

Use this extract as practice for Key Skill C3.2. Identify and compare the lines of reasoning of Lord Browne-Wilkinson and Lord Goff. Then write a brief summary of the two lines of argument.

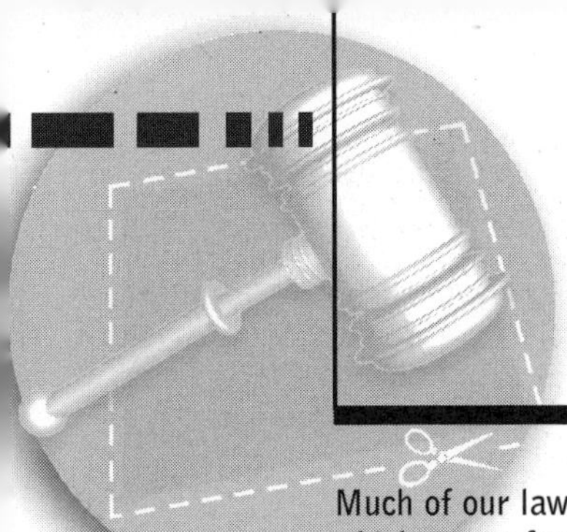

CHAPTER 3

LEGISLATION

Much of our law today is made by Acts of Parliament. These are also called statutes and the law which comes from them is referred to as statutory law. The procedure for an Act of Parliament to become law involves several stages in Parliament and there are often criticisms that Acts are too complicated and not clear enough. As parliamentary time is limited, other bodies are given the power by Parliament to make law. Law made in this way is delegated legislation.

Where there is a dispute about the meaning of an Act of Parliament or any delegated legislation, the courts will be asked to 'interpret' the law. The rules that the courts use on statutory interpretation are open to criticism. This section has exercises on law-making and on interpretation.

The exercises are:

- an extract from a report on the preparation of legislation
- looking at some sections from the Crime and Disorder Act 1998
- an extract on delegated legislation
- an extract from *R v Felix* where the literal rule was applied
- two extracts on the use of Hansard
- extracts from *DPP v Bull* where an number of different aids to statutory interpretation were considered
- extracts from *Jones v Tower Boot* where the purposive approach was applied.

EXERCISE 1 Acts of Parliament

Read the following extract from the *Report of the Committee on the Preparation of Legislation* (1975) and answer the questions below.

'6.1 Our terms of reference imply a widespread concern that much of our statute law lacks simplicity and clarity. This concern has been expressed to us in evidence by the judiciary, by bodies representing the legal and other professions, by the Statute Law Society, by non-professional bodies and by prominent laymen familiar with the problems of preparing legislation. First, let us try to assess the strength and substance of the criticism.

6.2 The complaints we have heard may be broadly grouped as follows:

(a) *Language*. It is said that the language used is obscure and complex, its meaning elusive and its effect uncertain.

(b) *Over-elaboration*. It is said that the desire for "certainty" in the application of legislation leads to over-elaboration.

(c) *Structure*. The internal structure of, and sequences of clauses within, individual statutes is considered to be often illogical and unhelpful to the reader.

(d) *Arrangement and amendment*. The chronological arrangement of the statutes and the lack of clear connection between various Acts bearing on related subjects are said to cause confusion and make it difficult to ascertain the current state of the law on any given matter. This confusion is increased by the practice of amending an existing Act, not by altering its text, (and reprinting it as a new Act) but by passing a new Act which the reader has to apply to the existing Act and work out the meaning for himself.'

Questions

1. What type of people have said that they are concerned about problems in statute law?

2. What are the main complaints about Acts of Parliament?
3. Why is it important that Acts of Parliament are easily understood?
4. Look at the following two sections of the Crime and Disorder Act 1998 and decide if any of the complaints given in the extract above could apply to them.

Crime and Disorder Act 1998, ss 25 and 26

'25. Powers to require removal of masks
(1) After subsection of section 60 (powers to stop and search in anticipation of violence) of the Criminal Justice and Public Order Act 1994 ('the 1994 Act') there shall be inserted the following subsection–

"(4A) This section also confers on any constable in uniform power–

(a) to require any person to remove any item which the constable reasonably believes that person is wearing wholly or mainly for the purpose of concealing his identity;
(b) to seize any item which the constable reasonably believes any person intends to wear wholly or mainly for that purpose."

(2) In subsection (5) of that section, for the words "those powers" there shall be substituted the words "the powers conferred by subsection (4) above".

(3) In subsection (8) of that section, for the words "to stop or (as the case may be) to stop the vehicle" there shall be substituted the following paragraphs–

"(a) to stop, or to stop a vehicle; or
(b) to remove an item worn by him,".

26. Retention and disposal of things seized
After section 60 of the 1994 Act there shall be inserted the following section–

"60A. Retention and disposal of things seized under section 60
(1) Any things seized by a constable under section 60 may be retained in accordance with regulations made by the Secretary of State under this section.

(2) The Secretary of State may make regulations regulating the retention and safe-keeping, and the disposal and destruction in prescribed circumstances, of such things.

(3) Regulations under this section may make different provisions for different classes of things or for different circumstances.

(4) The power to make regulations shall under this section shall be exercisable by statutory instrument which shall be subject to annulment in pursuance of a resolution of either House of Parliament." '

EXERCISE 2 Delegated legislation

Read the following extract from *Law – A Modern Introduction* by Paul Denham, and answer the questions below.

'Delegated legislation consists mainly of rules and regulations made by government ministers under the authority of an Act of Parliament. It is often convenient if Parliament hands the minister a partly blank cheque on which can be filled the relevant details. Very often those details are so technical in nature that it would be inappropriate to attempt to incorporate them into a single statute. Sometimes local government enjoys similar statutory authority – it may be allowed to make certain by-laws. On occasion public corporations such as the British Railways Board, may enjoy the powers of delegated legislation.

Delegated legislation may take different forms. One such method may be to make an Order in Council; other pieces of delegated legislation may take the form of rules or regulations . . .

The parent Act, that is the Act that gives authority for the statutory instruments to be made, may require the instrument to be laid before the House. If that is so the instrument will normally be subject to an affirmative of negative vote. A "negative" instrument will take legal effect if after forty days of being laid before the House no "prayer" to annul the instrument has been put to the House and carried. An affirmative vote means that MPs must approve the instrument.'

Questions

1. Who can make delegated legislation?
2. How are they given the power to make delegated legislation?
3. Why is it 'convenient' for delegated legislation to be made instead of an Act of Parliament?

4. What control does Parliament have over delegated legislation?

Look at s26 of the Crime and Disorder Act 1998, set out in Exercise 1.

5. Who has power to make delegated legislation under this section and on what type of thing?
6. To what type of vote is this delegated legislation subject?

EXERCISE 3 The literal rule

Look at the following case (*Felix v Director of Public Prosecutions* [1998] Crim. L.R. 657) and answer the questions below.

Facts

The defendant, Felix, was charged with leaving litter under s87 of the Environmental Protection Act 1990 when he left three cards (advertising the services of a prostitute) in a telephone box. The box had all three sides enclosed and a door on the fourth side but had a six-inch gap at the bottom of the box which was open to the air. The case rested on whether such a telephone box was a 'public open place' within the meaning of the Environmental Protection Act 1990.

Law

Section 87 of the Environmental Protection Act 1990 states:

'(1) Any person who throws down, drops or otherwise deposits in, into or from any place to which this section applies, and leaves anything whatsoever in such circumstances as to cause, or contribute to, or tend to lead to, the defacement of any place to which this section applies . . . shall be guilty of an offence.

(4) . . . "public open place" means a place in the open air to which the public are entitled or permitted to have access without payment; and any covered place open to the air on at least one side and available for public use shall be treated as public open place.'

Decision

The Queen's Bench Divisional Court decided that the telephone box was not a public 'public open place' under the first part of the definition in s 87(4) as it was not a place in the open air. It was also held that the telephone box did not come within the second part of the definition in s87(4) as it was not open on at least one side. It had three fixed sides and a door which was normally closed except when anyone was entering or leaving the box. The fact that there was a six-inch gap at the bottom was not enough to bring it within the definition of 'public open place'.

Questions

1. This decision was made looking at the literal meaning of the words in the Act. Explain the literal rule in statutory interpretation.
2. Explain whether you agree that in this case literally the words do not include such a telephone box.
3. Do you think the same decision would be made if the purposive approach to statutory interpretation was used?
4. Give the name and facts of another case in which the literal rule was used. Do you agree with the decision in the case?

Note that in Chapter 10 there is a further exercise about which courts were used in this case.

EXERCISE 4 The use of *Hansard* in statutory interpretation

Read this extract from the judgment in *Pepper v Hart* [1992] 3 WLR 1032 and answer the questions below

Judgment

LORD BROWNE-WILKINSON

'Statute law consists of the words that Parliament has enacted. It is for the courts to construe those words and it is the court's duty in so doing to give effect to the intention of Parliament in using those words. It is an inescapable fact that, despite all the care taken in passing legislation, some statutory provisions when applied to the circumstances under consideration any specific case are found to be ambiguous. One of the reasons for such ambiguity is that the members of the legislature in enacting the statutory provision may have been told the result those words are intended to achieve . . . In many, I suspect most, cases reference to Parliamentary materials will not throw any light on the matter. But in a few cases it may emerge that the very question was considered by Parliament in passing the legislation. Why in such a case should the courts blind themselves to a clear indication of what Parliament intended in using those words? The court cannot attach a meaning to words which they cannot bear, but if the words are capable of bearing more than one meaning why should not Parliament's true intention be enforced rather than thwarted? . . .

The purpose of looking at Hansard will not be to construe the words used by the minister but to give effect to the words used so long as they are clear . . .

I therefore reach the conclusion . . . that the exclusionary rule should be relaxed so as to permit reference to Parliamentary materials where: (a) legislation is ambiguous or obscure, or leads to an absurdity; (b) the material relied on consists of one or more statements by a minister or other promoter of the Bill together with such other Parliamentary material as is necessary to understand such statements and their effect; (c) the statements relied upon are clear. Further than this I would not at present go.'

Questions

1. What is *Hansard*?
2. Why is it useful to consider *Hansard* when the courts have to interpret a statute?
3. Explain in your own words the conditions that Lord Browne-Wilkinson imposed for when *Hansard* should be used for statutory interpretation.

EXERCISE 5 The problems of using *Hansard*

Read the facts and the law in the case of *R* v *Deegan* [1998] 2 Cr App R 121, then answer the questions below.

Facts

The defendant had a folding pocket-knife the blade of which was capable of being locked into an open position. He was charged with the offence of having 'a bladed article in a public place', contrary to s 139 of the Criminal Justice Act 1988.

Law

Section 139 of the Criminal Justice Act 1988 excludes 'folding pocket-knife' from the definition of 'bladed article'. The point the court had to decide was whether a folding pocket-knife with a blade that could be locked open came within the meaning of a 'folding pocket-knife' in which case the defendant would be not guilty.

To decide this the court looked at *Hansard* to try to discover the intention of Parliament. Having read the debates which took place between November 1987 and July 1988 when various amendments to the Criminal Justice Act 1998 were being considered, Lord Justice Waller said that *Hansard* showed that:

- at one stage it was intended that the sections should be made to expressly apply to a pocket-knife whose blade, however long, when opened locked automatically or could be locked automatically
- then there was then a decision not to make it so expressly apply and it was contemplated that the word 'pocket-knife' would exclude from the section 'locking pocket-knives'
- finally the word 'folding' was introduced in order to ensure that someone would not be allowed to produce from his pocket a sharp bladed instrument of three inches or less which had a flick effect or a gravity effect or slides out and can then be locked into place.

Lord Justice Waller then said that these statements were not clear in the sense required by *Pepper v Hart* because the phrase 'locking pocket-knifes' was an ambiguous phrase. To say that the court should attempt to define that phrase would be asking the court to go beyond its proper function. It would no longer be interpreting the intention of Parliament; instead it would be writing the legislation the court thought was reasonable.

In these circumstances their Lordships did not think that the conditions in *Pepper v Hart* were fulfilled, nor that it was legitimate to take into account the statements reported in *Hansard*.

Questions

1. In *R* v *Deegan*, what words were the judges trying to discover the meaning of?
2. What problems did the judges find when they looked at *Hansard*?
3. Why did they say that the conditions imposed by *Pepper v Hart* were not fulfilled?

EXERCISE 6 The mischief rule and aids to interpretation

In the case of *DPP v Bull* [1994] 4 All ER 411 the Court of Appeal considered various aids to interpretation. Read this extract and answer the questions below.

Facts

Bull was a male prostitute charged with an offence against s1(1) of the Street Offences Act 1959. This section says:

'It shall be an offence for a common prostitute to loiter or solicit in a public street or public place for the purposes of prostitution.'

The case was heard by a stipendiary magistrate at Wells Street Magistrates' Court. The magistrate dismissed the case on the ground that the words 'common prostitute' only applied to female prostitutes.

The prosecution appealed by way of case stated and the Queen's Bench Divisional Court had to decide whether the words were only meant to apply to women or could also cover male prostitutes.

Judgment

LORD JUSTICE MANN

'The submission for the appellant was that s1(1) of the 1959 Act is unambiguous and is not gender specific. Our attention was drawn to the following six factors which were relied upon. (i) The phrase in s1(1) "a common prostitute" was linguistically capable of including a male person. The *Oxford English Dictionary* (1989) includes within the possibilities for "prostitute", "a man who undertakes male homosexual acts for payment". (ii) Lord Taylor has recently said in *R v McFarlane*:

> "both the dictionary definitions and the cases show that the crucial feature in defining prostitution is the making of an offer of sexual services for reward."

(iii) Section 1(2) and (3) of the 1959 Act refer respectively to "a person" and "anyone". (iv) In contrast s2(1) refers specifically to "a woman" . . . (v) Since 1967 male prostitution has been in certain circumstances not unlawful and accordingly in the new environment it is open to the court to interpret s1(1) of the 1959 Act as being applicable to prostitutes who are male, "even if this was not the original intention of the provision". . . . (vi) Where Parliament intends to deal with gender specific prostitution it uses specifically the words "woman", "girl" or "her"...

It is to be observed that Mr Carter-Manning [counsel for the DPP] recognised that he could obtain no assistance from the gender provisions of s6 of the Interpretation Act 1978, because the provision that words importing the feminine gender . . . include the masculine is inapplicable to enactments such as the 1959 Act . . .

Mr Fulford's [counsel for Bull] main submission was that the court should avail itself of the report which led to the 1959 Act and of the Parliamentary debate upon the Bill for the Act. The availability of a report which led to an Act as an aid to interpretation is discussed in Bennion *Statutory Interpretation.* He cites *Fothergill v Monarch Airlines* (1980) where Lord Diplock said:

> "Where the act has been preceded by a report of some official commission or committee that has been laid before Parliament and the legislation is introduced in consequence of that report, the report itself may be looked at by the court for the limited purpose of identifying the 'mischief' that the Act was intended to remedy, and for such assistance as is derived from this knowledge in giving the rights purposive construction to the Act."

Section 1(1) of the Act was as a result of a recommendation in the *Report of the Committee on Homosexual Offences and Prostitution* [Wolfenden Committee Report]. The relevant chapter of the report leaves me in no doubt that the committee was only concerned with the female prostitute . . . It is plain that the "mischief'" that the Act was intended to remedy was a mischief created by women . . .

I have not sought to avail myself of the doctrine in *Pepper v Hart* because in my judgment and with the confirmation afforded by the Wolfenden Committee Report, the legislation is neither ambiguous, obscure nor productive of absurdity.'

Questions

1. What dictionary did the court look at for the definition of 'prostitute'? Is a dictionary an extrinsic or an intrinsic aid to interpretation?
2. In points (iii) and (iv) the court looked at other sections of the Act. Is this an extrinsic or an intrinsic aid to interpretation? Why were these other sections considered important?
3. Was the Interpretation Act 1978 any use in this case?
4. Why did the court not look at *Hansard*?

5. The court looked at the Wolfenden Committee Report. Why could it look at such a report? What limitations are there in statutory interpretation on using such a report?
6. Explain the mischief rule. Why was this rule relevant in this case?

EXERCISE

7 The purposive approach

In *Jones v Tower Boot Co Ltd* [1997] IRLR 168 the Court of Appeal considered the difference between the literal approach and the purposive approach. Read the following extract and answer the questions below.

Facts

Raymondo Jones worked for Tower Boot as a machine operative for one month. During this time he was subjected to a number of unpleasant incidents of racial harassment by fellow workers. These included his arm being burnt by a hot screwdriver, being whipped with a piece of welt and having metal bolts thrown at his head. He was also repeatedly called names such as 'chimp', 'monkey' and 'baboon'.

Law

It was clear that this was racial harassment by the fellow workers, but the point to be decided was whether the employers were liable for the acts of these employees. Section 32(1) of the Race Relations Act 1976 states that:

'Anything done by a person in the course of employment shall be treated for the purposes of this Act . . . as done by his employer as well as by him, whether or not it was done with the employer's knowledge or approval.'

The words 'course of employment' were the critical ones. In the law of tort this phrase has a well-established legal meaning, with the nub of the test being 'whether the unauthorised wrongful act is so connected with that which he was employed to do as to be a mode of doing it'.

The employers argued that this literal meaning of 'course of employment' should be used. This would mean that they were not liable for the racial harassment as burning and whipping another person could not be considered as an improper mode of performing authorised tasks.

Judgment

LORD JUSTICE WAITE CONSIDERED THE PRINCIPLES OF STATUTORY INTERPRETATION AND SAID:

'Two principles are in my view involved. The first is that a statute is to be construed according to its legislative purpose, with due regard to the result which it is the stated or presumed intention of Parliament to achieve and the means provided for achieving it (the "purposive construction"); and the second is that words in a statute are to be given their normal meaning according to the English language unless the context indicates that such words have to be given a special or technical meaning as a term of art (the "linguistic construction").

The legislation now represented by the Race and Sex Discrimination Acts currently in force broke new ground in seeking to work upon the minds of men and women and thus affect their attitude to the social consequences of differences between the sexes or distinction of skin colour. Its general thrust was educative, persuasive and (where necessary) coercive . . .

Since the getting and losing of work, and the daily functioning of the workplace, are prime areas for potential discrimination on grounds of race or sex, it is not surprising that both Acts contain specific provisions to govern the field of employment. Those provisions are themselves wide-ranging . . . There is no indication that Parliament intended in any way to limit the general thrust of the legislation.

A purposive construction accordingly requires s32 of the Race Relations Act 1976 to be given a broad interpretation. It would be inconsistent with that requirement to allow the notion of the "course of employment" to be construed in any sense more limited than the natural meaning of those everyday words would allow . . .

It would be particularly wrong to allow racial harassment on the scale that was suffered by the complainant . . . to slip through the net of employer responsibility by applying to it a common law principle evolved in another area of the law to deal with vicarious responsibility for a wrong doing of a wholly different kind. To do so would seriously undermine the statutory scheme of the Discrimination Acts and flout the purpose which they were passed to achieve.'

Questions

1. Explain what is meant by the purposive approach to statutory interpretation.
2. Explain what is meant by the 'linguistic' or literal approach to statutory interpretation.
3. Why did the Court of Appeal prefer the purposive approach in this case?
4. Give another case in which the purposive approach was used.
5. Give an example of a case in which the literal approach was used.
6. Discuss the advantages and disadvantages of the two approaches to statutory interpretation.

CHAPTER 4

EUROPEAN LAW

European law has become an important source of law since the United Kingdom joined the European Economic Community on 1 January 1973. The main institutions of the European Union are the Council of Ministers, the European Commission, the European Parliament and the European Court of Justice. The decisions of the European Court of Justice are binding in all member states. European law has had a major impact on many areas of our law.

This chapter has exercises on extracts from:

- the judgment in *Bulmer v Bollinger* on the effect of European law
- an article on the European Court of Justice
- the case of *Webb v EMO*
- a case on whether the UK could ban live calves from being exported to Europe
- a case on sex discrimination because of sexual orientation
- the Working Time Directive
- the case of *Gibson v East Riding* on the application of the Working Time Directive.

EXERCISE

1 The effect of EU law

Bulmer v Bollinger **[1974] 2 All ER 1226 was one of the first cases in which the effect of European law on the English legal system was considered. Read this extract from the judgment and answer the questions on it**

Judgment

LORD DENNING

'The first and fundamental point is that the Treaty [of Rome] concerns only those matters which have a European element, that is to say, matters which affect people or property in the countries of the Common Market besides ourselves. The treaty does not touch any of the matters which concern solely the mainland of England and the people in it. These are still governed by English law. They are not affected by the treaty. But when we come to matters with a European element, the treaty is like an incoming tide. It flows into the estuaries and up the rivers. It cannot be held back. Parliament has decreed that the treaty is henceforward to be part of our law. It is equal in force to any statute. The governing provision is s2(1) of the European Communities Act 1972. It says:

> "All such rights, powers, liabilities, obligations and restrictions from time to time created by or arising under the Treaties, and all such remedies and procedure from time to time provided for by or under the Treaties, as in accordance with the Treaties are without further enactment to be given legal effect or used in the United Kingdom shall be recognised and available in law, and be enforced, allowed and followed accordingly; and the expression 'enforceable Community right' and similar expressions shall be read as referring to one to which this subsection applies."

The statute is expressed in forthright terms which are absolute and all-embracing. Any rights or obligations created by the treaty are to be given legal effect in England without more ado. Any remedies or procedures provided by way of the treaty are to be made available here without being open to question . . .

In the task of interpreting the treaty, the English judges are no longer the final authority. They no longer carry the law in their breasts. They are no longer in a position to give rulings which are of binding force. The supreme tribunal for interpreting the treaty is the European Court of Justice at Luxembourg. Our Parliament has so decreed. Section 3 of the European Communities Act 1972 says:

> "(1) For the purposes of all legal proceedings any question as to the meaning or effect of any of the Treaties, or as to the validity, meaning or effect of any Community instrument, shall be treated as a

question of law (and, if not referred to the European Court) be for determination as such in accordance with the principles laid down by and any relevant decision of the European Court.

(2) Judicial notice shall be taken of the treaties, of the Official Journal of the Communities and of any decision of, or expression of opinion by the European Court on any such question as aforesaid...".'

Questions

1. Which Treaty lays down the original principles of European law?
2. Which Act of Parliament makes European law part of our law?
3. What is the effect of that Act of Parliament?
4. Which court is supreme in interpreting the Treaty?
5. Why is that court the final court for making decisions on EU law?

EXERCISE 2 Preliminary rulings from the European Court of Justice

This exercise is also based on *Bulmer v Bollinger* (see Exercise 1). In this part of the judgment Lord Denning considers the effect of referring cases to the European Court of Justice for preliminary rulings. Read the extract and answer the questions set.

Judgment

LORD DENNING

'... we must read article [234] of the treaty. It says:

"[1] The [European] Court of Justice shall have jurisdiction to give preliminary rulings concerning: (a) the interpretation of this Treaty; (b) the validity and interpretation of acts of the institutions of the Community; (c) the interpretation of the statutes of bodies established by an act of the Council, where those statutes so provide.

[2] Where such a question is raised before any court or tribunal of a Member State, that court or tribunal *may*, if it considers that a decision on the question is *necessary* to enable it to give its judgment, request the court of Justice to give a ruling thereon.

[3] Where any such question is raised in a case pending before a court or tribunal of a Member State, against whose decisions there is no judicial remedy under national law, that court or tribunal shall bring the matter before the Court of Justice."

That article shows that, if a question of interpretation or validity is raised, the European Court is supreme. It is the ultimate authority. Even the House of Lords has to bow down to it. If a question is raised before the House of Lords on the interpretation of the treaty – on which it is necessary to give a ruling – the House of Lords is bound to refer it to the European Court.'

Questions

1. On what three matters does the European Court of Justice have jurisdiction to make preliminary rulings?
2. When *may* national courts request a preliminary ruling?
3. When *must* national courts request a preliminary ruling?
4. Why does Lord Denning say that 'the European court is supreme'?

EXERCISE 3 The European Court of Justice

The following is an extract from 'The case for the European Court' by Lord Irvine of Lairg, Lord Chancellor, *The Times*, 28 April 1998. Read it and then answer the questions.

'Tomorrow I will be visiting the European Court of Justice in Luxembourg as part of my role as Lord Chancellor and Minister responsible for the justice system in the country currently holding the presidency of the European Union. Today, I take this opportunity to explain and pay tribute to the role played by the [European] Court of Justice in the development of the European Union ...

It is the court, perhaps more than any other European body, that has made the EU what it is today: not simply a loosely connected trade bloc, but a close knit international legal structure that exercises vital influence upon our policy and economy, and a dynamic influence upon our domestic law. The Treaty of Rome, by which the original EEC was established, refers only in passing to the role of the court. The court, it says, is to "ensure that the law is observed", but few could have anticipated the imagination and tenacity that would be brought to bear by the court in ensuring that it is.

The Treaty of Rome has always provided a mechanism under which member states who fail to comply with the obligations to which they have signed up can be brought before the Court of Justice at the behest of the Commission or another member state. However, the member states have lacked the political will for the policeman role while the Commission, which is significantly smaller in size than any of the larger government departments in this country, has limited resources for this thankless task. The response of the court to deficiencies in the enforcement of Community law has been to create a system by which each and every individual beneficiary of Community law rights can enforce those rights in the courts of his or her own domestic legal system. 2

In a series of landmark rulings, the court has given the foundation treaties for the EU a force and effect that goes far beyond that enjoyed by any other international agreement before or since. It decided that provisions of Community law could be relied upon directly by individuals in national courts and tribunals, and would take precedence over any conflicting provision of national law. Provisions of domestic law must be interpreted, so far as possible, in conformity with Community law, and recently the court has held that member states may be liable in damages if they fail to give effect to community law ... 3

The Commission continues in its enforcement role, but the vast majority of enforcement actions are brought by private attorney-generals – individual citizens who take legal actions in their domestic courts.'

Questions 7/11/05 hm/wk

1. The article refers to the European Court of Justice and the Commission. What are the other two major institutions in the European Union?
2. When was the original EEC established by the Treaty of Rome?
3. What role does the Commission play in ensuring that the law of the EU is observed by member states? Give a case example in which the Commission acted in this role.
4. What does the Treaty of Rome state about the role of the European Court of Justice?
5. Why does the Lord Chancellor state that the European Court of Justice is so important?
6. Explain one case in which the decision of the European Court of Justice affected the law in England and Wales.

EXERCISE 4 Applying European law in the English legal system

In the case of *Webb* v *EMO Air Cargo (UK) Ltd (No. 2)* [1995] IRLR 645 European law was important. Read what the judges in the House of Lords said and then answer the questions.

Judgment

LORD KEITH OF KINKEL

'... In brief, the appellant was engaged by the respondents with a view to replacing a pregnant employee, Mrs Stewart, during the latter's maternity leave. Shortly afterwards the appellant discovered that she too was pregnant, her baby being expected at roughly the same time as Mrs Stewart's, and the respondents dismissed her. She claimed that her dismissal constituted discrimination against her on the ground of sex, contrary to s.1 of the Sex Discrimination Act 1975. ... It appeared to your Lordships that it was necessary to obtain a preliminary ruling from the European Court of Justice upon the true construction of Article 2(1) of the Council Directive 76/207/EEC of the Council of the European Communities in order to see whether the dismissal of the appellant in the circumstances of this case was contrary to that Article, and if so to consider whether it was possible to construe the relevant provisions of the 1975 Act so as to accord with the ruling of the European Court.

Article 2(1) (of Directive 76/207/EEC) provides:

> "For the purposes of the following provisions, the principle of equal treatment shall mean that there shall be no discrimination whatsoever on the grounds of sex either directly or indirectly by reference in particular to marital or family status."

Article 5(1) (of Directive 76/207/EEC) provides:

> "Application of the principle of equal treatment with regard to working conditions, including the conditions governing dismissal, means that men and women shall be guaranteed the same conditions without discrimination on the grounds of sex."'

Questions

1. Under what Article of the Treaty of Rome would the House of Lords have referred the matter to the European Court of Justice for a preliminary ruling?
2. In his judgment, Lord Keith refers to Council Directive 76/207/EEC. Under which Article of the Treaty of Rome can directives be made?
3. What effect do directives have on national law in England and Wales?
4. Using Articles 2(1) and 5(1) of Council Directive 76/207/EEC set out above, consider whether the principle of equal treatment has been broken in the case of Mrs Webb.

EXERCISE 5 Restrictions on exports of calves

This exercise is based on the facts and decision in Case C–1/96 *R v Minister of Agriculture, Fisheries and Food, ex parte Compassion in World Farming* [1998] All ER (EC) 302. Study these and do the work set.

Facts

A Council Directive (91/629) laid down minimum standards as to the size of stall or box in which calves could be kept. This allowed the use of the 'veal crate' which was a box-like structure used to house a single calf. The use of such veal crates had, however, been banned in the UK from 1990. It was known that a large number of live calves who were exported to other Member States in Europe were then reared in veal crates.

Compassion in World Farming, an animal welfare group, asked the Minister of Agriculture, Fisheries and Food to prohibit or restrict the export of calves for rearing in veal crates. The Minister refused to do this, saying that he had no power to do this and that, even if he had, he was not minded to do so. Compassion in World Farming challenged his refusal by making an application to the Queen's Bench Divisional Court in the High Court for judicial review of the Minister's decision.

Law

Article 29 of the Treaty of Rome says that 'Quantitative restrictions on exports . . . shall be prohibited between member states'. However, there is a provision in Article 30 which says that Article 29 shall not preclude restrictions on exports justified on grounds of public morality, public policy or public security; or the protection of health and life of animals.

It was accepted that European law under Article 29 of the Treaty of Rome meant that normally the UK government could not restrict the exporting of animals. The query was whether Article 30 could allow a country to prohibit exports of calves. The Queen's Bench Divisional Court referred this point to the European Court of Justice for a preliminary ruling.

The European Court of Justice held that Article 30 could not be used in order to justify restrictions on the export of live calves, since the countries to which the calves were being exported were complying with Directive 91/629 on the minimum standards for the protection of calves.

Questions

1. Which Article of the Treaty of Rome gives the Council the power to make a directive?
2. Under which Article of the Treaty of Rome would the Queen's Bench Divisional Court have referred the case to the European Court of Justice?
3. Which Article of the Treaty of Rome prevents restriction on exports to other member states of the European Union? What is the aim of this Article?
4. Explain in your own words why the European Court of Justice ruled that the UK could not prevent calves being exported to other member states of the European Union.

DISCUSS

Is it right that decisions on welfare of animals and Britain's right to restrict exports are governed by European law in this way?

EXERCISE 6 Discrimination because of sexual orientation

Below are set out the facts and decision in Case C–249/96 *Grant v South-West Trains Ltd* [1998] All ER (EC) 193. Study these and do the work set.

Facts

Lisa Grant worked for South-West Trains Ltd. Her contract of employment granted free and reduced rate travel concessions to a legal spouse of an employee or to a common-law opposite sex spouse of an employee 'subject to a statutory declaration being made that a meaningful relationship has existed for a period of two years or more'. Lisa Grant applied for concessions for her female partner with whom she declared she had had a meaningful relationship for over two years. This application was refused on the ground that, for unmarried persons, concessions were only given for a partner of the opposite sex.

Lisa Grant claimed this refusal was sex discrimination.

Law

Article 139 of the Treaty of Rome sets out the principle of equal pay for men and women. Under Article 139 'pay' means 'the ordinary basic or minimum wage or salary and any other consideration, whether in cash or in kind, which the worker receives, directly or indirectly, in respect of his employment from his employer'. The tribunal hearing the discrimination claim referred the question of whether the refusal in this case could be discrimination under Article 139.

The European Court of Justice ruled that as the condition in the contract of employment that a worker had to live in a stable relationship with a person of the opposite sex applied regardless of the sex of the worker. This meant that concessions would be refused to a male person living with a male just as to a female worker living with a female. Since the condition applied in the same way to female and male workers, it was not discrimination directly based on the sex of the worker.

Questions

1. Why are concessionary fares in this case within the meaning of 'pay'?
2. What effect do Treaty Articles have on the law in England and Wales?
3. Explain in your own words why the refusal to allow concessionary fares in this case was held not to be discriminatory.
4. Name and explain a case in which there was discrimination under Article 139.

EXERCISE 7 The Working Time Directive

This exercise is based on the Working Time Directive. Part of the directive is set out below. Read it and then answer the questions.

'COUNCIL DIRECTIVE 93/104/EC

of 23 November 1993

concerning certain aspects of the organisation of working time

THE COUNCIL OF THE EUROPEAN UNION,

Having regard to the Treaty establishing the European Community, and in particular Article [138] thereof,

Having regard to the proposal from the Commission,

In co-operation with the European Parliament,

Having regard to the opinion of the Economic and Social Committee,

Whereas Article [138] of the Treaty provides that the Council shall adopt, by means of directives, minimum requirements for encouraging improvements, especially in the working environment, to ensure a better level of protection of the safety and health of workers; . . .

HAS ADOPTED THIS DIRECTIVE

SECTION 1

SCOPE AND DEFINITIONS

Article 1

Purpose and scope

1. This Directive lays down minimum safety and health requirements for the organization of working time.

2. This Directive applies to:

(a) minimum periods of daily rest, weekly rest and annual leave, to breaks and maximum weekly working time; and

(b) certain aspects of night work, shift work and patterns of work.

3. This Directive shall apply to all sectors of activity, both public and private, . . . with the exception of air, rail, road, sea, inland waterway and lake transport, sea fishing, other work at sea and the activities of doctors in training . . .

SECTION II

MINIMUM REST PERIODS – OTHER ASPECTS OF THE ORGANIZATION OF WORKING TIME

Article 3

Daily rest

Member States shall take the measures necessary to ensure that every worker is entitled to a minimum daily rest period of 11 consecutive hours per 24-hour day.

Article 4

Breaks

Member States shall take the measures necessary to ensure that, where the working day is longer than six hours, every worker is entitled to a rest break . . .

Article 5

Weekly rest period

Member States shall take the measures necessary to ensure that, per each seven-day period, every worker is entitled to a minimum uninterrupted rest period of 24 hours plus the 11 hours daily rest referred to in Article 3.

Article 6

Maximum weekly working time

Member States shall take the measures necessary to ensure that, in keeping with the need to protect the safety and health of workers: . . .

2. The average working time for each seven-day period, including overtime, does not exceed 48 hours.

Article 7

Annual leave

1. Member States shall take the measures necessary to ensure that every worker is entitled to paid annual leave of at least four weeks in accordance with the conditions for entitlement to, and granting of, such leave laid down by national legislation and/or practice.'

Questions

1. Which European Institution enacted (passed) this directive? Briefly explain the role of this institution.
2. Who proposed the directive? Briefly explain the role of this institution.
3. Which other European institutions were consulted? Briefly explain the role of each of these.
4. What does this directive apply to?
5. Which types of work are excluded from the effect of the directive?

EXERCISE 8 Applying the Working Time Directive

In *Gibson v East Riding of Yorkshire District Council, The Times*, 12 February 1999, Mrs Gibson claimed that she should be able to rely on the Working Time Directive. Read this case and then answer the questions.

'A swimming instructor employed by a local authority, who was paid an hourly rate and was not paid during school holidays, was entitled to four weeks' paid annual leave under the Working Time Directive (93/104/EC) (OJ 1993 1307/18) which was directly enforceable by her.

The Employment Appeal Tribunal so held when allowing an appeal by Mrs Lorraine Gibson from a decision of a Hull industrial tribunal in January 1998, that she could not rely on the provisions of the directive to claim holiday entitlement and that the claim under section 13 of the Employment Rights Act 1996, that her employers, the East Riding of Yorkshire District Council, had made unlawful deductions from her wages by not paying her for annual leave, failed.

The applicant had appealed on the ground that the industrial tribunal had erred in law in failing to apply article 7 of the directive which provided that every worker was entitled to paid leave of at least four weeks and which was directly enforceable by the applicant against the council as an emanation of the state.

MR JUSTICE MORISON said . . .

It was the duty of the court in applying national law to ensure fulfilment of the obligation arising from a directive to achieve the result envisaged by the directive, since a directive was binding on all the authorities of the member states, including, for matters within their jurisdiction, the courts; see *Marleasing SA v La Commercial International de Alimentation SA* (Case C–106/89) ([1990] ECR 1413).

Although directives had direct effect they did so only in relation to employees of an emanation of the state. That was because the directive itself was a provision directed to national governments and the state, or a state related employer could not take advantage of its own failure to introduce legislation into domestic law which fully gave effect to the provisions of the directive . . .

The directive was concerned with the further harmonisation of health and safety conditions within the Community, ensuring that those conditions should not be subordinated to purely economic considerations, and granting minimum annual periods of rest in order to ensure the safety and health of community workers.'

Questions

1. Which Article of the Treaty of Rome gives the European Council power to issue directives to member states?
2. Against whom does a directive have 'direct effect'?
3. Explain what is meant by the phrase 'direct effect'.
4. Why was the concept of 'direct effect' important to Mrs Gibson's case?

CHAPTER 5

LAW REFORM

The law needs to be kept up to date; as society changes and so must the law. The law also needs to be changed when it is realised that a particular law is not working. There are influences from many sources for changes to be made to the law: the Government's political commitments; individual Members of Parliament; pressure groups and official law reform bodies. The Law Commission was set up to review the law and propose changes. This section deals mainly with the work of the Law Commission and the problems of law reform.

There are extracts from:

- a passage on influences on law reform from a textbook
- the Law Commission home page on the Internet
- the 36th Annual Report of the Law Commission
- an article by the chairman of the Law Commission
- *B v DPP*, a case in which the judges pointed out the difficulties created because of lack of reform.

EXERCISE 1 Different influences on law reform

The following is an extract from *Law – A Modern Introduction*, by Paul Denham, setting out a number of different influences which may lead to law reform. Read it and do the work below.

'Law can never be seen in isolation from its connected parts. Indeed parliamentary law owes its origins to various influences. In the first place the most obvious is the party factor. Political parties are broad coalitions of similar interests. A party's election manifesto will give some indication of further legislative intention. If elected to power, the party that then forms the government is expected to implement most of those promises . . . Most legislation passed by Parliament is introduced by the government: much of it will be politically controversial and will be opposed by the Opposition parties . . . This is what might be termed "politician's law".

Secondly, a range of pressure groups attempts to persuade government ministers, civil servants and MPs to introduce certain legislation. Pressure groups are basically of two types – interest or sectional groups and promotional or casual groups. The first attempts to defend the interests of a certain section of the community, for example, the CBI, trade unions, the second promotes a particular cause, for example, Liberty, the League against Cruel Sports . . .

Thirdly, the ordinary backbench Member of Parliament has a limited chance to introduce his own legislation. The best way is to gain one of the 20 or so places in the annual ballot in the Commons for Private Member's Bills, although usually an MP needs government support if he is to have any chance of success. Once an MP has drawn a place [in the ballot] he is likely to find himself under considerable pressure from individuals and pressure groups to introduce a particular Bill. Thus the Housing (Homeless Persons) Act 1977 [a Private Member's Bill] owed something not only to government backing but also to the activities of Shelter (the campaign for the homeless) . . .

Fourthly it is often the Civil Service itself and statutory bodies like the Law Commission which put proposals to the government. This will frequently be non-controversial in the political sense – in other words it might be called "lawyers" law'. For example, reforms in such areas as company law, the law of tort, the law of contract and criminal justice often fall into such a category.'

Questions

1. What four influences on law reform are mentioned in this extract?
2. Which of these four is likely to have the biggest impact on which laws are passed through Parliament? Why is this so?

3. Explain the difference between 'politicians' law' and 'lawyers' law'.
4. The extract mentions four pressure groups. Which ones are they?
5. What is meant by 'backbench Member of Parliament'? What makes it unlikely that such a person will succeed in getting a law passed by Parliament?

RESEARCH

Draw up a list of pressure groups other than the ones mentioned in this extract. Choose one and use a search engine to find its site on the Internet. Look at the website and try to discover what changes to the law it would like to be made.

EXERCISE 2 The Law Commission

The following is the way the Law Commission describes itself and the type of reform in its Home Page on the Internet (January 2003). Read it and answer the questions below.

What is the Law Commission?

The Law Commission is the independent body set up by Parliament in 1965 (along with a similar Commission for Scotland) to keep the law of England and Wales under review and to recommend reform when needed. Our law is a combination of the common law – decisions of judges of the higher courts – and of statute law enacted or authorised by Parliament; sometimes those decisions and statutes may go back many centuries.

Substantial reform of the law is a task for Parliament. But proposals for reform may well not be satisfactory unless they are preceded by research and by wide consultation with experts and with those who may be affected by the reforms. Our job is to carry out this research and consultation, and to modernise, improve and simplify the law by formulating proposals on a systematic basis for consideration by Parliament.

Reform of What?

The Law Commissions Act requires the Commission to keep "all the law" under review. In choosing the projects on which to work we are guided by the views of judges, lawyers, government departments and the general public, who tell us of the difficulties they have experienced in applying the law or in seeking legal remedies. We take account of the importance of the issues involved and their suitability for consideration by the Commission, as well as the availability of resources.

The main areas of law on which we work include trust and property law, criminal law, contract, tort, commercial law, the law of landlord and tenant and damages.

A full list of all the Commission's consultation papers and reports, together with the legislation resulting from them is available on the Internet. Some examples of such legislation are the Land Registration Act 2002, providing for electronic conveyancing and revolutionising the land registration system; the Trustee Act 2000, modernising aspects of the law of trusts; the Family Law Act 1996, changing the law of domestic violence; the Computer Misuse Act 1990, introducing new criminal offences about the misuse of computers; the Children Act 1989, rewriting the whole of the law on children; the Consumer Protection Act 1987, covering liability for defective products; and the Family Law Reform Act 1987, removing he disadvantages attached to illegitimacy.

Questions

1. In the opening paragraph the article states that our law is a combination of the common law and of statute law. Explain what is meant by:
   (a) common law
   (b) statute law.
2. Give an example of:
   (a) a statute law
   (b) a law which comes from the common law.
3. Which Act of Parliament sets out the Law Commission's role?
4. Explain the role of the Law Commission.
5. What are the main areas of law the Law Commission researches?
6. How does the Law Commission decide which areas of law to research?
7. Why is the Law Commission's work important?

RESEARCH

1. Use the Internet to discover more about the Law Commission. Its website is at www.lawcom.gov.uk
2. The article lists laws that have resulted from Law Commission work. Choose one and find out more about the changes it made to the law.

EXERCISE 3 The effectiveness of the Law Commission

Each year the Law Commission publishes a report on its work. The following is an extract from the 36th Annual Report for the year 2001. Read it and do the work below.

'3.2 At the beginning of 2001:

(i) Nine of our reports had been accepted by the Government in full or in part and legislation had yet to be introduced; and
(ii) 12 other reports of ours awaited by decisions by the Government.

3.3 At the end of 2001:

(i) One new Law Commission reforming bill was accepted by the Government and introduced into Parliament and one other was in effect implemented by the courts [in a case decision] and an Act implementing one of our reports on Trustees Powers and Duties was brought into effect.
(ii) 12 of our reports had been accepted by the government during or before the year in full or in part and legislation had yet to be introduced.
(iii) 15 other reports of ours awaited decisions by the Government ...

Government Decisions on Our Reports in 2001

DOUBLE JEOPARDY

3.6 The Government has announced that there will be legislation which would make it possible to retry someone who has been acquitted of murder where there is compelling new evidence of guilt. This was one of the main recommendations in our report Double Jeopardy and Prosecution Appeals, though the Government have not yet indicated whether it accepts all the recommendations we made.

Current Position of Some of the Law Commission Reports Awaiting Implementation

3.7 At the end of 2001 there were some 27 reports which awaited implementation. Some have been accepted by the Government and await legislative opportunities, some await decision by the Government. For some there are good reasons why the Government should not give a decision at present e.g. because of the link with the recommendations of the Company Law Review. For others we shall continue to urge the Government to make progress.'

Questions

1. What was the position of reports by the Law Commission at the beginning of 2001?
2. Explain whether this position was better or worse than at the end of 2001.
3. How, and by whom, are Law Commission reports normally implemented?
4. What problems are there in implementing Law Commission reports?
5. Discuss whether it is important that Law Commission reform recommendations are implemented.

RESEARCH

The extract mentions 'double jeopardy'. At the end of 2002, the Government included reform of the double jeopardy rule as part of the Criminal Justice Bill 2002. Use the Internet to discover whether this Bill is now an Act of Parliament (try www.hmso.gov.uk/acts.htm) and whether the double jeopardy rule has been reformed by it.

EXERCISE 4 The views of the Chairman of the Law Commission

This exercise is based on 'Without commitment, law reform is a pipe dream', by the chairman of the Law Commission, Mr Justice Carnwath, *The Times*, 15 June 1999. Read it and answer the questions below.

'The commission's work programme has huge variety and depth. There are some 20 completed reports awaiting implementation. Each focuses on an area of law chosen in consultation with the Government seen to be in need of reform. Each project also represents a big investment of public resources, including detailed research of the existing law, public consultation and a final report accompanied by draft legislation.

The missing link, as my predecessors regularly complained is a systematic procedure to put that work to practical effect. Although historically 70 per cent of the Law Commission's reports have led eventually to legislation, the timing has been unpredictable and the process haphazard. "Joined-up government", whatever that means, has not yet reached us.

The Holy Grail of the Commission, for which my predecessors have been searching for at least 20 years, is codification of the criminal law. There is little dispute as to its need and the principle is backed by the Home Secretary and the Lord Chief Justice.

Senior judges condemn the cost, injustice and delay caused by uncertainty in the criminal law. Yet that mixture of political and legal muscle has not yet been able to break the legislative logjam. A political commitment to codification of the criminal law, with a programme to achieve it over this and the next Parliament, would be the ultimate prize of my term of office.

The problem at its starkest is illustrated by our proposals to reform the Offences Against the Person Act 1861. This "out-moded and unclear Victorian legislation" (Jack Straw's [the Home Secretary's] words) is one of the workhorses of the criminal law, responsible for 80,000 cases a year.

It is a tired and confused old workhorse, and our proposals to replace it (published in 1993) were widely welcomed. Six years and half a million cases later, they remain unimplemented. The principles were accepted by Mr Straw in a consultation paper early last year, but there is still no final decision, let alone commitment to legislate.

Such problems are not confined to the criminal law. One of our most important projects is the review, with the Land Registry, of the law of land registration. This was the subject of a consultation paper last year. A draft Bill will be published later this year, but again the timing of any legislation is unknown. Land registration may not be a subject to grip the average reader but it affects everyone who buys or sells a house. If implemented, the proposals would cut the cost and delays of housebuying and pave the way for electronic conveyancing.'

Questions

1. What position did the writer hold at the time this article was written?
2. How many reports of the Law Commission had not been implemented at the date of the article?
3. Why is there a problem with implementation?
4. What two particular areas of law are highlighted in the article as being in need of reform?
5. Explain why it is important to reform those two areas.

RESEARCH

Look at the Law Commission's website (www.lawcom.gov.uk) to discover:

1. Who is the current Chairman of the Law Commission?
2. Whether the laws referred in the article have now been implemented by the Government.

EXERCISE 5 The problems of unreformed law

The following is an extract from the case of *B* v *DPP* [1998] All ER 265 at 276. It is not about the decision in the case but about the lack of law reform in this area. Read the extract and answer the questions below.

Point of law being decided

The judges had to decide whether a mistaken belief about the age of the victim of an offence under section 1(1) of the Indecency with Children Act 1960 could make the defendant not guilty. The problem was that the Act did not state clearly what the *mens rea* (mental element) of the crime was.

Judgment

BROOKE LJ

'I am only adding a judgment of my own because this three-judge court has just spent a day and a half at the taxpayer's expense exploring the highways and byways of our laws on sexual offences simply because Parliament has not explained to us the mens rea requirement for some of those offences in clear simple terms . . .

In 1978 the Law Commission, under the chairmanship of Cooke J, published its *Report on the Mental Element in Crime*, Law Com No 89) in which it drew Parliament's attention to the chaotic state of the law relating to mens rea in criminal offences and made recommendations for its reform. In 1984 the Criminal Law Revision Committee, under the chairmanship of Lawton LJ, supported by a star-studded cast of experts in the administration of the criminal law, published its

Fifteenth Report (Sexual Offences) (Cmnd 9213) in which it made its recommendations for clarifying the law on the mens rea requirement for those offences. In 1989 the Law Commission, under the chairmanship of Beldam J, published *A Criminal Code for England and Wales* (Law Com No 177) in which it included the unimplemented recommendations of the Criminal Law Revision Committee and demonstrated in Ch II of Part II of the Code how easy it is to make the mens rea requirement for each offence transparently clear once the necessary policy choices have been made. Despite this cascade of expert advice, Parliament continues to legislate in this area on an ad hoc piecemeal basis, and declines to set aside the time to make the necessary policy choices as to the mens rea requirement in relation to the changes of law it enacts, let alone the many parts of the law it leaves unaltered. Hour after expensive hour has to be spent in the courts and elsewhere puzzling over these matters.'

Questions

1. To which two law reform bodies does the judgment refer?
2. Briefly explain the role of these two law reform bodies.
3. Why does the judge draw attention to the work of the law reform bodies?
4. What problems are created by lack of law reform?

OVERVIEW I

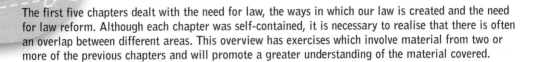

A REVIEW OF CHAPTERS 1–5

The first five chapters dealt with the need for law, the ways in which our law is created and the need for law reform. Although each chapter was self-contained, it is necessary to realise that there is often an overlap between different areas. This overview has exercises which involve material from two or more of the previous chapters and will promote a greater understanding of the material covered.

EXERCISE 1 Law and morality, the role of judges and the role of Parliament

This is an extract from the judgment in *Airedale NHS Trust v Bland*. There is another extract from this case in Chapter 1 which sets out the facts of the case. This extract is concerned with who should create new law where issues of ethics and morality are involved. Read it and answer the questions below.

Judgment

LORD BROWNE-WILKINSON

'Where a case raises wholly new moral and social issues, in my judgment it is not for the judges to seek to develop new, all embracing, principles of law in a way which reflects the individual judges' moral stance when society as a whole is substantially divided on the relevant moral issues. Moreover, it is not legitimate for a judge in reaching a view as to what is for the benefit of the one individual whose life is in issue to take into account the wider practical issues as to allocation of limited financial resources or the impact on third parties of altering the time at which death occurs.

For these reasons, it seems to me imperative that the moral, social and legal issues raised by this case should be considered by Parliament. The judges' function in this area of the law should be to apply the principles which society, through the democratic process, adopts, not to impose their standards on society. If Parliament fails to act, then judge-made law will of necessity through a gradual and uncertain process provide a legal answer to each new question as it arises. But in my judgment that is not the best way to proceed.

The function of the court in these circumstances is to determine the particular case in accordance with the existing law, and not seek to develop new law laying down a new regimen. The result of this limited approach may be unsatisfactory, both in moral and practical terms, but it is for Parliament to address the wider problems which the case raises and lay down principles of law generally applicable to the withdrawal of life support systems.'

Questions

1. Why does the judge in this case say that it is not for judges to develop new law?
2. Why is it suggested that it is better for Parliament to act?
3. What does the extract consider to be the judges' function?
4. Why is judge-made law described as a 'gradual and uncertain process'?
5. Using case examples, explain how judges have 'made' law.

EXERCISE 2 Binding precedent and the role of judges

This exercise is based on the judgment by the Queen's Bench Divisional Court in *C (a minor) v DPP* [1996] AC 1. It is linked to Exercises 3 and 4 which follow.

Background information

At the time of this case, children between the ages of 10 and 14 were legally presumed not know that they were doing wrong. (This was known as the presumption of *doli incapax*.) But, if there was evidence that a child of this age did know that his act was seriously wrong, then this presumption was rebutted. This meant that the child could be convicted of the crime concerned. However, there had to be extra evidence that the child knew that what he was doing was seriously wrong; evidence of the acts which made up the actual offence was not enough for this. The rule was a very old one. *Blackstone' Commentaries on the Laws of England* (1769) pointed out that it had stood at least since the time of Edward III (1327–77).

Facts

C was a 12-year-old boy who was seen by police officers holding the handlebars of a motorbike while another boy tried to force off the chain and padlock which secured it. When the police officers approached, the boys ran off. C was charged with interfering with a motorbike with the intention that an offence of theft should be committed. C was convicted and appealed to the Queen's Bench Divisional Court. His lawyers argued that the prosecution had not produced any evidence that he knew that what he did was seriously wrong and so had not rebutted the presumption of *doli incapax*.

Judgment

In the Queen's Bench Division the appeal was dismissed. The judges held that the presumption of *doli incapax* was no longer part of the law.

LAWS J

'It is not surprising that this presumption took root in an earlier era, when the criminal law was altogether more draconian. When Blackstone wrote (1769), young children along with adults suffered capital punishment, and for offences much less grave than homicide. Blackstone gives an instance of a boy of eight hanged for firing two barns. Little wonder that at a time when criminal guilt led to such ferocious retribution, the law developed a means by which mercy was exceptionally extended to child defendants. But the philosophy of criminal punishment has, very obviously, changed out of all recognition since those days. This presumption has no utility whatever in the present era. It ought to go.'

Laws J discussed three reasons why the court might be persuaded not to abolish the rule. These were:

1. That the court's decision would have retroactive effect. In other words they would be changing the legal rules effective at the time of the defendant's acts.
2. That the presumption was of such long standing in the law that it should only be changed by Parliament (or at least by a decision of the judges in the House of Lords).
3. That the Queen's Bench Divisional Court was bound by the doctrine of precedent to adhere to the presumption.

Of this last point, Laws J said:

'This is the most important argument, because the rules as to *stare decisis* provide a crucial counterpoint to the law's capacity for change: apparently established principles are not to be altered save through the measured deliberation of a hierarchical system. First instance courts do not, on the whole, effect root and branch changes to legal principle, since if they were permitted to do so legal certainty, which is at least as important as legal adaptability, would be hopelessly undermined. But the Divisional Court is in a peculiar position. In point of hierarchy, it is a first instance court, an arm of the Queen's Bench Division. But it is also an appellate court for cases like the present; and in such cases there is no appeal from its decisions save to the House of Lords . . .

It is clear on authority that the Divisional Court has the power to depart from its own previous decisions: *R v Greater Manchester Coroner, ex p Tal* [1985] QB 67. The rule is that the court will follow a decision of a court of equal jurisdiction unless persuaded that it is clearly wrong. It is, perhaps, not plain what is added by the adverb "clearly": it can mean no more in my view than that judicial comity and the obvious need for conformity in decisions of the higher courts create a legitimate pressure in favour of consistent results at the Divisional Court level . . .'.

Questions

1. Why did Laws J think that the presumption of *doli incapax* had come into existence?
2. What are the three reasons given as to why the Queen's Bench Divisional Court might have refused to change the law?
3. Explain the rules of binding precedent in respect of the Queen's Bench Divisional Court.
4. Do you think that the court was right to decide that the presumption of *doli incapax* was no longer part of the law?

EXERCISE 3 Precedent, judicial law-making and the role of Parliament

This is an extract from the judgment of the House of Lords in *C v DPP* in the House of Lords (see previous exercise). Read it and answer the questions.

Judgment

LORD LOWRY

'My Lords, the point of this appeal is: "Whether there continues to be a presumption that a child between the ages of 10 and 14 is *doli incapax* and, if so, whether that presumption can only be rebutted by clear positive evidence that he knew that his act was seriously wrong, such evidence not consisting merely in the evidence of the acts amounting to the offence itself . . .".'

Lord Lowry considered whether it was right for the House of Lords to create law. He put forward the following guidelines on judicial law-making:

1. If the solution is doubtful, the judges should beware of imposing their own remedy.
2. Caution should prevail if Parliament has rejected opportunities of clearing up a known difficulty or has legislated while leaving the difficulty untouched.
3. Disputed matters of social policy are less suitable areas for judicial intervention than purely legal problems.
4. Fundamental legal doctrines should not be lightly set aside.
5. Judges should not make a change unless they can achieve finality and certainty.

The House of Lords allowed the appeal. It decided that the presumption of *doli incapax* could not be changed by it. It was a matter which was 'a classic case for parliamentary investigation, deliberation and legislation'.

Questions

1. Compare the House of Lords' decision with that of the Queen's Bench Divisional Court in Exercise 2. Why did the two courts come to different decisions?
2. Comment on the guidelines on judicial law-making suggested by Lord Lowry.
3. Explain why it may be considered better for Parliament to change the law.

EXERCISE 4 Parliamentary law-making and statutory interpretation

Soon after the decision in *C v DPP* (see Exercises 2 and 3) Parliament altered the law regarding the rule of *doli incapax* in the Crime and Disorder Act 1998. Look at the following and answer the questions below.

Section 34 of the Crime and Disorder Act 1998 states:

'The rebuttable presumption of criminal law that a child aged 10 or over is incapable of committing an offence is hereby abolished.'

When this Act was going through Parliament the Solicitor-General said, during the Second Reading of the Bill:

'The possibility is not ruled out, where there is a child who has genuine learning difficulties and who is genuinely at sea on the question of right and wrong, of seeking to run this as a specific defence. All that the provision does is remove the presumption.'

***Hansard*, House of Lords, 16 December 1997, column 596**

Questions

1. This extract refers to the Second Reading of the Bill. What is a Bill? What other stages does a Bill go through in Parliament?
2. If there was any problem interpreting the words of s34 of the Crime and Disorder Act 1998, explain why the comment made by the Solicitor-General might be relevant.

DISCUSS

Should the *doli incapax* rule have been abolished?

ACTIVITY

Using the Internet, find the report in *Hansard* on a Bill that is currently going through Parliament.

EXERCISE 5 Acts of Parliament, statutory interpretation and European law

The following is an extract from the first of a series of articles by Francis Bennion on statutory interpretation. Read the extract and answer the questions below.

'I start with a basic concept, the legal meaning of an enactment. But first I should explain what an enactment is, for it is a term of art we shall often use. Bentham said that a law is an assemblage of propositions. An enactment is a proposition or an assemblage of propositions laid down in an Act or other legislative text. Its usual effect is that, when the facts of a case fall within an indicated area called the factual outline, specified consequences called the legal thrust ensue.

There are many types of enactment. For the purposes of this discussion I take as an example the Criminal Damage Act 1971, s.1(1). This specifies several offences. By omitting irrelevant words we can express one of these offences as follows:

> "A person who without lawful excuse damages any property belonging to another, being reckless as to whether such property would be damaged, shall be guilty of an offence."

This then is a typical "enactment". The interpreter's duty is to arrive at the legal meaning of a relevant enactment, that is the meaning it has in law. As Chief Baron Pollock said, "it is our duty to ascertain the true legal meaning of the words used by the legislature". Many factors bear on this meaning, and it may not turn out to be the same as the grammatical or literal meaning. Finding it must be done in accordance with the rules, principles, presumptions and canons governing statutory interpretation . . .

Put shortly, the legal meaning is the one that corresponds to the legislator's intention in framing the enactment. Lord Radcliffe said that "the paramount rule remains that every statute is to be expounded according to its expressed intention". This rule has been criticised as artificial. It sits uncomfortably with modern developments such as the European Communities Act 1972 ss.2 and 3 to construe United Kingdom enactments so as to fit Community law wherever possible and the forthcoming requirement, under cl.3 of the Human Rights Bill now before Parliament, to do the same in relation to the European Convention on Human Rights. Yet the original legislator's intention is still the touchstone, and must remain so.'

Questions

1. Explain what is meant by an 'enactment'.
2. The article gives one example of an enactment: give another example.
3. The article refers to 'an Act or other legislative text'. What is meant by 'other legislative text'?
4. What is the courts' (or interpreter's) role in regard to enactments?
5. Briefly explain how the courts go about finding out the 'legislator's intention'.
6. What important effect does the European Communities Act 1972 have on statutory interpretation?
7. The final part of the extract (written in 1998) refers to 'the Human Rights Bill now before Parliament'. That Bill is now the Human Rights Act 1998. What important effect does this Act have on statutory interpretation?

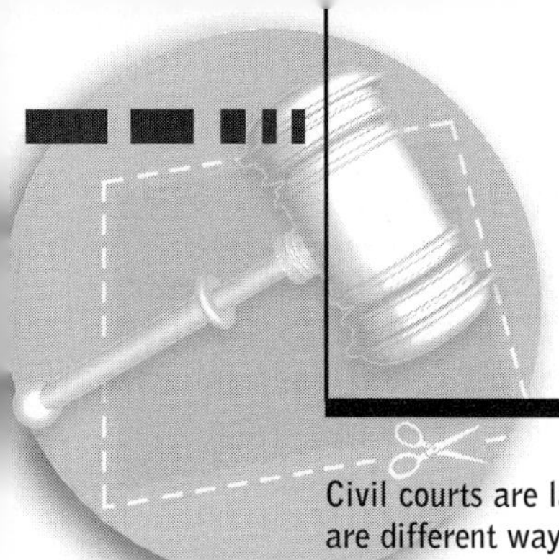

CHAPTER 6

CIVIL COURTS

Civil courts are largely concerned with resolving disputes between individuals and/or businesses. There are different ways of dealing with cases in court depending on the amount of money claimed. Taking a court case can be an expensive, long drawn-out, worrying experience. There have been many reviews of and research into the problems of civil cases. Major reform of the civil courts was made in 1999, bringing in most of the measures suggested in the Woolf Report.

This section includes extracts from various sources. These are on:

- the Woolf reforms
- research into the effects of the Woolf reforms
- the use of fast-track procedure
- cases in the Queen's Bench Division
- delays in the courts
- problems of enforcing a judgment
- scenarios to test understanding of the court structure.

EXERCISE

1 The Woolf reforms

This extract sets out the main reasons, aims and reforms of the Woolf Report. Read it and answer the questions below.

'In April 1999, major reforms were introduced into the civil courts of England and Wales. They were designed to remedy the shortcomings identified by Lord Woolf in his report, *Access to Justice* [Woolf 1996]. These shortcomings included excessive and unpredictable cost, delay and complexity. With cases run by the parties rather than managed by the courts, litigation was perceived as being too adversarial.

Lord Woolf identified principles that should underpin the civil justice system. The system should be just, fair, proportionate, understandable and responsive to those who use it. It should deal with cases with reasonable speed. The system should also provide as much certainty as the nature of the case allows and be effective, adequately resourced and organised.

Reforms were aimed at each stage of the litigation process. For the pre-action stage, Lord Woolf proposed protocols to 'enable the parties to obtain information earlier and promote settlement' [Woolf 1996, p.5]. Other key features of the new system included a unified set of Civil Procedure Rules, claimant offers to settle and the use of single joint experts. Cases would be allocated to one of three tracks – small claims, 'fast track' and 'multi-track' – according to their value and complexity. They would be managed by the courts to ensure they were dealt with justly and proportionately.

Taken from *More Civil Justice? The impact of the Woolf reforms on pre-action behaviour* by Goriely, Moorhead and Abrams (2002)

Questions

1. What main problems in the civil justice system did Lord Woolf identify?
2. What key principles did Lord Woolf think should underpin the civil justice system?
3. What were the main reforms made to the system?
4. What is meant by the 'pre-action' stage?
5. What did Lord Woolf propose for this stage and with what aim?
6. When cases go to court, to what tracks are they allocated?
7. What are the normal financial limits for each of those tracks?

EXERCISE 2 The impact of the Woolf reforms on pre-action behaviour

This extract comes from the same source as that in Exercise 1. This sets out part of the summary of research findings into the reforms made to the civil justice system. Read it and answer the questions below.

'Most practitioners regarded the Woolf reforms as a success. The reforms were liked for providing a clearer structure, greater openness and making settlements easier to achieve. Claimant offers under Part 36 of the Civil Procedure Rules were singled out for praise; claimants saw them as a way of obtaining a response from the defendant, while defendants appreciated them for setting an upper limit to the bargaining range.

. . .

There were four main areas of criticism. The first was the lack of sanctions on those who failed to act reasonably in their pre-action negotiations. Secondly, expert evidence is a subject that continues to provoke controversy. Many solicitors continue to believe that they should "own" their experts and they resented the moves towards joint experts. Thirdly, . . . interviewees frequently highlighted perceived failings within the courts. Respondents criticised the courts for inefficiency and delay.

Finally, defendants complained that the Woolf reforms had failed to reduce the cost of litigation.'

Taken from *More Civil Justice? The impact of the Woolf reforms on pre-action behaviour* by Goriely, Moorhead and Abrams (2002)

Questions

1. What were the main changes made by the Woolf reforms?
2. What did respondents in the survey like about the reforms?
3. What was seen as one of the most useful reforms? What was liked about this reform?
4. What were the main criticisms of the reforms?

EXERCISE 3 The fast track

The following extracts are taken from a report on a simulation of 12 cases with 15 solicitors and one District Judge. This was done in order to try to discover how the new fast-track procedures in the County Court would work.

'When asked how they perceived the main aims of the Fast Track in advance of the simulation, all participants emphasised speed and cost. Typical comments were:

> "Ensure that litigation is prosecuted diligently, quickly and economically";
>
> "Minimum time; minimum costs".

Some elaborated their replies by linking speed to efficiency and cost to proportionality. For example:

> "Justice without delay and at a proportional cost to what is at stake";
>
> "To provide an efficient, cost effective court system to provide greater access for people to the legal system".

Around these core agreed elements was a scattering of other aims identified by one or more individuals. These were:

- Focusing on key issues;
- Improving the public's perception of civil justice and access;
- Providing more case management;
- Limiting experts/documents in discovery;
- Improving the quality of justice with smaller value claims;
- Openness between parties pre-action;
- Identifying issues sooner;
- Expediting the post-issue process.

The profile of responses after the simulation was similar but more varied. The consensus about the importance of speed and cost held firm but some new aims were added to the original list:

- Client input and information to client;
- Increased co-operation with the court;
- Clarifying rules;
- Compromise rather than adversarial approach;
- Fairer allocation of court's time;
- Greater emphasis upon the needs of the client.

This suggests that the simulation had successfully promoted learning about the changed relationship of practitioners to the court and a more team-focused approach to litigation . . .

Reactions to the idea of the pro-active District Judge

There was a general welcome to the concept of the pro-active District Judge but some concern that all District Judges would be able to respond effectively. The general view was that District Judges were more likely to be able to appreciate the practical problems of running cases than Circuit Judges who largely being barristers were not used to organising cases from beginning to end. There was very little support for lawyers in Fast Track work being able to retain control of the pace and extent of procedures.

> "I don't think there is a problem there because most District Judges are ex solicitors. They have worked in private practice, they know what it is like to deal with the cases hands on and I generally find that most District Judges are very pragmatic people. They are very realistic. I think sometimes they become exasperated with the way that cases are just rambling on." (A defendant personal injury solicitor)

> "It's got its advantages and its disadvantages – the fact that parties in the past have been able to flout court orders left right and centre and not comply with a first order, putting the other party to the expense of having to go back and get perhaps a final order – that regime wasn't satisfactory. And now, yes, there certainly will be more incentive for parties to comply with court directions the first time round. But the imposition of directions from a District Judge who hasn't had the opportunity really to look at the case and who's also taking into account the state of the court list and the court's resources may mean that inappropriate directions are given that adversely affects the parties . . .". (Defendant commercial lawyer)'

***Report of the Fast Track Simulation*, Lord Chancellor's Department, Research Series No. 9/98, (December 1998) Nottingham Law School**

Questions

1. Which report, published in 1996, had recommended that procedures in the civil courts be changed?
2. What problems did this report identify in the civil justice system?
3. What improvements did the participants in the simulation think that fast-track procedure will bring?
4. Which improvement do you think is the most important? Give reasons for your answer.
5. Explain the role of a District Judge in a County Court.
6. What new role does the fast-track procedure give District Judges? What are the advantages and disadvantages of this?

EXERCISE 4 Cases in the Queen's Bench Division

Read this extract on the type of cases and the procedure in the Queen's Bench Division and answer the questions below.

Jurisdiction

There is a basic rule that cases of less than £15,000 value may not be litigated in the Queen's Bench Division. Between £15,000 and £50,000 they may be, but unless there is some other distinguishing factor, cases at this level are more likely than not to be transferred out – but they may not be – clinical negligence and other professional negligence claims, claims for malicious prosecution or false imprisonment, claims against the police and Human Rights Act claims for example are normally regarded as complex enough to be retained. Claims of around £50,000–£70,000 value may be transferred out but that will depend on subject matter and complexity.

Type of work

All common law claims not appropriate for the Technology and Construction Court or Commercial Court – particularly contract and negligence claims, Fatal Accidents Act claims, claims for malicious prosecution or false imprisonment, defamation claims, claims against the police and Human Rights Act claims.

Basic issue procedure

Claim forms may be issued in person or by post and can be served by the court or by post or by the claimant.

Allocation

When a defence is filed Allocation Questionnaires are sent out and parties are asked to try to agree proposed directions in Form PF52 ... When the Allocation Questionnaires are returned the file is placed in front of the assigned Master. Almost always he will set a date immediately for a case management conference though he may give directions regarding standard disclosure and inspection and the issue of any applications that have been mentioned by the parties as likely. This is really the crux of the Queen's Bench management regime. The idea is to get the parties in as quickly as possible so that the progress of the action can be timetabled and a trial window set.'

Taken from 'A guide to the Queen's Bench Division', Master Stephen Whitaker, *New Law Journal*, 10 January 2003

Questions

1. Under what value can cases not be dealt with in the Queen's Bench Division?
2. What is the position for cases of the value £15,000 to £50,000?
3. What type of cases are heard in the Queen's Bench Division?
4. How is a claim started?
5. Once a defence is filed, what will happen?
6. Who deals with the pre-trial matters in the Queen's Bench Division?
7. What is the important point about case management?

EXERCISE 5 Delays in the courts

The following figures are taken from the *Judicial Statistics* for 2001. Below, there are questions on these figures for you to answer.

County Court – Average waiting time between start of proceedings and start of the trial for 2001

Small claims	**Main County Court**
28 weeks	73 weeks

Queen's Bench Division of the High Court – Average time in weeks between start of proceedings and start of the trial for the years 1994 to 2001

1994	**1995**	**1996**	**1997**	**1998**	**1999**	**2000**	**2001**
177	161	179	178	178	174	164	173

Questions

1. Which court is the slowest to hear cases?
2. Which type of case is dealt with quickest by the courts?
3. What is the worst delay shown by these figures?
4. Do the figures show that the Woolf reforms (which came into effect in April 1999) have improved matters in the Queen's Bench Division?
5. What problems does delay cause for the people making claims in court?

EXERCISE 6 Enforcement of court judgments

Read the source material and answer the question below.

Background

Even where a claimant takes a case to court, wins and gets a judgment against the other party, this does not mean that their problems are over. There are major difficulties in getting money from the losing party in a court case.

'1.1 The distinction between debtors who "can't pay" and debtors who "won't pay" a judgment debt is crucial in any debate on enforcement. Creditors do not want to waste time and money taking action against debtors who do not have the means to pay a debt. Equally, debtors who genuinely cannot pay must be protected from over-zealous creditors. A proper identification of "can't pay" debtors would also free up court resources for the pursuit of those resisting payment. . . .

2.5 The current enforcement system relies heavily on obtaining information about a debtor's circumstances from the debtor himself, through the N9 Statement of Means enquiry, and the oral examination. In many cases, the information requested is either not forthcoming – because the debtor deliberately refuses to provide it, or simply avoids acknowledging the need to take action through fear, ignorance or indifference – or the information provided is incomplete or inaccurate.

2.6 The current system can leave creditors wondering whether there was any point in obtaining a judgment of the court if the judgment was then unenforceable because of lack of information about a debtor's circumstances. It has also led many creditors to believe, often mistakenly, that the only possible method of enforcement open to them was a warrant of execution. In many cases had a fuller picture of a debtor's circumstances been available, creditors might have been able to make a more careful assessment of, and often a quite different choice about, how to enforce a judgment, with a greater likelihood of success. It is clear that better targeted enforcement action would be in the best interests of both debtors and creditors. The panels concluded, therefore, that the solution lay in enabling the courts to play a more proactive role in obtaining information about debtors though access to alternative sources of information.'

Taken from Enforcement Review Consultation Paper 2: *Key principles for a new system of enforcement in the civil courts*, Lord Chancellor's Department, May 1999

Questions

1. What is meant by a 'judgment debt'?
2. Why is it important to distinguish between those who 'can't pay' and those who 'won't pay' a judgment debt?
3. What difficulties are there for a successful claimant who wants to enforce a judgment debt?
4. What methods are there of enforcing judgment debts?

EXERCISE 7 Which court?

The following is a series of mini scenarios about people who want to make a claim in court. Advise each person as which court (or track) they should use.

1. A bought a washing machine costing £450 from a local shop. The machine has never worked properly and A wants to claim the cost of the machine from the store.
2. B was knocked down while walking across a pedestrian crossing. Both his legs were broken in the accident and he was unable to work for six months. He has been advised that his claim is worth about £80,000.
3. C is a builder who has built a garage for a customer at a cost of £12,000. The customer has not paid and C wants to start a court case for the money.
4. D injured his back at work because of faulty machinery. He has been advised that his claim is worth about £25,000.
5. E, an athlete, wants to claim against a local newspaper for defamation because it published an article which falsely stated that E took performance-enhancing drugs.

CHAPTER 7

ALTERNATIVE METHODS OF DISPUTE RESOLUTION

It is not necessary to 'go to court' in order to resolve a dispute. In fact, taking a case in court should be thought of as the last resort when nothing else will work. The difficulty of taking cases in court has led to the development of other methods of resolving disputes. The most traditional of these is arbitration, which is governed by the Arbitration Act 1996, but there are other alternative dispute resolution methods, in particular, conciliation and mediation. There are also tribunals in which many thousands of cases are heard each year. Tribunals run parallel with the court system, hearing cases which cannot be dealt with by a court. There are different tribunals to deal with different types of claim.

This section has exercises on different types of dispute resolution. These are based on:

- a report of a conference on ADR
- a pilot mediation scheme at the Central London County Court
- ADR and the Civil Procedure Rules
- arbitration
- online dispute resolution
- research into tribunal hearings.

EXERCISE 1 Alternative dispute resolution

The following is an extract about a conference on ADR. Read it and answer the questions below.

'Last Friday, November 13, was the Centre for Dispute Resolution (CEDR)'s eighth birthday. CEDR's Biennial Conference took place a couple of days earlier on November 1. The subject under discussion was Alternative Dispute Resolution (ADR), something to which CEDR is firmly committed.

Professor Karl Mackie, Chief Executive of CEDR, opened the meeting in upbeat mood. ADR, he said, is an alternative to the two established and traditional methods of dispute resolution, namely litigation and arbitration. As such, "it offers the best way to reduce costs and improve the reputation of the civil litigation system".

The keynote speech was delivered by Lord Irvine, the Lord Chancellor, who welcomed ADR as the best way of reaching a settlement and of streamlining the civil justice system. "ADR", he continued, "guarantees that everyone has access to the justice that he or she requires ... It is compatible with the broader aims of reform of the justice system that we are seeing today."

Lord Irvine cited the way in which minor disagreements can all too easily escalate into major stressful conflicts. He hailed ADR as an effective and valuable option in seeking redress, which can save time and money for both the litigants and for the court.

Some people are still resistant to it, but that's probably for no other reason than the fact that ignorance breeds fear. There's nothing like going through with the experience to convince someone of its benefits, and there was an impressive number of converts – judges, solicitors, barristers, insurance companies – who were all present at the conference to testify to its value.

So how does it work? The most powerful and widely used technique in ADR is mediation, which helps disputants to reach a negotiated, legally binding outcome. It's not the easy option.

It's a tough process, which offers the forum for a negotiated broad brush resolution of a dispute. Essentially, it provides a safe framework in which parties can start to talk and to work towards a settlement, under the guidance of a neutral, independent mediator, who brings negotiating, problem-solving and communication skills to the process.

No two mediations are the same, but the steps are broadly similar, along the following lines. Preliminary contact between the parties and the mediation organisation (or mediator) to:

- agree to mediation
- agree terms of mediation (date, duration, location etc.)
- agree on a named mediator.

Limited, brief written summaries of the case are submitted by the parties in advance. These serve several purposes. They inform the mediator; and focus the parties on the real issues.

There is an initial joint meeting, at which the mediator clarifies the process and establishes the ground rules; the parties present a summary of their case to each other; the issues are clarified.

Private, confidential meetings (known as caucuses) between the mediator and each party separately to:

- examine the important issues and needs of each party
- discuss the options for settlement. . . .

Most mediations last between one and two days. While saving time and money is probably the major consideration, there's something else that gets saved – aggravation.

This can all too easily lead to the destruction of a business relationship when it hits a costly and sticky patch. An adversarial process may reach a settlement of the issues but it is hardly likely to alleviate any bitterness. Mediation avoids the sour grapes and often enables the satisfactory continuation of a worthwhile business relationship.

Mediation is voluntary in the sense that it usually takes place as a result of the parties agreeing to enter the mediation process. It is non-binding until an agreement is reached, when it is put in writing and signed by all parties, when it becomes an enforceable contract. Up until that moment, both parties may walk away from the mediation, but people seldom do.'

Taken from 'Alternative dispute resolution instead of trial by ordeal', *New Law Journal*, 20 November 1998

Questions

1. Which organisation was holding this conference?
2. What advantages of ADR are given in the extract?
3. Explain how mediation normally works.
4. What other ways are there of settling disputes?

RESEARCH

Find out more about the Centre for Dispute Resolution.

EXERCISE

2 Mediation

Read the source material and answer the questions below.

Backgound

In 1996 a pilot mediation scheme was established in the Central London County Court for non-family civil disputes with a value over £3,000. A three-hour session with a trained mediator was offered in 4,272 cases at a cost of £25 per party. The pilot scheme ran for two years.

Demand

The rate at which both parties accepted mediation offers remained at about five percent throughout the life of the scheme and despite vigorous attempts to stimulate demand. Demand was virtually non-existent among personal injury cases, although these comprised almost half of the cases offered mediation. Contract, goods/services disputes and debt cases had the highest levels of demand although the joint acceptance rate was less than ten percent. The joint demand for mediation was *lowest* when both parties had legal representation. Acceptance of mediation was highest among disputes between businesses. Interviews with solicitors rejecting mediation revealed:

- lack of experience and widespread ignorance of mediation among the legal profession;
- apprehension about showing weakness through accepting mediation within the context of traditional adversarial litigation;

- evidence of litigant resistance to the idea of compromise, particularly in the early stages of litigation . . .

Evaluation of mediators and mediation process

The overwhelming motivation for mediation was to save time and legal costs. Few parties or solicitors had any experience of mediation or any knowledge of the process. The vast majority of litigants and solicitors made positive assessments of the mediation process. Confidence in mediators was generally high, although less so when cases failed to settle.

The characteristics most valued by litigants were:

- the opportunity to state their grievance and focus on the issues in the disputes;
- to participate fully in a process relatively free from legal technicality;
- the qualities of the mediators.

Solicitors particularly welcomed:

- the speed of the process;
- the opportunity to review the case with a neutral third party;
- the concentration on commercial realities;
- the opportunity to repair damaged business relationships.

Most mediated settlements were perceived by litigants to have been fair, although fairness was often assessed against the cost and time of continued litigation.

Negative assessments by parties centred on:

- deficiencies in mediators' knowledge of the law and issues in dispute;
- undue pressure to settle and bullying by mediators;
- mediators being *insufficiently* directive.'

Taken from *The Central London County Court Pilot Mediation Scheme, Evaluation Report*, Lord Chancellor's Department, Research Series No. 5/98 July 1998

Questions

1. Explain what is meant by 'mediation'. What other methods of alternative dispute resolution are there?
2. In what percentage of cases in the Central London County Court pilot scheme was the offer to mediate accepted?
3. Does the extract give any indication of why the acceptance rate was so low?
4. What are the advantages and disadvantages of mediation shown by this report?

EXERCISE 3 ADR and the Civil Procedure Rules

This article looks at the emphasis on ADR in the Civil Procedure Rules. Read it and answer the question below.

'What do we mean by ADR? The glossary to the Civil Procedure Rules describes ADR as *"Collective description of methods of resolving disputes otherwise than through the normal trial process."*

This will include all the various methods by which disputes can be resolved without resorting to conventional litigation. What is really contemplated are those methods which are essentially negotiation. The parties find their own solution to a dispute but probably use a mediator to help them get there. It needs to be remembered, however, that there are numerous other forms of ADR, many of which are more akin to an arbitration procedure, where a third party imposes a judgment on the parties. The litigator will have to assess the scope for ADR according to the nature of the dispute and the client's objectives.

Encouraging the use of ADR – carrot and stick

The carrot – the overriding objective recited in Rule 1 of the [Civil Procedure] Rules is to enable the court to deal with cases justly. The court's duty to manage cases recited at Rule 1.4 includes at 1.4(2)(e) "*encouraging the parties to use an alternative dispute resolution procedure if the court considers that appropriate and facilitating the use of such procedure*".

Rule 26.4 provides that a party may make a written request for the proceedings to be stayed while the parties try to settle the case by ADR or other means. Under Rule 26.4(2), the court must (if the parties wish it), and can of its own volition, stay proceedings for a month. Under Rules 26.4(3), this stay can be extended for as long as the court sees fit.

The stick – Rule 44.5(1) provides that the court is to have regard to all circumstances in deciding whether costs incurred were proportionate, reasonably incurred and reasonable in amount. One of the matters specifically to take into account is "*the efforts made, if any, before and during the proceedings in order to try and resolve the dispute.*" A party who fails, without good reason, to explore ADR may therefore suffer a costs penalty.

There are some difficulties with this. What is to stop a party asserting a wish to resolve a dispute by ADR and then, in reality, refusing to negotiate during the ADR procedure? A mediator would be unlikely to be prepared to articulate a judgment against one party for not co-operating during the mediation. But the duty is clear – to make a genuine effort to resolve a dispute by negotiation.'

Taken from 'ADR after Woolf', Paul Leigh-Morgan, *The Legal Executive Journal*, May 1999

Questions

1. What is the definition of ADR given in this article?
2. In what way do the Civil Procedure Rules encourage the use of ADR?
3. What difficulties does the article suggest there may be?
4. Why is it important to encourage the use of ADR rather than using the courts?

EXERCISE 4 Arbitration

This article looks at the rules in the Arbitration Act 1996. Read it and answer the questions below.

'The Arbitration Act 1996 received the Royal Assent on 17 June [1996]. Its main provisions came into force on 31 January 1997.

The new rules apply to any arbitration dispute arising after 31 January, whatever the date of the original arbitration agreement. Section 1 states the principles of the Act:

(a) to obtain a fair and impartial resolution of disputes without unnecessary delay or expense;
(b) to allow parties to agree on how their disputes are to be resolved, subject only to such safeguards as are necessary in the public interest; and
(c) to limit interference from the court . . .

The Act defines an "arbitration agreement" to be an agreement to refer present or future disputes to arbitration (whether the disputes are contractual or not). Section 5 requires any arbitration agreement to be made of evidence in writing . . .

Most arbitration agreements will stipulate how arbitrators are to be appointed, and the time within which this is to be done and what is to happen if the parties cannot agree on who is to be appointed. If the agreement does not cater for a stalemate, section 18 allows either party to apply to a court for directions for the appointment of an arbitrator. If appropriate, the court can make the appointment itself.

Section 33 then makes it each arbitrator's overriding duty:

(a) to act fairly and impartially, giving each party a reasonable opportunity to put its case and to deal with that of its opponent; and,
(b) to adopt procedures suitable to the circumstances of the case, avoiding unnecessary delay or expense, so as to provide a fair means of resolving the issues.

Subject to this it is for the parties and the arbitrators to decide all procedural and evidential matters.

This might include: whether formal pleadings are to be used; disclosure requirements; whether strict rules of evidence shall be applied; and whether there should be oral evidence or written submissions . . .

Unless the parties have agreed otherwise, arbitrators have all the powers of a judge; to issue a declaration on any matter; to order the payment of money; to direct a party to do or refrain from doing anything.'

'Arbitration under the Arbitration Act 1996', Charles Ward, *The Legal Executive Journal*, April 1997

Questions

1. Explain the principles of the Arbitration Act 1996 in your own words.
2. What is an arbitration agreement?
3. How are arbitrators chosen?
4. Explain an arbitrator's duty in your own words.

5. What powers does an arbitrator have?
6. What makes arbitration different from other methods of ADR?
7. What advantages does arbitration offer over a court hearing?

EXERCISE 5 Online dispute resolution

This exercise is about using the Internet for dispute resolution. Read the extract and answer the questions below.

'The main dispute resolution methodologies employed are blind-bidding, online arbitration and online mediation.

Blind-bidding

Blind-bidding is one of the most commonly used dispute resolution services provided online. In a nutshell the system works in the following way: in "bidding rounds" parties make submissions of either monetary offers (in settlement) or monetary demands, which are not disclosed to their negotiating counterpart, but rather compared by computer. If the offer and demand match, fall within an agreed range or overlap (i.e. where the offer is more than the demand) then the case will be settled at the agreed level, or mid-way between the offer and demand, or if there is an overlap, at the level of the demand. If the claim is settled, the parties will be notified online or by mail.

Online arbitration

Online arbitration is in essence the same as "documents only" arbitration procedures, except that the process takes place online. The parties' view of the conflict and supporting evidence is submitted online and an arbitrator appointed by the service provider after reviewing the evidence and perhaps taking further representations from the parties, grants an award via a secure online server.

Online mediation

In an online mediation transaction, the process typically begins by one party completing a confidential online form which identifies the parties to, and nature of, the dispute and their desired outcome. The online service provider then contacts the other party to gain their agreement to mediate. If both parties agree to the mediation an agreement outlining the ground rules for the process is executed between the parties. The mediator then communicates by text with the two parties either at the same time or separately in an attempt to assist the parties craft their own resolution to the dispute.'

Taken from 'ODR: the new kid on the block', Bryan Clark, *New Law Journal*, 15 November 2002

Questions

1. What are the three main methods of ADR which are used online?
2. Explain in your own words what is meant by 'blind-bidding'.
3. What is meant by 'documents only' arbitration?
4. What is meant by an award in arbitration?
5. What advantages does arbitration have over other methods of ADR?
6. Why might people prefer to used online mediation to other mediation services?

EXERCISE 6 Tribunals and the use of legal representation

This extract comes from a report on research into tribunal hearings. It looks at whether claimants should have a representative, for example a lawyer or a trade union official, at tribunal hearings. Read it and answer the questions below.

'Representatives regard representation as vital in all tribunals. Their view is based on perception of legal complexity, the imbalance of power between the parties at the hearings, whether inquisitorial or adversarial, and the inability of appellants to advocate their own case. Their view was also, importantly, influenced by a unanimous belief that no matter how well-intentioned tribunals might be, it was impossible to compensate for lack of representation.
Representatives felt that lack of representation placed a great burden of responsibility on tribunals. Some felt that it was undesirable that tribunals should be expected both to adjudicate and to represent the appellant at the same time. Many considered this to be a theoretically impossible approach to the conduct of appeal hearings, and, in any case, a practical impossibility. Tribunals cannot spend the time

necessary to elicit relevant information from the undifferentiated stream in which most appellants present their stories. Nor can they always know, in advance of hearing the evidence, what questions should be asked. The opinions of representatives was largely confirmed in observation of hearings.

There was consistency in the views expressed by tribunals regarding the contribution of good representation to hearings. The experience of tribunals was that good representation resulted in properly investigated cases, the provision of the correct sort of evidence, coherent and succinct isolation of relevant material and presentation of facts. Good representatives also assisted the tribunal by researching the law and presenting relevant cases to the tribunal. In sum, the view of tribunal was that good representation always made their job easier.

There was no consistency between tribunals in their views on the extent to which representation was necessary at their particular hearings, or on their ability to compensate for lack of representation. Immigration adjudicators and members of mental health review tribunals were the most likely to assert that representation was always desirable. Chairs of social security appeal tribunals and industrial [employment] tribunals were divided in their views. The majority of chairs believed that they could compensate for lack of representation.'

Taken from *The Effectiveness of Representation at Tribunals*, H Genn and Y Genn, Faculty of Law, Queen Mary College, University of London (1989)

Questions

1. What types of tribunal are mentioned in this extract?
2. Choose one sort of tribunal and explain the types of cases that it hears.
3. Tribunals are generally regarded as 'do-it-yourself' places. What arguments does this extract give for having a representative when making a claim in a tribunal?
4. What are the advantages and disadvantages of tribunals?

CHAPTER 8

POLICE POWERS

It is necessary for the police to have powers to investigate crime but, at the same time, the rights of individuals have to be protected. The main Act setting out police powers to stop and search, to search premises, to arrest and detain people is the Police and Criminal Evidence Act 1984 (PACE). Under this Act, Codes of Practice on how the police should use their powers are published. There are also provisions in other Acts, especially the Criminal Justice and Public Order Act 1994, which placed limits on the right of suspects to remain silent during police interviews.

The extracts in this section are based on:

- crime statistics
- Code of Practice A (stop and search)
- ss 24 and 25 of PACE
- research into rights of detainees at police stations
- the right to silence.

EXERCISE 1 Recording crime

This extract makes comparisons between crime figures provided by the British Crime Survey (BCS) and police crime figures. Read it and look at the bar chart and answer the questions below.

The Extent of Crime According to Police and BCS Figures

The BCS count in the comparable subset is close to four times higher than the recorded crimes. Put another way, this means that only 25% of crimes against private individuals and their households end up in the recorded crime count.

There are two main reasons for the difference between the BCS and the recorded crime counts. First, many crimes are not reported to the police; and second, not all those that are, are recorded in equivalent offence categories or recorded at all. Because reporting and recording rates vary across offence types, so do the resulting gaps between the BCS and police counts.

The BCS asked victims why they did not report incidents to the police.

- For most crimes the main reason for not reporting was that the incident was too trivial, there was no loss or the police could not do much about it (70 per cent for all comparable crime), followed by the incident being considered a private matter and had been dealt with by the victim (25 per cent of all comparable crime).
- For violent crime many victims did not report a crime as they considered the issue to be a private matter and dealt with it themselves (45 per cent).

FACTORS INFLUENCING POLICE RECORDING OF CRIME

The number of crimes that are recorded by the police are dependent on, firstly, the victim or a representative of the victim bringing that crime to the attention of the police or on the crime coming to the attention of the police through some other means (such as the police officer being present at the time), and then whether that incident is determined as being a recordable offence within categories laid down by the Home Office.

Taken from *Crime in England and Wales 2001/02,* Home Office Statistical Bulletin 07/02. London: Home Office

Bar chart comparing reported and recorded crime

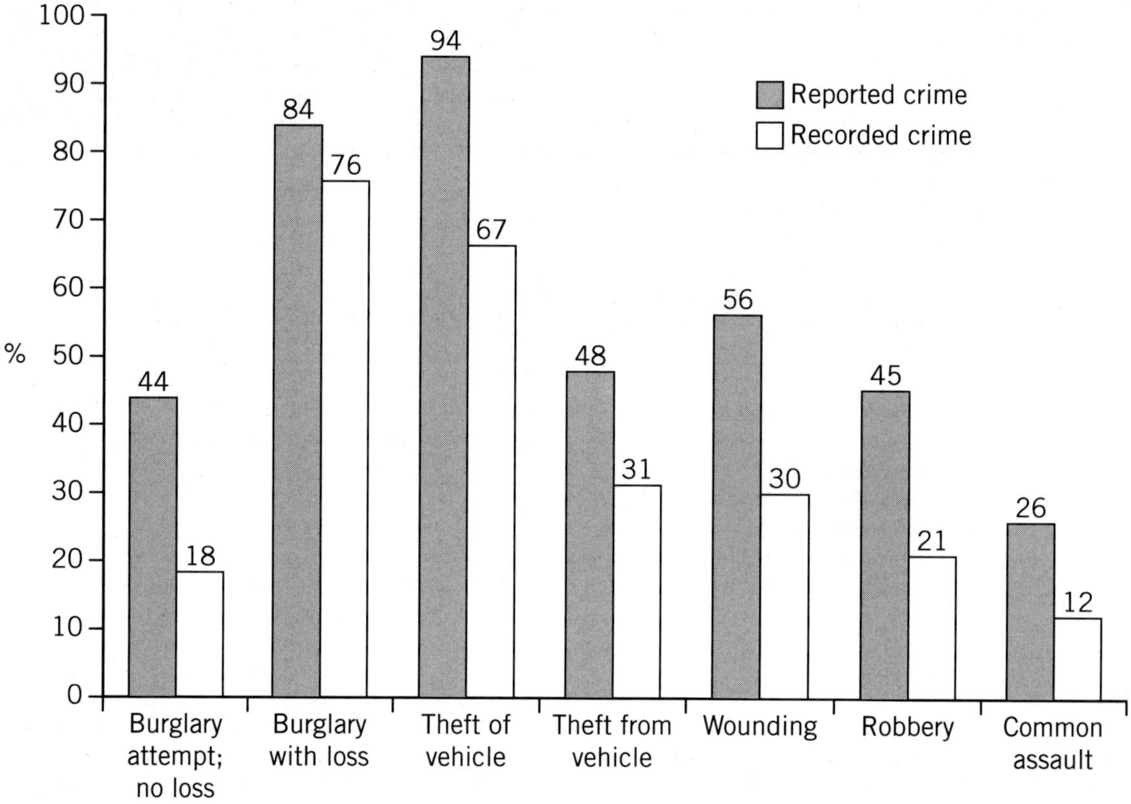

Based on figures in Home Office Statistical Bulletin 07/02

Questions

1. What percentage of crimes is recorded by the police?
2. Why is there a large difference between the amount of actual crime and the amount reported to the police?
3. Which crime is most likely to be reported to the police?
4. Which crime is least likely to be reported to the police?
5. Which type of reported crime is most likely to be recorded by the police?
6. Which type of reported crime is least likely to be recorded by the police?
7. Why are there differences in the number of crimes recorded by the police?

EXERCISE 2 Stop and search powers

This is a small part from the Code of Practice for the Exercise by Police Officers of Statutory Powers of Stop and Search (Code of Practice A). Read it and answer the questions below.

'Powers requiring reasonable suspicion

1.6 Whether a reasonable ground for suspicion exists will depend on the circumstances in each case, but there must be some objective basis for it. An officer will need to consider the nature of the article suspected of being carried in the context of other factors such as the time and the place, and the behaviour of the person concerned or of those with him. Reasonable suspicion may exist, for example, where information has been received such as a description of an article carried or of a suspected offender; a person is seen acting covertly or warily or attempting to hide something; or a person is carrying a certain type of article at an unusual time or in a place where a number of burglaries or thefts are known to have taken place recently. But the decision to stop and search must be based on all the facts which bear on the likelihood that an article of a certain kind will be found.

1.6A For example, reasonable suspicion may be based upon reliable information or intelligence which indicates that members of a particular group or gang, or their associates, habitually carry knives unlawfully or weapons or controlled drugs.

1.7 Reasonable suspicion can never be supported on the basis of personal factors alone without supporting intelligence or information. For example, a person's colour, age, hairstyle or manner of dress, or the fact that he is known to have a previous conviction for possession of an unlawful article, cannot be used alone or in combination with each other as the sole basis on which to search that person. Nor may it be founded on the basis of stereotyped images of certain persons or groups as more likely to be committing offences.'

1.7AA However, where there is reliable information or intelligence that members of a group or gang habitually carry knives unlawfully or weapons or controlled drugs, and wear a distinctive item of clothing or other means of identification to indicate membership of it, the members may be identified by means of that distinctive or other means of identification.

Questions

1. Explain, in your own words, situations in which reasonable suspicion may exist.
2. Explain, in your own words, factors which cannot be used as grounds for reasonable suspicion.
3. When is the wearing of a distinctive item of clothing sufficient to give rise to reasonable suspicion?
4. Would a police officer be justified in stopping and searching in the following circumstances?
   (a) Oscar, aged 16, is walking down a residential street at 2 o'clock in the morning. He has with him a large holdall. The police officer recognises Oscar and knows that he has previous convictions for burglary.
   (b) A police officer is told by a member of the public that Jenny has a knife in her coat pocket. Jenny is stopped when walking in a park at midday.
5. Discuss whether the two sections of the Code of Practice in the extract strike an adequate balance between allowing the police power to investigate possible crimes and protecting the liberty of the individual.

this book is hilariously out of date on police powers use your handout from 2/12/06

EXERCISE 3 Powers of arrest – arrestable offences

The main power of arrest is given by s24 of PACE. The key parts of this section are given below. Study them and then answer the questions below.

Section 24 (1) The powers of summary arrest conferred by the following subsections shall apply–

(a) to offences for which the sentence is fixed by law;
(b) to offences for which a person of 21 years of age or over (not previously convicted) may be sentenced to imprisonment for a term of five years . . . and;
(c) to offences to which subsection (2) below applies,

and in this Act 'arrestable offence' means any such offence.

[Subsection (2) lists a variety of different offences including taking a vehicle without authority (s12 Theft Act 1968); going equipped for stealing (s25 Theft Act 1968); and any offences under the Football (Offences) Act 1991]

. . .

(4) Any person may arrest without a warrant–

(a) anyone who is in the act of committing an arrestable offence;
(b) anyone whom he has reasonable grounds for suspecting to be committing such an offence.

(5) Where an arrestable offence has been committed, any person may arrest without a warrant–

(a) anyone who is guilty of the offence;
(b) anyone whom he has reasonable grounds for suspecting to be guilty of it.

(6) Where a constable has reasonable grounds for suspecting that an arrestable offence has been committed, he may arrest without a warrant anyone whom he has reasonable grounds for suspecting to be to be guilty of the offence.

(7) A constable may arrest without a warrant–

(a) anyone who is about to commit an arrestable offence;
(b) anyone whom he has reasonable grounds for suspecting to be about to commit an arrestable offence.

Questions

1. Explain what is meant by an 'arrestable offence'.
2. What differences are there under this section between a police officer's powers of arrest and those of an ordinary citizen?
3. The phrase 'reasonable grounds for suspecting' are used throughout this section. Explain and comment on this phrase.
4. Explain whether the following people have been lawfully arrested:
   (a) Zack is arrested when a police officer saw him break a window of a car. In fact, it was his own car and he broke the window because he had locked his car keys inside the car.
   (b) Yvonne is arrested outside a shop by a store detective who thought that he saw her put a box of chocolates into her shopping bag. Yvonne denies taking any chocolates and when her bag is searched there are no chocolates in it.

EXERCISE 4 Powers of arrest – general arrest conditions

Section 25 of PACE sets out general arrest conditions which allow a police officer to arrest someone for an offence which is not an arrestable offence under the definition in s24. Study this section and then answer the questions below.

Section 25 (1) Where a constable has reasonable grounds for suspecting that any offence which is not an arrestable offence has been committed or attempted, or is being committed or attempted, he may arrest the relevant person if it appears to him that service of a summons is impracticable or inappropriate because any of the general arrest conditions are satisfied.

(2) In this section 'the relevant person' means any person whom the constable has reasonable grounds to suspect of having committed or having attempted to commit the offence or of being in the course of committing or attempting to commit it.

(3) The general arrest conditions are–

(a) that the name of the relevant person is unknown to, and cannot be readily ascertained by, the constable;
(b) that the constable has reasonable grounds for doubting whether a name furnished by the relevant person as his name is his real name;
(c) that–
   (i) the relevant person has failed to furnish a satisfactory address for service; or
   (ii) the constable has reasonable grounds for doubting whether an address furnished by the relevant person is a satisfactory address for service;
(d) that the constable has reasonable grounds for believing that arrest is necessary to prevent the relevant person–
   (i) causing physical injury to himself or any other person;
   (ii) suffering physical injury;
   (iii) causing loss of or damage to property;
   (iv) committing an offence against public decency; or
   (v) causing an unlawful obstruction of the highway;
(e) that the constable has reasonable grounds for believing that an arrest is necessary to protect a child or other vulnerable person from the relevant person.

Questions

1. How are offenders who commit non-arrestable offences normally brought to court?
2. Explain why it is necessary for the police to have the right to arrest for a non-arrestable offence in the circumstances under subsections (3) (a), (b) and (c).
3. Explain why the right to arrest is important in the circumstances under subsections (3) (d) and (e).

EXERCISE 5 Detention at the police station

This extract is taken from research into detention of people at police stations. It explains how that research was carried out and comments on two main points: (1) the use of appropriate adults and (2) legal advice. Read the extract and answer the questions below.

'The research was conducted at 25 police stations in ten forces. The study used three forms of data collection: observation in police custody areas; analysis of custody records; and the administration of questionnaires to investigating officers. The main findings were as follows:

- Nearly one in five of detainees were juveniles (19%). The vast majority of these had an appropriate adult attend the police station while they were in custody. Well over half of appropriate adults attending police stations were parents or guardians, and just under a quarter were social workers.
- Two per cent of detainees were initially treated as mentally disordered or handicapped. Appropriate adults attended in about two-thirds of these cases. Social workers most frequently acted as appropriate adults.
- It was rare for custody officers to provide guidance to appropriate adults, while those acting in this role rarely asked for an explanation of what was required of them.
- Social workers were more supportive towards the suspect and more co-operative with the police when acting as appropriate adults than family members, who could express high levels of hostility and distress.
- Detainees are increasingly likely to request legal advice while in custody. Four out of ten suspects asked for legal advice, with a notable increase found among juveniles.
- Although 40 per cent of suspects *requested* legal advice only 34 per cent of suspects actually *received* legal advice while in custody. The most common reasons for legal advice not being received were because suspects: changed their minds about needing legal advice; were released before an advisor arrived: or agreed to see a solicitor later in court rather than at the police station. No cases were found where custody officers had delayed access to legal advice on the basis that it might hinder investigations.
- Compared to previous studies, the proportion of unqualified "legal representatives" giving advice to the suspects appears to have declined, with a corresponding rise in the number of solicitors giving advice and the introduction of "accredited representatives". Accredited representatives were the most likely to give advice when a suspect's own legal advisor had been requested.
- Just under half of all suspects interviewed by the police received legal advice while in custody. The rate at which legal advisors attend police interviews has risen compared to previous studies.'

Taken from *In police custody: police powers and suspects' rights under the revised PACE codes of practice*, Home Office Research Study 174

Questions

1. Who is entitled to have an appropriate adult present when interviewed at a police station?
2. Which Code of Practice gives the right to an appropriate adult?
3. What did the research discover about the use of appropriate adults?
4. Which section of PACE gives the right to legal advice when detained at a police station?
5. What did the research discover about the use of legal advice by detainees compared to previous studies?
6. Why did only 34 per cent of detainees actually receive legal advice?
7. What other rights do those detained at a police station have?

EXERCISE 6 The right to silence

The extract in Source 1 comments on the possible link between having a legal adviser present at a police interview and the change to the law on the 'right to silence'. Read it and study the figures in Source 2 and answer the questions below.

Source 1

'The presence of a legal adviser during police questioning is seen by some commentators as providing an important form of support for suspects (Sanders et al., 1989). More specifically, research has suggested that suspects are more likely to exercise the right of silence when a legal adviser is present; this may be due to advice given or more general support gained from the adviser's presence . . .

Comparison with previous studies indicates a pronounced rise in legal advisers attending police interviews. Brown (1989) found that legal advisers attended all police interviews in only 12 per cent of cases – one-third of the level found in the current study. This large increase in attendance is only partly due to the rise in requests for legal advice . . .

One explanation for this increase concerns the changes to the right of silence. It is reasonable to suggest that legal advisers are now more likely to decide their presence is required during interviews in order to steer their clients through police questioning. . . .

A specific comparison of suspects' use of the right of silence before and after the introduction of the new provisions is possible with reference to an earlier piece of research.

Reductions in the use of silence were found to be greatest among suspects receiving legal advice. This may be a result of legal advisers warning their clients about the consequences of remaining silent under the new provisions.'

Source 2

The following table compares suspects' use of the right to silence before and after the change in the law.

	Refused to answer all questions	**Refused to answer some questions**	**Answered all questions**
Pre-1994	10%	13%	77%
1997 study	6%	10%	84%

Both sources have been adapted from *In police custody: police powers and suspects' rights under the revised PACE codes of practice,* Home Office Research Study 174

Questions

1. Which Act limited the right to silence?
2. What effect may it have if a defendant fails to mention something which he later relies on at his trial?
3. What effect does the research indicate that this change in the law has had?
4. Why is it important that a suspect has a legal adviser present during questioning?

DISCUSS

Should people detained by the police have the right to remain silent without the risk of adverse inferences being made at any subsequent trial?

CHAPTER 9

PRE-TRIAL MATTERS IN CRIMINAL CASES

After the police have charged a person with a crime there are various matters that are considered before the case is finally tried. One of the most important points to be decided is whether the defendant should be released on bail while waiting for the court hearing. Other matters include the disclosure of evidence between prosecution and defence. For offences triable either way there is also the decision on where the case will be tried. Finally the role of the Crown Prosecution Service, and the Director of Public Prosecutions, who is the head of the CPS, is important as they can decide to drop a case or reduce the offence charged to a lesser one. All these matters have been the subject of a lot of criticism.

The first three extracts in this section are all from a Home Office Research Study into bail; the others are taken from various articles. The exercises are about:

- when and who makes the decision about granting bail
- the consequences of the decision to grant bail
- making the decision to grant bail
- the problems of disclosure of evidence
- the role of the DPP and the Crown Prosecution Service
- problems in the system
- private prosecutions.

EXERCISE 1 When and who makes the decision about granting bail

This extract is from Home Office research into the granting of bail. Read it and answer the questions below.

'In England and Wales, the majority of decisions about the granting of bail before trial arise at three points: when a suspect has been arrested by the police but the evidence available is not sufficient for charges to be brought; when a suspect has been arrested and charged with an offence; and when the court has decided to adjourn the hearing of a case to another date. The first two of these decisions are made by the police: the third is made by the magistrates.

When a suspect has been arrested but the police do not have sufficient evidence to charge him with an offence, they can either release him without charge or, if they wish to seek more evidence before deciding whether to charge, they can release him with the requirement that he returns to the police station on a given date. This second alternative is usually called bail to return to the police station. It differs from the other types of bail considered in this report in that, once the initial questioning is concluded, the police have no option of holding the suspect in custody.

After a suspect has been charged with an offence, the police must decide whether he (the "defendant") should be held in custody overnight to appear at the next available magistrates' court, or whether he can be released on bail with the requirement that he appears at the court on a given date. ... The information on which this decision is based will be obtained from the defendant himself, from the arresting police officer, possibly from statements by witnesses to the offence, and from the Criminal Records Office on the defendant's past record. At this stage, the police may also make a recommendation to the Crown Prosecution Service (CPS) as to whether the defendant should be refused bail at his first appearance in court ...

When the defendant appears at court, the case might be dealt with immediately, in which case no further pre-trial decisions are needed. In many cases, however, this is not possible and the court will adjourn the proceedings to a future date. When they adjourn a case, the magistrates must decide whether to remand the defendant on bail or in custody until the next hearing. They will first hear any recommendations by the CPS prosecutor, usually in the form of any "objections to bail" which the CPS wish to make. The defence lawyer will then be given the opportunity to make representations to the magistrates before their decision is made.'

Taken from *Remand decisions and offending on bail: evaluation of the Bail Process Project*, (1998) Home Office Research Study 184

Questions

1. At what points in a criminal case is bail considered?
2. Who makes the decision as to whether bail should be granted?
3. What is different about 'bail to return to the police station'?
4. When is a decision about bail not needed at the Magistrates' Court?
5. If bail is an issue at the Magistrates' Court, who and what procedure is involved?

EXERCISE 2 Grounds for and the consequences of the decision on granting bail

Read this extract on the grounds for granting bail (taken from the same source as that for Exercise 1) and answer the questions below. Note that the next exercise is related to this one.

'The grounds on which the police can refuse bail after charge to a defendant are set out in section 38 of the Police and Criminal Evidence Act 1984 (PACE). The grounds on which the court can refuse bail are set out in schedule one of the Bail Acts 1976. The most important grounds are that, if released on bail, the defendant would be likely to:

- fail to appear at the next court appearance
- commit an offence while on bail
- interfere with the witnesses who will be giving evidence against him or otherwise obstruct the course of justice.

In making their decision or recommendation, the police, CPS and court are required to assess the risk that any of the above will occur. If they lean too far on the side of leniency, the result may be that more people will fail to appear at court (hence avoiding justice), more offences will be committed by persons on bail (causing nuisance or positive danger to the public), and/or more witnesses will be intimidated.

On the other hand, if the decision-makers lean too far on the side of severity, more people are likely to be remanded in custody who would not have 'failed bail' if they had been given the chance. The result will be more people will lose their liberty and the prison population will be increased (at some considerable cost) with no consequent benefit to the public.

It is important therefore that decision-makers should try to target those who would fail to appear at court, offend on bail or interfere with witnesses, and remand those persons and those only in custody.'

Questions

1. Which Act sets out when the police are entitled to refuse bail?
2. Which Act governs the courts' decisions on bail?
3. Explain in your own words the grounds on which bail can be refused.
4. Why is the decision on whether or not to grant bail important?

EXERCISE 3 Making decisions on granting bail

This exercise follows on from the previous one and it is necessary to read both extracts in order to answer the questions below.

'Analyses of nearly 4,000 court remand decisions suggested that the factors which had the most bearing on the decision were:

- address status (whether the defendant was homeless or not)
- the type of offence currently charged (grouped into "more serious" and "less serious"[1])
- bail history (any previous instances of absconding or breaching bail conditions, or whether the defendant was already on bail when charged with the current offence)
- whether the defendant had served a custodial sentence (this appeared to be the most important aspect of the criminal record)

- employment status
- gender (a marginal effect only).

The rate [of remanding in custody] varied from two per cent to five per cent of defendants who were charged with "less serious" offences, had no bail history and had not served a custodial sentence in the past, to 64 per cent for persons charged with "more serious" offences and had no fixed address.'

[1] For the purpose of this analysis 'more serious' offences were burglary, robbery, GBH, indictable/either way sex offences and drug trafficking. All others were categorised as 'less serious' offences.

Questions

1. Which is the main Act which sets out the law on bail?
2. What is the key presumption in that Act?
3. What factors does the Act state should be taken into account when decisions about bail are made?
4. Look at the list of factors which affected bail decisions in the study. To what extent are these the same factors as set out in the Act?
5. Which factor(s) do you think should be the most important?

RESEARCH

The Criminal Justice Bill 2002 (which is likely to become law in late 2003) proposed some amendments on the law of bail. Find out what amendments have been made. Try searching for the new Act at www.hmso.gov.uk/acts.htm

EXERCISE 4 Disclosure of evidence

In the 1970s and 1980s there were many miscarriages of justice which might have been avoided if the prosecution had revealed to the defence that they had evidence which supported the defendant's innocence. This article points out the risk of similar problems recurring. Read it and answer the questions below.

'Last week a rape trial in Nottingham Crown Court was stopped by the judge and the teenage defendant acquitted when it was discovered that a crucial videotape taken from a CCTV camera in a nightclub foyer, which proved the defendant's innocence, had not been disclosed. After hearing a detective state on oath that he had overlooked the relevant parts of the tape, Judge John Hopkin described the circumstances as lamentable, demanding "a full explanation" from the Chief Crown Prosecution Solicitor . . .

In the 1992 case of the Taylor sisters – convicted of the murder of a rival lover – it was never disclosed at trial that a witness had told the police that one of the two women seen near the place of the crime was black. Both Taylor sisters are white.

The Director of Public Prosecutions, David Calvert-Smith, QC, gave a warning last week about the risk of a return to the sort of miscarriages of justice that were seen in the 1970s and 1980s. Since the Criminal Procedure and Investigations Act 1996, police and the prosecution have been holding back material that could help the defence case. The risk is not only of innocent defendants being convicted: a loss of trust in the police and prosecution could lead to guilty defendants being acquitted. There is clear evidence that the Act is not working . . .

Before the Act came into force, police sent to the prosecutor copies of all the material that was not going to be part of the case, as well as the material that was. Since the Act, the prosecutor has received only copies of documents that the police disclosure officer believes should be given to the defence. The Law Society said it was unrealistic to give a policeman responsibility for identifying material that may help the defence.

Against this background, Mr Straw [the Home Secretary] is to proceed against the right of a defendant to elect jury trial for a swath of middle-ranking offences. As a result, many more cases will be tried in the Magistrates' Court where information about the prosecution case given to the defendant is limited and the trial process less rigorous.

In the Crown Court, all evidence by the prosecution is given to the defence at an early stage, allowing it a better chance of identifying missing material . . . There is no similar requirement to provide copies of the prosecution evidence if the trial is to be held in the Magistrates' Court.'

Taken from 'The dangers of keeping a jury in the dark', Michael Mathews, *The Times*, 25 May 1999

Questions

1. The article highlights the need for all material in police possession to be available to the defence. What examples are given showing why this is important?
2. Which Act changed the law on disclosing material held by the police?
3. What was the change that this Act made?
4. What points does the writer make about the way in which the current law on disclosure operates?
5. What is the key difference regarding evidence between cases in the Crown Court and cases in the Magistrates' Court?
6. What new factor makes this difference even more important?

EXERCISE 5 The roles of the Director of Public Prosecutions and the Crown Prosecution Service

Read the following article and answer the questions below.

'The office of the Director of Public Prosecutions is almost 120 years old. But for only one tenth of that time has the holder been head of the Crown Prosecution Service. That service itself is facing considerable change and a big part of that will be in the role, nature of responsibilities and skills required of the DPP.

For more than a century after the first DPP was appointed in 1880, he and his department were concerned solely with the prosecution of the most important and difficult criminal offences. Throughout this period, the task of conducting most of the criminal prosecutions in England and Wales remained in the hands of the police.

Although the work of the DPP's department was of increasing importance, including the prosecution of the most complex or sensitive cases, the department handled only a small proportion of prosecutions instituted by the police. And it remained small. In the early 1980s the DPP had a total staff of about 180. This changed in 1986 when the CPS was created. The DPP became head of the new service, charged with taking over the conduct of most criminal proceedings against 1.3 million defendants instituted by the police, dealing with offences ranging from the gravest to the least serious.

The DPP has overall responsibility, with 6,000 staff, for this work. In addition, the change in 1986 was not simply a vast increase in the size and the workload of the organisation. The department and the way it operated were then wholly new and thus quite unlike the old DPP's department.

The Prosecution of Offences Act 1985 was intended to create a prosecuting service which would be funded by the national exchequer. It would apply national standards to the prosecution process, but would deliver its product, the effective but fair prosecution of offences, at local level throughout the country, operating through local offices.

The history of the CPS over the 12 years of its life shows that the two aspects intended by the 1985 Act, reconciliation of the national and local elements in the equation were not easy to achieve. To ensure that national standards are applied to the prosecution decisions throughout the country, some system of period checks and inspection is necessary.

But the problem is that the greater the impact of national headquarters, the less scope there is for those making the decisions and conducting the prosecutions locally to exercise their own judgment and initiative and local knowledge.

There have been real achievements in the past 12 years which are rarely acknowledged: the establishment of a national, independent, professionally run prosecution service; the formulation and promulgation of a national code for Crown prosecutors; and the establishment in co-operation with the police and other agencies, of common policies in important aspects of the criminal justice process, such as charging standards and guidelines for the care of witnesses.

The process of creating a national service has now reached a point where we can be reasonably satisfied that this half of the equation is in place. This is less true of the devolution of responsibility for the conduct of prosecutions to the local level.'

'Crown head with a new leading role', Sir Iain Glidewell, *The Times*, 16 June 1998

Questions

1. What is the role of the DPP? How has this role changed?

2. Which Act established the CPS?
3. Before the creation of the CPS, who had responsibility for conducting criminal proceedings?
4. What advantages are there in having the CPS handle all prosecutions?

EXERCISE

6 Private prosecutions

Although the Crown Prosecution Service deals with prosecutions, there is also a right for an individual to bring a private prosecution. The following article examines this right. Read it and answer the questions below.

'Before the first police force was established in 1829, almost all prosecutions – with the exception of matters affecting the state – were brought by individuals. Nowadays, most private prosecutions are either theft prosecutions brought by shop-owners against shoplifters, or assault victims prosecuting their alleged assailants.

Traditionally, the police have always been reluctant to interfere in cases of trivial assault where assailant and victim are known to each other. It is left to complainants to bring their own proceedings in the Magistrates' Court if they feel sufficiently aggrieved. Indeed, before the Criminal Justice Act 1988, such proceedings could only be instituted by victims.

A third category of private prosecutions is brought by individuals who feel let down by the system. The tragic case of Stephen Lawrence is an example. The parents of murdered teenager, Stephen Lawrence, brought their own prosecution for the murder of the youths whom they suspected of killing their son. The Crown Prosecution Service (CPS) had previously refused to prosecute, on the grounds that the evidence was not strong enough to achieve a conviction.

Ultimately, the CPS were proved right. After the prosecution witnesses had given their evidence, the judge stopped the trial saying that there was no evidence which could prove beyond reasonable doubt that the defendants were the assailants.

The right for private individuals to bring prosecutions is now expressly preserved by section 6 of the Prosecution of Offences Act 1985, which established the CPS, and which states that nothing in the Act shall preclude anyone from instituting any criminal proceedings or conducting any criminal proceedings to which the Director of Public Prosecution's duty to take over the conduct of the proceedings does not apply ...

While the victim of a crime, or, indeed, anyone else, may have the right to prosecute, is prosecution always the best way forward, or are there other proceedings which may be more appropriate? What is the prosecutor's objective in bringing the prosecution?

For the CPS, this question does not arise. It is its statutory function to prosecute offences where there is a reasonable prospect of conviction, and where it is in the public interest to bring the proceedings.

For private individuals, the motivation is more complex. Shop proprietors may prosecute shoplifters to protect their businesses from other shoplifters. Assault victims may gain satisfaction from seeing their assailant punished by the courts. A successful motoring conviction may provide a sound basis for an accident-damage claim against the errant driver. However, the overriding purpose of prosecution is never to provide redress for individuals – but redress for the state – although the criminal courts have limited power to award compensation to a victim of crime ...

Legal aid is not available to someone who wishes to bring a private prosecution ... There are other practical difficulties in bringing private prosecutions.

Unlike the police, private prosecutors have no power to arrest and question suspects, enter and search premises, or inspect documents. There may be a problem in getting evidence. Unlike the state, the private prosecutor may not have an open-ended budget. It may cost no more than a few hundred pounds to prosecute for common assault in the Magistrates' Court, particularly if the defendant pleads guilty. It cost [one private prosecutor] tens of thousands of pounds for a jury trial in the Crown Court. Even after she won her case, only a fraction of those costs were recoverable from her assailant.'

Taken from 'Private Prosecutions', Charles Ward, *The Legal Executive Journal*, July 1998

Questions

1. What is the function of the CPS?
2. Which Act preserves the right to bring a private prosecution?
3. What categories of people are most likely to bring private prosecutions?
4. For what reasons may someone decide to bring a private prosecution?
5. What problems do private prosecutors face?

CHAPTER 10

CRIMINAL COURTS

There are two main courts in which criminal cases are tried. These are the Magistrates' Court and the Crown Court. The decision on which one of these courts is used depends on the crime committed by the defendant. There are three categories of offence: summary cases which can only be tried in the Magistrates' Court; offences triable either way, which may be tried in either court; and indictable offences which must be tried at the Crown Court. One of the main issues is on how the decision as to where offences triable either way are tried is made. This is seen as important because a jury is used to decide the verdict in cases at the Crown Court.

As well as the courts in which a trial is held, it is also necessary to know about the rights of appeal in criminal cases. The defendant has more rights to appeal against being convicted than the prosecution has to appeal against an acquittal. This is another area in which there has been debate.

Finally, there is the problem of miscarriages of justice and the role of the Criminal Cases Review Commission.

The exercises in this section are on:

- trial in the Crown Court versus trial in the Magistrates' Court
- the results of cases dealt with at the Crown Court
- appeal routes from the Magistrates' Court
- prosecution rights of appeal
- youth courts
- the Criminal Cases Review Commission.

EXERCISE 1 Should more cases be dealt with in the Magistrates' Court?

The following is taken from an article which considers arguments for and against increasing the length of sentence which the magistrates have power to impose. Read the article and answer the questions below.

'The Government has indicated a desire to reduce the number of cases that are dealt with in the Crown Court. Inevitably this will result in an increase in the number of cases dealt with in the Magistrates' Court. One of the ways in which this may be achieved is by reducing the number of offences that carry a right to elect trial by jury. Another way is to extend magistrates' powers to sentence to imprisonment. This would reduce the number of cases in which the magistrates decline jurisdiction or commit to the Crown Court for sentence on the grounds that their powers to sentence to up to six months' imprisonment may be inadequate for the offence.

The arguments in favour of the change claim that this would be in the interests of justice; but one suspects that the real motivation for the proposals is more to do with cost and efficiency. But whilst there may be perceived financial advantages, there are a number of disadvantages which must be considered before any such change in the balance of work between the Magistrates' Court and the Crown Court is effected.

Presently there is an incentive for defendants, who are at risk of being convicted, to plead guilty in the Magistrates' Court because of the limit to the length of sentence of imprisonment which may be imposed. If magistrates have the power to imprison up to 12 months' imprisonment, then the perceived gap between the likely sentence which may be imposed in the Crown Court and that in the Magistrates' Court will be narrowed, with the consequence that the defendant may decide that he or she is better off electing and being dealt with in the Crown Court.

There are many safeguards apparent (at least to the defendant) in proceedings in the Crown Court compared to those in the Magistrates' Court. The division of roles between judge and jury, and the representation of both prosecution and defence by specialist advocates are but two examples. The justification for these safeguards, at least in part, is that defendants who face receiving serious penalties – such as a sentence of imprisonment in excess of six months – should feel that they have had a fair trial.

Whilst there is a need for both Magistrates' Court and Crown Court jurisdiction, the division between the two is rightly that between non-serious and serious matters. The dividing line has been formed by the limit on the power to sentence to imprisonment. If this limit is to be interfered with, there must be an awareness of the undermining of confidence in the system as a whole.

In the Crown Court, experienced professional judges pass sentence. Sentencing in the Crown Court tends to be consistent throughout England and Wales, whilst research has shown that sentences passed in one Magistrates' Court vary considerably to those passed in another. The frequency of the imposition of custodial sentences can vary from 3% in one Magistrates' Court to 17% elsewhere. It seems likely that extending magistrates' powers to sentence to longer periods of imprisonment will lead to more inconsistency, and thus less confidence in magistrates' jurisdiction.'

'The Magistrate Debate: Increasing powers', Scott Ingram, *The Magistrate*, February 1999

Questions

1. What types of cases can be tried at either the Magistrates' Court or the Crown Court?
2. In what two ways is it suggested that the number of cases dealt with in the Crown Court could be reduced?
3. For what reasons should the number of cases at the Crown Court be reduced?
4. The article states that there are many safeguards in proceedings in the Crown Court. What safeguards does the article give?
5. For what other reasons might a defendant prefer to be tried in the Crown Court to the Magistrates' Court?
6. Do you agree that magistrates should be given greater powers to imprison defendants? Give reasons for your answer.

EXERCISE 2 Magistrates' Court or Crown Court?

This extract is taken from the Government White Paper *Justice for All* (2002). Read it and answer the questions below.

'4.19 About 95% of all criminal cases are dealt with in the magistrates' court, locally and quickly. This benefits defendants, victims and witnesses. We are not convinced that there is a strong enough case to justify introducing a new "intermediate tier" court, as was recommended by Sir Robin Auld. We believe that the benefits this would provide can be achieved in other ways. We will legislate to increase magistrates' sentencing powers to 12 months, and to allow us to increase them up to a maximum of 18 months, depending on the results of evaluations, and taking account of any necessary additional training requirements.

4.20 Some types of case, known as "either-way" cases, may be dealt with in either the Crown Court, where they would receive jury trial or the magistrates' court. They may go to the Crown Court either because the magistrates decide that the appropriate sentence on conviction could exceed their sentencing powers (presently up to 6 months' imprisonment for adult defendants) or because the defendant elects jury trial. In practice, most of these types of cases are dealt with by magistrates – 87% in 2000, with 9% going to the Crown Court because the magistrates declined to take the case and 4% because the defendant elected. The proportion of these cases that are heard by magistrates has increased in recent years. In over half of the either-way cases that do go to the Crown Court and in which the defendant pleads or is found guilty, magistrates could have given the sentence.'

Questions

1. This extract speaks of 'either-way cases'. Explain what is meant by this phrase and give two examples of such offences.
2. In 2000, what percentage of either-way cases was heard at the Crown Court?
3. Why did these cases go to the Crown Court?
4. Some offences have to be tried at the Magistrates' Court. What are these called?
5. Up to 2003, what was the maximum sentence magistrates could give for one offence?
6. What is the proposed increase in magistrates' sentencing powers?
7. What effect would you expect this to have on the number of either-way cases going to the Crown Court? Give reasons for your answer.

EXERCISE 3 Disposal of cases at the Crown Court

Bar chart showing result by percentage of cases disposed of in the Crown Court in 2001

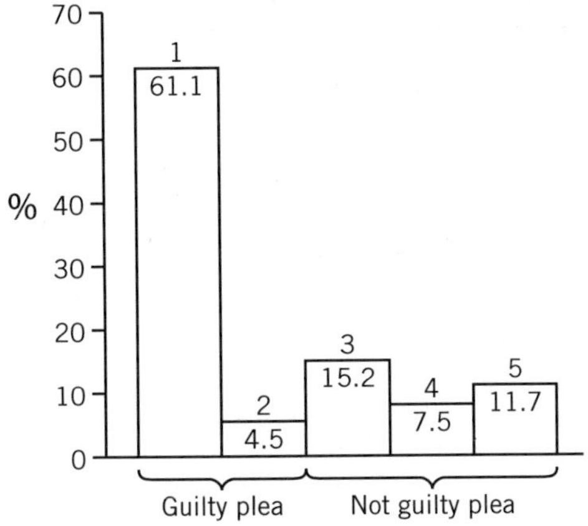

1. Defendant pleads guilty to all charges
2. Defendant pleads guilty to some charges
3. Judge discharges or directs acquittal
4. Jury acquit
5. Jury convict

Questions

1. Give examples of the types of cases which are heard at the Crown Court.
2. From the graph, what is the most common way for a case to be disposed of in the Crown Court?
3. Give the percentage of cases in which the defendant pleaded not guilty.
4. When a defendant pleads not guilty, are they more likely to be convicted or acquitted?
5. What is the most common way for a defendant to be found not guilty?
6. When a jury makes the decision, are they more likely to convict or acquit?

EXERCISE 4 Appealing from the Magistrates' Court

The following piece outlines the courts that the case in *Felix v Director of Public Prosecutions* (1998) went to. Study it and answer the questions.

Felix was charged with leaving litter, contrary to s87 of the Environmental Protection Act 1990. This particular offence is a summary offence. The case was tried in the Marylebone Magistrates' Court. Felix was found guilty. He appealed to the Knightsbridge Crown Court where his appeal was dismissed. He then appealed to the Queen's Bench Divisional Court by way of case stated. At this court his appeal was allowed and his conviction quashed.

Note: more detail on the facts and the law in the case are given in Chapter 3 Exercise 3

Questions

1. What is meant by 'summary offence'?
2. Who would have tried the case at the Marylebone Magistrates' Court?
3. When Felix appealed to the Knightsbridge Crown Court, who would have decided that appeal?
4. What is an appeal by way of case stated?
5. When the Queen's Bench Divisional Court quashed the conviction, it would have been possible for the prosecution to appeal against this. To which court would that appeal be and what conditions are there on such an appeal?

EXERCISE 5 Should the prosecution have more rights of appeal?

Key parts of s36 of the Criminal Justice Act 1972 regarding the prosecution rights after an acquittal are set out in this exercise. Study the section and answer the questions.

s36 (1) Where a person tried on indictment has been acquitted . . . the Attorney General may, if he desires the opinion of the Court of Appeal on a point of law which has arisen in the case, refer that point to the court, and the court shall, in accordance with this section, consider the point and give their opinion on it. . . .

(3) Where the Court of Appeal have given their opinion on a point referred to them under this section, the court may, of their own motion or in pursuance of an application on that behalf, refer the point to the House of Lords if it appears to the court that the point ought to be considered by that House. . . .

(7) A reference under this section shall not affect the trial in relation to which the reference is made or any acquittal in that trial.

Questions

1. Which Act of Parliament allows the prosecution to refer a point of law?
2. Who makes the reference for the prosecution?
3. To which court is the reference made?
4. Can the point then be referred to any other court? If so, which court?
5. Does the decision on the point of law have any effect on the person who was acquitted?

RESEARCH

Find a case in which a reference was made under the Criminal Justice Act 1972.

EXERCISE 6 Further rights of appeal after an acquittal

This exercise looks at ss54 and 55 of the Criminal Procedure and Investigations Act 1996. These sections give very limited rights to the prosecution to apply for an acquittal to be quashed. Study the sections and answer the questions below.

s54 (1) This section applies where–

(a) a person has been acquitted of an offence, and
(b) a person has been convicted of an administration of justice offence involving interference with or intimidation of a juror or a witness (or potential witness) in any proceedings which led to the acquittal.

(2) Where it appears to the court before which the person was convicted that–

(a) there is a real possibility that, but for the interference or intimidation, the acquitted person would not have been acquitted . . .

the court shall certify that it so appears.

(3) Where a court certifies under subsection (2) an application may be made to the High Court for an order quashing the acquittal, and the Court shall make the order if (but shall not do so unless) the four conditions in section 55 are satisfied. . . .

s55 (1) The first condition is that it appears to the High Court likely that, but for the interference or intimidation, the acquitted person would not have been acquitted.

(2) The second condition is that it does not appear to the Court that, because of lapse of time or for any other reason, it would be contrary to the interests of justice to take proceedings against the acquitted person for the offence of which he was acquitted.

(3) The third condition is that it appears to the Court that the acquitted person has been given a reasonable opportunity to make written representations to the Court.

(4) The fourth condition is that it appears to the Court that the conviction for the administration of justice offence will stand . . .

Questions

1. When does this Act apply?
2. To which court is an application made under these provisions?
3. What can that court do and why is this important?
4. Explain in your own words the four conditions which must be satisfied before the court acts.

EXERCISE 7 Youth Courts

This extract is taken from the Government White Paper, *Justice for All* (2002). Read it and answer the questions below.

'4.35 Since 2000 the youth court, operating within the magistrates' court structure, has been able to deal with a wider range of defendants and where necessary order up to two years' detention as part of arrangements for giving the best chance for a young offender to mend his or her ways. Despite this, some 5,000 young defendants still go to the Crown Court for trial each year – about 1,000 from the youth court and a further 4,000 committed for trial with an adult from the adult magistrates' court.

4.36 The youth court is more suitable for young people, because it is a specialist court and its style has been progressively modified to ensure young defendants and their parents properly understand and engage in the process. By contrast, in the Crown Court the presence of a jury as the focus for the trial makes it difficult to involve young people properly. We therefore propose to provide for strengthened youth courts to deal with young offenders accused of serious crimes. Juveniles facing such charges without adult co-defendants would be dealt with by the youth court, presided over by a judge, with two experienced lay magistrates in support.'

Questions

1. Within which court structure does the Youth Court operate?
2. Who normally sits to hear cases in the Youth Court?
3. What is the maximum sentence that can be imposed by the Youth Court?
4. At what other court may some young offenders be tried? Why would they be sent to this court?
5. Why is the Youth Court more suitable for hearing cases involving young offenders?
6. What proposal does the Government have for trying young offenders accused of serious crimes?
7. Do you agree with the change proposed by the Government? Give reasons for your answers.

EXERCISE 8 The role of the Criminal Cases Review Commission

This article was written by a member of the Criminal Cases Review Commission (CCRC) and sets out the role of the CCRC. Read the article and answer the questions below.

'The Criminal Cases Review Commission was established in January 1997. Our task is to investigate suspected miscarriages of justice and refer, to the appropriate appeal court, those cases which have a real possibility of succeeding. Our jurisdiction covers both summary and indictable offences in England, Wales and Northern Ireland, and we can consider both sentence and convict.

The Commission began handling casework from 31 March 1997, when it took over responsibility from the Home Office and Northern Ireland Office. By the end of September 1998, a year and a half into the Commission's working life, the total number of applications stood at 1,986. It had completed 532 and referred 21 to the Court of Appeal for new hearings.

The Commission had been born out of events in the late 1980s, when public concern about the criminal justice system reached unprecedented levels. A series of high profile miscarriages of justice cases turned the spotlight on the investigation and prosecution of criminal offences. On 14 March 1991, the day that the Birmingham Six were released, the then Home Secretary announced the establishment of a Royal Commission on Criminal Justice to be chaired by Viscount Runciman of Doxford.

Central to the Royal Commission's work was an examination of the effectiveness of the criminal justice system in securing the conviction of the guilty and the acquittal of the innocent. When it reported to Parliament, in July 1993, the Royal Commission made a great many recommendations, including the establishment of an independent body to consider suspected miscarriages of justice, to arrange for their investigation where appropriate, and to refer to the Court of Appeal those cases meriting further consideration by the Court.

The legislation creating the Criminal Cases Review Commission and setting out its role and powers is the Criminal Appeal Act 1995. This establishes the new body as an executive non-departmental public body whose members are appointed by the Queen. The Commission is independent from government and the judiciary, and is given extensive powers to carry out investigations.

The Act adds three further responsibilities to the principal one of reviewing suspected injustices. These are: investigating matters at the direction of the Court of Appeal to assist the Court in its determination of a case; providing assistance to the Home Secretary on matters relating to a Royal Pardon; and referring cases to the Home Secretary where the Commission feels a Royal Pardon should be considered.'

'A Necessary and Welcome Body', David Kyle, *The Legal Executive Journal*, December 1998

Questions

1. Which report had recommended the setting up of an independent body to consider suspected miscarriages of justice?
2. Which Act of Parliament set up the Criminal Cases Review Commission?
3. Who had previously had responsibility for the investigation of suspected miscarriages of justice?
4. What important difference is there between the Criminal Cases Review Commission and its predecessor?
5. What are the main responsibilities of the Criminal Cases Review Commission?

EXERCISE 9 The way the Criminal Cases Review Commission works

This exercise is based on the same article as in Exercise 8. This part explains how the Criminal Cases Review Commission works. Read the extract and answer the questions below.

'Broadly speaking, we allocate cases for investigation and review in date order of receipt. Our objective, however, is to have a sensible and effective means of according priority to cases which deserve accelerated treatment, taking into account a range of factors such as whether the applicant is in custody, the state of health of people significantly involved in the case, and the possibility of evidence deteriorating or being lost . . .

Occasionally it will be possible for the Commission to reach a decision based on the information given in the application form or other correspondence, but more often we will need to call for further information or carry out our own investigation.

This is where the Commission enjoys a particular status within the British criminal justice system. Unlike other bodies, our role is to take an inquisitorial approach rather than the usual adversarial stance.

To assist its investigative role, the Commission has been given wide-ranging powers to conduct investigations. Section 17 of the [Criminal Appeal Act 1995] allows the Commission access to all the material relating to a case which is held by public bodies if this is necessary for the purpose of the Commission's investigation and review . . .

If a case calls for special knowledge – for example, about forensic science, engineering, medicine, handwriting, psychology or video analysis – we can instruct an expert to look at the evidence and report on it.

When the nature of the investigation requires it, the Commission can request the appointment of an investigating officer from another body. This will usually be an investigating police officer, given that the police have resources and expertise in the field of criminal investigation and, in some circumstances, they may be able to exercise powers which they enjoy and the Commission does not, for example have the power to search premises. Although concern has been expressed in some quarters about this part of the Commission's work, our experience to date has been very encouraging . . .

The person working on the review will continue to explore the issues raised by the applicant, together with any other issues that may be identified during its progress, until confident that a decision may be made. What we are looking for is that evidence or point of law which in our judgment produces a real possibility that the Court of Appeal would not uphold a conviction or sentence should we refer the case.'

'A Necessary and Welcome Body', David Kyle, *The Legal Executive Journal*, December 1998

Questions

1. On what basis does the Commission decide to allocate cases for investigation?
2. What powers does it have to assist with its investigations?
3. What type of points will it look at?
4. Who can it ask to help with investigations and why?
5. What is the Commission seeking to establish in a case?

RESEARCH

Use the Internet to find out more about the Criminal Cases Review Commission. Their website is at www.ccrc.gov.uk.

EXERCISE 10 Evaluation of the Criminal Cases Review Commission

Read the following article and answer the questions below.

'James Hanratty was hanged 37 years ago for the notorious A6 murder. Yesterday his case – one of the longest running alleged miscarriages of justice – was referred by the Criminal Cases Review Commission back to the Court of Appeal for a second look. The referral is a victory for his solicitor, Geoffrey Bindman, who has campaigned for over 20 years for the case to be reopened. It is also a timely decision by the Commission itself as it celebrates its second birthday.

The Commission, set up after a series of miscarriages of justice had rocked the system, has always insisted that its performance can best be judged after two years. It began work on April 1, 1997. How successful has it been?

The purpose of the Commission was to take over from the Home Office the handling of alleged wrongful convictions. It has received 2,325 submissions. Of these 100 have now been given the thumbs down; and it has referred the convictions of 36 men – including another posthumous case, that of Derek Bentley – and two women to the appeal court.

Many cases have been rejected because they do not meet the appropriate criteria (generally, because they have not exhausted the appeal process). More than 1,000 are still under consideration. These figures encapsulate the story so far, a mixed one of success and continuing problems. On the one hand 38 referrals of serious criminal cases in two years compares extremely favourably with what the Home Office managed when the re-evaluation of cases was still its responsibility. On the other, there is a lengthy wait for applicants who are now told not to expect work on their cases to start for two years. . . .

Traditionally, there were three areas of concern about miscarriages of justice. Why did they first occur? Why did the Court of Appeal so often fail to rectify them? And why was the Home Office so reluctant to refer contentious cases back to appeal?

The creation of the Commission looked at just the last of these, though in practice it may also have had an impact on the second. Of the Commission-referred cases which have so far been heard at appeal, all but two have been successful, suggesting some deference on the part of the Court of Appeal to the Commission's exhaustive work. By contrast three of the last cases referred to appeal by the Home Secretary were turned down at appeal.'

'Why the wheels of justice grind so slowly', Bob Woffinden, *The Times*, 30 March 1999

Questions

1. Why was the Criminal Cases Review Commission set up?
2. How successful has it been in its first two years?
3. What main problem is there with referring a case to the Commission?
4. To what extent does the creation of the Commission deal with all the worries about miscarriages of justice?

RESEARCH

Find out the most recent figures for cases referred to the Court of Appeal by the Criminal Cases Review Commission. This should be available on its website, www.ccrc.gov.uk.

CHAPTER 11

SENTENCING

There are two main areas to know and understand in this topic. The first is the aims of sentencing: that is, why are offenders punished and what is the sentence intended to achieve. Secondly, it is important to know the different types of sentence that the courts can use when dealing with offenders.

During the past ten years or so, sentencing of offenders has been on the political agenda with the government concerned to show that they are 'tough on crime'. As a result, several Acts of Parliament have been passed. Much of the law on sentencing was brought together in the Powers of Criminal Courts (Sentencing) Act 2000, with additional sentencing powers in the Criminal Justice and Court Services Act 2000. In 2002 the Government White Paper, *Justice for All*, proposed major changes to sentencing and this is likely to be made law under the Criminal Justice Bill 2002, which was still going through the stages in the House of Commons at the time of writing this (April 2003).

This section contains exercises on the following:

- extracts from Home Office Research Study 187/98 on sentencing aims and reoffending
- guidelines on sentencing burglars
- a newspaper article on sentencing 'phone muggers'
- research on youth referral orders
- extracts from a law report in *R v Goodwin* on the approach of the courts to sentencing young offenders involved in violent crime
- changes proposed in *Justice for All* (2002)
- the use of drug testing in the criminal justice system.

EXERCISE 1 Aims of sentencing

This extract is from research into the effect of sentences. Read it and study the graph and then answer the questions which follow.

'Sentencing by courts is used to fulfil a variety of purposes simultaneously:

- deterrence;
- incapacitation;
- rehabilitation;
- fairness and equity;
- retribution; and,
- maintaining confidence in the criminal justice system.

On occasions one of these objectives will predominate. More often sentencers seek to balance different objectives. Reconviction rates over the years have told a consistent story: any apparent differences between sentences, in terms of their impact on re-offending rates, are largely the result of other factors, such as the age and criminal history of the offender. There is also increasing evidence of a link between drug usage and other forms of crime. Criminal punishment does have a deterrent effect, although it is not clear how much extra deterrence can be achieved by increasing the severity of punishment. For this to happen, potential offenders need to be aware that the risks have changed and it appears that this is often not the case.

Custody is the most expensive disposal, and is no more successful at preventing offenders obtaining further convictions than other forms of disposals. But it protects the public from the risk of further harm from the offender while the imprisonment lasts, and satisfies the public need for retribution in respect of serious offences.

Reconviction rates within two years for those released from prison between 1987 and 1995 and adjusted[1] rates for those commencing community penalties[2] during this period

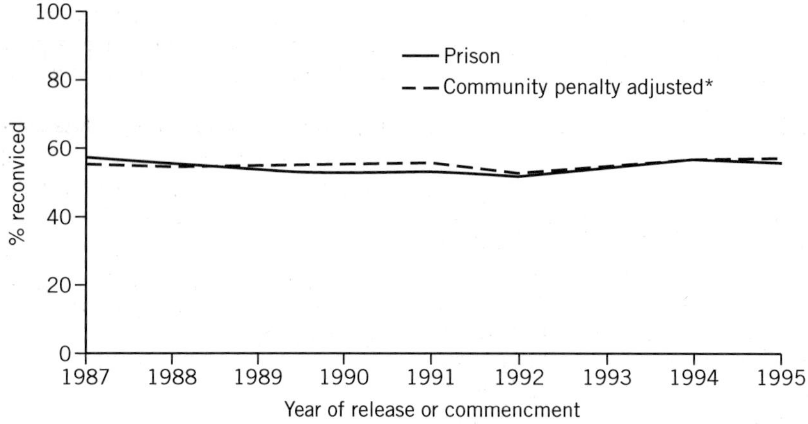

Notes:
1. Adjusted to account for differences in the characteristics of offenders and for pseudo-reconvictions.
2. Figures for community penalties include combination orders from 1993 onwards and for 1995, are based only on commencements in the first quarter of the year.

Both sources taken from *Reducing offending, an assessment of research evidence on ways of dealing with offending behaviour*, Home Office Research Study 187/98

Questions

1. Briefly explain each of the different sentencing aims in the bulleted list.
2. What does the extract identify as the aim(s) of imprisonment for offenders?
3. What is meant by 'reconviction rates'?
4. Considering both the graph and the extract, what conclusions can you reach about the effectiveness of different types of sentences in preventing offenders from re-offending?

EXERCISE 2 Guidelines on sentencing burglars

In 2002 the Court of Appeal issued guidelines on sentencing those convicted of burglary for the first time. Read this extract from the judgment in that case and do the work at the end.

Lord Woolf

'Burglary was an offence which gave rise to particular public concern. For that reason the Sentencing Advisory Panel had commissioned research into public attitudes to sentencing. The panel had also been influenced by section III of the Powers of Criminal Courts (Sentencing) Act 2000.

A degree of caution had to be exercised when using the results of a survey of members of the public. When the court framed or revised sentencing guidelines, one, but only one of the considerations it was required to have regard to was the need to promote public confidence in the criminal justice system.

Among the other requirements was the cost of different sentences and, importantly, their relative effectiveness in preventing re-offending.

There was an extremely high level of re-offending by those released from prison for offences such as domestic burglary. The Prison Service accepted that there was little it could achieve in the way of turning offenders from crime during the course of a sentence of up to 12 months.

Also the present crowded state of the prison system had resulted in extensive use of executive release for those sentenced to four years or less . . .

The court proposed that . . . the initial approach should be to impose a community sentence subject to conditions that ensured that the sentence was an effective punishment and one which offered action on the part of the Probation Service to tackle the offender's criminal behaviour and, when appropriate, would tackle the offender's underlying problems such as drug addiction.

If, and only if, the court was satisfied that the offender had demonstrated by his or her behaviour that punishment in the community was not practicable, should the court resort to a custodial sentence.'

Taken from *R v McInerney, R v Keating, The Times*, 20 December 2002

Questions

1. What is the role of the Sentencing Advisory Panel?
2. What matters does the Court of Appeal say they must take into account when issuing sentencing guidelines?
3. What is the problem in sending offenders to prison for periods of up to 12 months?
4. What is the court's recommendation for sentencing a first-time burglar?
5. The extract mentions 'section III of the Powers of Criminal Courts (Sentencing) Act 2000'. This sets out minimum sentences for those convicted of burglary for the third time. Explain what is meant by a 'minimum sentence'.
6. Discuss what aims should be the most important when a sentence is imposed for burglary.

RESEARCH

Carry out a survey on what sentences people think should be imposed for
(a) a first-time burglar and
(b) a persistent burglar.

EXERCISE 3 Sentences for phone muggers

This exercise is based on a newspaper article. Read it and do the work set below.

'Britain's most senior judge declared war on mobile phone muggers today by calling for them to face five years or more in jail.

Lord Justice Woolf said that stiffer sentences were needed to combat Britain's fastest growing street crime which is running at one million attacks a year.

He said the new sentences should apply irrespective of the youth of the robber or whether he has any previous convictions. Muggers were preying on young and vulnerable victims and persistent thieves should expect even higher sentences because the courts had no alternative to a "robust sentencing policy".

Lord Woolf said that street robberies of mobile phones were particularly worrying "because of the effect they have on the victims and the fact that they undermine the criminal justice system".'

'Law Chief orders five years in prison for fastest growing crime', Paul Cheston, *The Evening Standard*, 29 January 2002

Questions

1. How serious a crime do you think robbery of a mobile phone is?
2. Should the type of victim have an effect on the sentence given for a crime?
3. Do you agree that stiffer sentences should apply 'irrespective of the youth of the robber or whether he has any previous convictions'? Give reasons for your answer.
4. Compare the recommendations for sentences for first-time robbery of a mobile phone with the sentencing guidelines for first-time burglary in Exercise 2. Explain whether you think the two are justified.

EXERCISE 4 Referral orders for young offenders

The exercise is based on research into referral orders. Read the extract and answer the questions which follow.

'The referral order was introduced in the Youth Justice and Criminal Evidence Act 1999 as a new primary sentencing disposal for 10–17 year olds pleading guilty and convicted for the first time by the courts. Underpinning referral orders is for the panel to reach agreement with an offender on a programme of behaviour, the principal aim of which is the prevention of future re-offending. Referral orders are also intended to introduce the principles underlying restorative justice into the process. Panels, made up of volunteer representatives of the community and one

Youth Offending Team (YOT) member, agree a "contract" with the young offender. These contracts include reparation to the victim or wider community and programmes of activities designed primarily to prevent further offending.[1]

Young offenders and their parents

- The young people were generally happy with their experience of attending an initial panel meeting. The majority felt the purpose of the meeting was fully explained to them (72%) and they understood what was going on at that meeting (91%).
- Over two-thirds of young people said they had a clearer idea of how people had been affected by their offence after attending the panel meeting.
- Three quarters of young people agreed that their contract was useful . . . and an even larger number (78%) agreed that it had helped keep them out of trouble.

Contracts

- The most common compulsory element in all contracts was some from of reparative activity (40%). This was followed by offending behaviour work (9%), attending supervision/assessment sessions with a YOT officer (6%), exploring employment and career options (6%), and education (5%) and victim awareness work (5%). Education and reparation also formed the most common voluntary elements in contracts.
- The most common form of reparation was community reparation (42%), followed by written apology (38%), indirect reparation (10%), direct reparation to victim or the payment of compensation (7%) . . .
- The most common YOT activities were meetings with a YOT officer (20%), attending offending behaviour sessions (17%), anger management sessions (13%), drugs/alcohol awareness sessions (9%), victim awareness sessions (8%), and attending courses on the consequences of violent behaviour (3%).
- Young people completed the contract successfully in three-quarters of cases where a panel had met. Higher completion rates were associated with shorter orders, fewer elements in the contract and the type of offence committed.

[1] Taken from the Foreword by David Moxon.

Newburn, T., et al. (2002) *The Introduction of Referral Orders into the Youth Justice* System, Home Office Research Study 242. London: Home Office

Questions

1. Which Act introduced referral orders as a method of sentencing?
2. For what age group of offenders is the referral order available?
3. Who is present at a panel meeting?
4. What is a 'contract' in a referral order?
5. What are the most common elements in a contract?
6. Choose two of these elements and explain what activities they may contain.
7. How useful do the young people involved think their contract was?
8. Explain why a contract may prevent future offences by the young person.

EXERCISE 5 Sentencing of young offenders

Read the summary of the case facts and the extracts from the judgment by Lord Bingham in the cases of *R* v *Goodwin*; *R* v *O'B*; *R* v *H*, *The Times*, 28 December 1998 and use them for discussion.

Facts

The Court of Appeal reviewed the sentence in three separate cases of youths charged with an offence of wounding with intent to grievous bodily harm (s18 Offences Against the Person Act 1861)

Goodwin, aged 18, had become confrontational at a party and attacked a guest by throwing a beer glass which broke in the victim's face, causing severe cuts and permanent scarring. The court increased his sentence from 15 months' detention to two years' detention.

O'B, aged 17, after a fight with another teenager who had been provocative, returned to the scene with a knife and inflicted near-fatal injuries on the victim. The court quashed a combination order of 80 hours' community service and 18 months' probation and substituted a sentence of three years' detention.

H, aged 16, had challenged a schoolmate to a fist fight. After some fighting, the victim called the fight off and on turning away was stabbed in the back, suffering serious injuries and permanent scarring.

H had been made the subject of a supervision order, but the Court of Appeal quashed this and substituted a custodial sentence of two and a half years.

Judgment

LORD BINGHAM, LORD CHIEF JUSTICE

'An offence against section 18 had always been regarded as of great seriousness reflected in the maximum penalty of life imprisonment. . . . The seriousness with which section 18 offences were regarded was also evident in the fact that a section 18 offence ranked as "a serious offence" for the purposes of section 2 of the Crime (Sentences) Act 1997 with the consequence that the second conviction obliged the court, in the absence of exceptional circumstances, to impose a life sentence.

In sentencing young offenders the court would of course have regard to the welfare principle . . . the younger the offender the less the justification in treating him exactly as if he were an adult.

It had to be recognised that an effective means of protecting the public in the future was to reform a criminal whether young or old.

Sentencers had, however, always to bear in mind that the welfare of the young offender was never the only consideration. When an offender, however young, deliberately inflicted serious injury on another there was a legitimate public expectation that such an offender would be severely punished to bring home to him the gravity of the offence and to warn others of the risk of behaving in the same way.

If such punishment did not follow, public confidence in the administration of the criminal law was weakened and the temptation arose to give offenders extra-judicially the punishment which the processes of law had not given.

In speaking of the public, the victim and those close to him were not forgotten. If the punishment of the offender did little to heal the offender's wounds there could be little doubt that inadequate punishment added insult to injury.'

DISCUSS

1. Should young offenders be treated differently from adult offenders?
2. Should a crime of violence always be punished by a custodial sentence?

EXERCISE 6 Proposed changes in sentencing

In 2002 the Government proposed changes to the sentences available. Read the extract and answer the questions below.

'5.19 We will legislate to give sentencers a better framework within which to tailor sentences to the offender and the offence.

The new sentences in the framework, in summary are:

- **Customised Community Sentence** – all the sentence would be served in the community. All existing community sentences would be available together in a new sentence, allowing sentencers to fit the restrictions and rehabilitation to the offender.
- **Custody Plus** – a short prison sentence followed by a community programme. A prison sentence of up to 3 months followed by a period of compulsory supervision in the community, within an overall sentence envelope of up to 12 months.
- **Custody Minus** – a short prison sentence will be suspended [for up to 2 years] and the offender will undertake a community sentence. Breach of the community sentence will result in imprisonment.
- **Intermittent Custody** – a new approach in which a prison sentence and community sentence are served intermittently. A prison sentence would be served for example at weekends whilst the community programme is served through the week.
- **Prison sentence of 12 months and over** – half served in prison, half in the community. Automatic release will be at the half way point, with licence conditions extending until the end of the community sentence period.

...

5.21 The Government will introduce a community sentence which will replace the individual community penalties and give sentencers a menu of options which can be combined to form a single sentence These will build on existing provisions and will include:

- compulsory, unpaid work
- offending behaviour programmes
- education and training, especially basic skills
- drug testing, treatment and abstinence requirements
- intensive community supervision
- curfew or exclusion restrictions
- residence requirements
- participation in restorative justice schemes

5.22 The Government believes that existing short-term custodial sentences, where the offender is released from prison at the halfway point of sentence, often with no community support or supervision afterwards are usually ineffective. Short custodial sentences with no support or supervision after release do not allow the correctional services to do any meaningful behavioural or rehabilitation work with offenders and re-offending rates for short-term prisoners are high.'

***Justice for all*, Cm 5563**

Questions

1. Why did the Government want to replace individual community penalties? What advantages will the new system have?
2. What is the problem with short custodial sentences?
3. What is meant by 'Custody Plus'?
4. Why is Custody Plus preferable to the previous short-term custodial sentences?
5. Explain in your own words what is meant by (a) custody minus and (b) intermittent custody.
6. Comment on the aims of the new sentencing framework.

EXERCISE 7 Drug testing in the criminal justice system

It is believed that many crimes are committed because of drug addiction. This extract considers the use of drug testing at various stages in the criminal justice system. Read and answer the questions below.

'The Criminal Justice and Court Services Act 2000 gave the police the power to drug test detainees in police custody and courts the power to order drug testing of offenders under the supervision of the probation service. For the police, this involves drug testing of individuals charged with a trigger offence. For probation, drug testing of offenders is specified for those who have received one of the following:

- a court request to conduct a Pre-sentence Test
- a drug abstinence order
- a drug abstinence requirement attached to a community sentence
- drug testing as a condition of release from prison on licence.

The aims of the new initiative are to deter drug misuse and related offending whilst under criminal justice supervision and to identify offenders who should be receiving treatment and monitoring their progress. . . .

It is too early to tell whether drug testing is having an impact on sentencing and bail decisions. All three sites [in the pilot study] have experienced some difficulty in terms of:

- notification of test results to courts so that they can have a bearing on bail decisions and sentencing
- the identification by probation and courts of all individuals who meet the criteria for drug testing.

Of 106 tests taken by the probation service, 61 showed that the offender tested positive for cocaine and/or heroine.

Options to widen the coverage of the scheme which have been suggested include extending the scheme to:

- other offences such as handling, attempts and prostitution linked to drug misuse
- 16–18 year olds – the police have suggested that the deterrent effect could work well for individuals who have yet to become addicted.

Adapted from Mallander, J., Roberts, E. and Seddon, T. (2002) *Evaluation of drug testing in the criminal justice system in three pilot areas,* Home Office Findings 176. London: Home Office

Questions

1. Which Act gave powers to drug test offenders?
2. When can the probation service ask an offender to take a drug test?
3. What is the aim of drug testing offenders?
4. What problems have the pilot areas discovered?
5. Do you agree that the power should be extended to cover 16–18 year olds? Give reasons for your answer.

OVERVIEW II

A REVIEW OF CHAPTERS 6–11

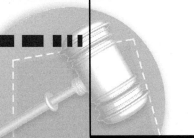

The exercises in this section combine different areas of work in Chapters 6–11. It is advisable that you work through those chapters before you tackle any work in this overview section.

EXERCISE 1 Litigation, ADR or negotiation

This extract looks at statistics on the number of claims in the civil courts and the number of cases dealt with by ADR. Read it and answer the questions below.

'The Queen's Bench Division of the High Court deals with common law business, actions relating to contract and tort. It operates through the central office of the Royal Courts of Justice in London and also through district registries. Published figures reveal a staggering drop in claims over the past 11 years. The number of writs [claims] and originating processes issued in the central office in 1990 was 125,000 and in the district registries 245,000. In 2001 those figures had reduced to 5,100 and 16,000 respectively. It is interesting to note that the biggest reduction in claims occurred before the Woolf reforms came into effect in April 1999 . . .

Has the loss of work in the Queens Bench Division been compensated for by an increase in claims in the County Courts? They have been given jurisdiction to hear larger cases, so one might reasonably expect the number of claims commenced to have grown. They have not. In 1990 there were just over 3.3 million claims issued, both for money and for the recovery of land. By 1999 that had dropped to two million and was 1,739,000 for 2001 . . .

It is clear, then, that in the past ten years there has been a significant reduction in the number of civil disputes referred to the courts.

Has mediation, with support form the judiciary, grown to take the place of formal dispute resolution? Figures from the Centre for Effective Dispute resolution suggest not. In 1999, 468 disputes were referred to it. In 2000 the figure was almost identical, but in 2001 it had reduced to 338.

Are disputes instead being arbitrated, with parties preferring the confidentiality and party control afforded by the process? Reference to the number of new matters referred to the London Court of International Arbitration shows that referrals in the past five years have numbered between 52 and 87, with the total last year running at 71.

What can one make of this? Conversations I have had with directors of companies confirm that businesses are much more cautious about embarking on formal proceedings than they used to be. There is an increased awareness of the importance of maintaining relationships with those they do business with and there is more effort put into resolving disputes on a commercial basis and less in adopting macho claims tactics for their own sake.

There is much more realisation that large disputes can be distracting to staff to the detriment of the company. Potential claimants are well aware of the issue of potential irrecoverable costs, even if they win. The emphasis now is on negotiation, often tough, but driven by a determination to reach a conclusion that is commercially acceptable.'

Taken from 'It's good to talk – rather than sue', Justin Ede, *The Times*, 26 November 2002

Questions

1. What type of cases are heard in the Queen's Bench Division?
2. What type of cases are heard in the County Court?

3. Explain what is meant by 'mediation'.
4. Explain what is meant by 'arbitration'.
5. What figures support the point that there has been a move away from using the courts?
6. Why does the article suggest that mediation and arbitration are not dealing with more cases?
7. Explain the advantages to a business of negotiating rather than using formal ADR or taking a court case.

EXERCISE 2 Problems in the criminal justice system

This extract is taken from the Government White Paper, *Justice for All* (2002). Read it and answer the questions below.

'1.1 The criminal justice system exists to fight and reduce crime and to deliver fair, efficient and effective justice on behalf of victims, defendants and the community. It must convict the guilty, acquit the innocent, and in the penalties it imposes, punish offenders and reduce offending. Better practical support for victims and witnesses is crucial and all the criminal justice system agencies – from the police to the Crown Prosecution Service, to the courts, the Prison and National Probation Services and the Youth Justice Board – need to make victims and witnesses a higher priority. The criminal justice system must retain the confidence of the public that it is effective in the fight against crime and in the delivery of justice.

1.5 Unfortunately, too many people do escape justice. This is the "justice gap", namely the gap between the number of offences recorded by the police and the number of offences where an offender is brought to justice. During 2001–02 recorded crime totalled 5.5 million. The police only successfully detected 23% of these offences, that is 1.29 million. Of these detected cases there were the following outcomes:

- Charge/summons 0.78 million
- Cautions 0.21 million
- Taken into consideration 0.11 million
- No further action 0.2 million.

1.6 In relation to those who do enter the criminal justice system:

- 12% of those bailed to appear at court fail to do so;
- nearly a quarter of defendants commit at least one offence whilst on bail – rising to 38% of offenders under 18;
- only 55% of contested case files are properly compiled: and
- the Crown Prosecution Service has to discontinue 13% of cases passed to it by the police.'

Questions

1. (a) List the various roles of the criminal justice system.
   (b) Choose one of these roles and explain why you think it is important.
2. (a) Name four agencies of the criminal justice system.
   (b) Choose one of these agencies and briefly explain its role.
3. What is meant by the 'justice gap'?
4. In detected cases, what is the most usual outcome?
5. What does it mean when an offender is cautioned?
6. Paragraph 1.6 sets out various statistics about the criminal justice system. Choose one of these and explain what problems may arise from it.

EXERCISE 3 The Youth Court

This extract explains some of the principles in dealing with young offenders. Read it and answer the questions below.

'The statutory provisions and guiding principle

The principal aim of the youth justice system is set out in section 37(1) of the Crime and Disorder Act 1998. It shall be the principal aim of the youth justice system to prevent offending by children and young persons.

Subsection 2 of section 37 imposes a statutory duty on the court to have regard to the principal aim. In addition to any other duty to which they are subject it shall be the duty of all persons and bodies carrying out functions in relation to the youth justice system to have regard to that aim.

THE DUTY TO HAVE REGARD TO WELFARE

The statutory duty in section 44 of the Children and Young Persons Act 1933 continues to apply to sentencing in the youth court: *Every court in dealing with a child or young person who is brought before it, either as an offender or otherwise shall have regard to the welfare of the child or young person, and shall in a proper case take steps for removing him from undesirable surroundings, and for securing that proper provision is made for his education and training.*

Welfare issues are likely to arise in the context of offender mitigation but they must be considered in the light of the principal aim to prevent offending. They do not imply that young people cannot help their behaviour simply because of their social circumstance. Observance of section 44 by the court should not "excuse" offending behaviour, or stop young offenders being confronted with their actions and being required to take responsibility for them.

An intervention ordered by the court with a view to preventing offending and helping a young offender become a responsible adult clearly promotes that young person's long term welfare.

THE COURT'S TASK

The court's task is, through a process of reasoning, to make an Order (or Orders) which is:

- A proportionate response to the persistence and seriousness of the offending.
- Is an intervention which in its judgement tackles the factors associated with the child or young person's offending behaviour and is most likely to prevent future offending.
- Has a proper regard to the offender's welfare.'

Taken from the *Youth Court Bench Book*, published by the Judicial Studies Board

Questions

1. What ages of offenders does the Youth Court deal with?
2. Who sits on the panel in a Youth Court?
3. What is the principal aim of the youth justice system?
4. What statutory duty is there on the Youth Court?
5. (a) Give six types of order that can be made by the Youth Court.
   (b) Choose two from your list and explain how these may fit the criteria in the bulleted list at the end of the extract.
6. What is the role of the Judicial Studies Board?

EXERCISE 4 Statistics on race and the criminal justice system

The following is a summary of some of the statistics for 2000–01. Read this and do the work below.

'686,000 stops and searches were recorded on persons by the police under a range of legislation, including the Police and Criminal Evidence Act (PACE), of which 10% were of black people, 5% Asian and 1% "other" ethnic origin. Police forces varied widely in their numbers for recorded stops and searches. Published research by the Home Office has indicated that resident population figures give a poor indication of the population observed in public places when and where police carry out searches, and therefore do not give a good basis for assessing ethnic biases in officer search practice. However, these statistics remain important in describing the overall experiences of stop and searches among ethnic minority communities with black people 7 times more likely to be stopped and searched than white people.

An estimated 1.3 million arrests for notifiable offences took place, of which, 7% were of black people, 4% Asian and 1% "other" ethnic origin. Arrests for black people, Asians and 'other' ethnic groups rose by 5%, 8% and 10% respectively last year, while the number of white people arrested fell by 2%. Black people were 4 times more likely to be arrested than white or other ethnic groups. White people showed a higher likelihood of being arrested for burglary and criminal damage, black people for robbery and both black and Asians for fraud, forgery and drugs.

The police cautioned an estimated 209,200 persons for notifiable offences of which 6% were black people, 5% Asian and 1% "other" ethnic origin. Relative to the number of people arrested, the cautioning rate was slightly higher for white people (16%) and Asians (17%) than for black people (13%). An offender's eligibility for a caution depends upon a number of factors including the circumstances of an offence and whether they admit to the offence.

Information collected from six pilot areas on magistrates' court decisions indicated that, excluding those defendants committed to the Crown Court for trial, white defendants were more likely to be convicted (64%) than black or Asian defendants (53% and 54%).'

Taken from *Statistics on Race and the Criminal Justice System,* a Home Office publication under s95 of the Criminal Justice Act 1991 London: Home Office.

Questions

1. Explain what powers the police have under PACE to stop and search.
2. Explain what powers the police have under PACE to arrest a suspect.
3. What is meant by 'cautioned' in the third paragraph?
4. The last paragraph mentions 'defendants committed to the Crown Court for trial'.
   (a) What type of offences can be tried at the Crown Court?
   (b) When a defendant pleads not guilty, who decides whether he is guilty or not?
5. Who tries cases in the Magistrates' Court?

RESEARCH

Research the most recent statistics on the use of 'stop and search' powers. Try the Home Office website www.homeoffice.gov.uk.

EXERCISE 5 Women and the criminal justice system

This extract gives information about offending by women. Read it and answer the questions below.

'Arrests and police disposals

- 16% of those arrested for notifiable offences are women but the proportion is higher for fraud and forgery (27%) and theft and handling (22%)
- Research suggests that following arrest, women are more likely than men to be cautioned and are less likely to have their cases classified as "No Further Action" or be charged. This partly reflects the fact that women are more likely than men to admit their offences and to be arrested for less serious offences
- According to statistics, female offenders are more likely than men to be cautioned for indictable offences.

Sentencing

- Women are more likely than men to be discharged or given a community sentence for indictable offences and are less likely to be fined or sentenced to custody
- Women sentenced to custody receive shorter sentences on average than men.

The top eight offences for women sentenced to custody in 2001 were:

- theft from shops (2,400 women sentenced to custody)
- fraud (490)
- wounding (460)
- production, supply and possession with intent to supply a class A controlled drug (450)
- summary motoring (430)
- burglary of all kinds (330)
- handling stolen goods (320)
- robbery (320).

Recent figures suggest that the rise in sentenced prison receptions for women is driven by a *more severe* response to *less severe* offences.

The *rate of increase* of women being given a custodial sentence at Magistrates' Courts is higher than at the Crown Court.'

Taken from Home Office (2002) *Statistics on Women and the Criminal Justice System*, a Home Office publication under s95 of the Criminal Justice Act 1999, London: Home Office

Questions

1. What are the two most common crimes for women to commit?
2. Why are women more likely than men to be cautioned'?
3. What is an indictable offence?
4. For indictable offences, what differences in sentencing are there between men and women?
5. Look at the list of offences for which women were most likely to be sentenced to custody. With reference to the aims of sentencing, explain whether you think that these are offences for which there should be a custodial sentence.
6. Explain what type of offences are tried in:
   (a) the Magistrates' Court
   (b) the Crown Court.
7. Why might the last two points in the extract be considered to be surprising trends?

CHAPTER 12

THE LEGAL PROFESSION

There are two types of legal professional in England and Wales. These are solicitors and barristers. Their training and roles are different. The legal profession as a whole has been the subject of criticism and there have been changes made, especially under the Courts and Legal Services Act 1990 and the Access to Justice Act 1999. There are also likely to be on-going changes. Areas for discussion include whether barristers should continue to have the main rights to take cases in court (this is referred to as the right of audience), the problems faced by women in the profession and the problems over complaints about the professions and how these are handled.

The exercises in this section are based on:

- the training of solicitors
- the role of solicitors
- problems of training to be a barrister
- Queen's Counsel
- women in the legal profession
- complaints about lawyers.

EXERCISE 1 Solicitors' training

This extract is taken from a publication by the Law Society. Read it and answer the questions below.

The 3 main routes to qualification as a solicitor

The Law Society prescribes the legal education and training required to qualify as a solicitor in England and Wales. All students must complete both the academic and vocational stages of the training . . .

The academic stage of training is obtained by either:

1. The Law Degree Route or
2. The Non-Law Degree Route or
3. The Non-Graduate Route

The vocational stage of training is obtained by:

1. Completing the Legal Practice Course, and
2. Serving a Training Contract (equivalent to 2 years full-time) if following Routes 1 and 2 above, and
3. Completing a Professional Skills Course

The profession is very competitive and entry is not guaranteed to those with law degrees, CPE or LCP. Economic circumstances alone can mean that training places within the profession are subject to market forces which can fluctuate.

Taken from *The Student's Guide to Qualification as a Solicitor*, The Law Society, 2002

Questions

1. What is the role of the Law Society in legal training and education?
2. What are the other main roles of the Law Society?
3. What is meant by the 'Non-Law Degree Route'? On this route, as well as a degree, what other qualification must a would-be solicitor obtain?
4. Briefly describe the Non-Graduate Route.
5. What is the Legal Practice Course?
6. What is meant by a 'training contract'?
7. What difficulties may face those who have completed all their qualifications?

EXERCISE 2 The role of solicitors

The following information is taken from a careers brochure produced by the Law Society. Read it and answer the questions below.

The role of solicitors

The role of today's solicitor can be very varied and challenging. Solicitors have direct contact with their clients, providing specialist legal advice and assistance and may represent them in the lower courts. Solicitors do not normally represent clients in the higher courts, however with additional training they can acquire the right to do so. In the highest courts cases are prepared by solicitors, but advocacy is undertaken by barristers.

There are over 80,000 solicitors practising in England and Wales and their work varies enormously. A solicitor's job is to provide clients (members of the public, businesses, voluntary bodies, charities etc.) with skilled legal advice and representation, including representing them in court. Most solicitors work in private practice, which is a partnership of solicitors who offer services to clients. Others work as employed solicitors for Central and Local Government, the Crown Prosecution Service, the Magistrates' Court Service, a commercial or industrial organisation or other bodies. If you become a solicitor, you can choose the kind of environment which suits you best.

Key facts about the solicitors' profession

- As at 31 July 2000, 72,769 solicitors held practising certificates, an increase of 4.1% on the previous year.
- 66,445 (80.3%) of solicitors holding practising certificates work in private practice; the remainder work mainly in commerce and industry and the public sector.
- Women now account for 36.6% of solicitors with practising certificates. Whereas since 1990 the total number of solicitors holding practising certificates has grown by 51.2%, the number of women holding practising certificates more than doubled, having increased by 136.7%.
- In the year ending 31 July 2000, 7,793 students enrolled with the Law Society. Of these students 60.3% were women and 22.0% were drawn from the ethnic minorities.
- There were 5,285 new traineeships registered in the year 1 August 1999 to 31 July 2000. This is an increase of 9.5% on the level recorded last year.
- Of new trainees registered, 56.9% were women and 15.8% of trainees with known ethnicity were drawn from the ethnic minorities.
- As at 31 July 2000, 1075 solicitors had gained rights of audience in the higher courts.

Taken from *Becoming a solicitor*, The Law Society

Questions

1. Briefly describe the role of a solicitor in private practice.
2. What is meant by 'advocacy'?
3. The extract states that solicitors may represent clients in lower courts. Which courts are these?
4. Which Act first allowed solicitors to apply for the right to represent clients in the higher courts?
5. Apart from working in private practice, where may a solicitor work?
6. What percentage of solicitors holding practising certificates work in private practice?
7. What do the statistics show about the number of women in the profession?

EXERCISE 3 Problems for would-be barristers

This extract comes form an article by a former metropolitan magistrate, who was asked by two students on the Bar Vocational Course to make their views on the problems for Bar students known. Read it and answer the questions below.

'It was regarding the financial aspect that two students, a man and a woman, approached me. They knew that I wrote for *New Law Journal* and wanted their views to be made known there ... So I told them to write out what they had to say and to give it to me. They did so in headings ...

They headed their thoughts: "Notes for the *NLJ*. The Bar A Realistic Outlook": When you join an Inn of Court you have a 30 per cent chance of becoming a barrister. 1,300–1,400 people will graduate on the Bar Vocational Course in 1999. Of these 750–800 will be successful in obtaining pupillages in 1999/2000.

For all of these there will be just 350 tenancies available.

Commencing with the BVC is equivalent to taking out a mortgage! The fees for the BVC are £6,300 for provincial providers and in the region of £7,000 for London-based providers. On average, students who look to banks for funding will, if lucky enough to get the loan, end up £20,000 in debt. The debt will hang over their heads until the year 2010–2012. For CPE students the cost of the CPE fees will also be incurred. The figures will also be much higher for those students who already have student loans and will obviously escalate due to the standard contribution of £1,000 to their tuition fees.

The debt does not end here. Many pupillages are unfunded and those which are funded are funded by way of a grant/loan. Thus earning during the pupillage period is obtained and does not cover living expenses suitably. Never mind meeting loan repayments which may average £170 per month.

The greatest danger lies in restriction of the profession. It will be restricted to those who can afford it – an elitist Bar. Already it is an oversubscribed cause with opportunities becoming few and far between. However, curtailing the number of applicants may not be the answer.'

Taken from 'The Future of the Bar', Eric Crowther, *New Law Journal*, 29 January 1999

Questions

1. What is the Bar Vocational Course?
2. What is meant by 'pupillage'?
3. In the context of this article, what is meant by 'tenancies'?
4. Why are would-be barristers likely to have debts?
5. Why is important that the profession should not be elitist?

RESEARCH

The article states that 'many pupillages are unfunded'. There are proposals that this will change in 2003. Find out:
(a) are pupillages now funded?
(b) is there a minimum annual amount paid? If so, what is the amount?

EXERCISE 4 Queen's Counsel

This extract is about the appointment of Queen's Counsel. Read it and do the work below.

'4.1 Queen's Counsel (sometimes known as "Silks") are appointed by the Queen on the recommendation of the Lord Chancellor. The rank of Queen's Counsel is essentially a mark of distinction as an advocate . . .

4.5 The Lord Chancellor only recommends for appointment as Queen's Counsel those practitioners, regardless of gender, ethnic origin, sexual orientation, marital status, political affiliation, religion, disability or professional background, who display the following attributes to a degree which marks them out as leaders of the profession, that is to a standard comparable to those appointed Queen's Counsel in the same or analogous type of practice.

Advocacy

Outstanding ability as an advocate, to a standard to be expected of Queen's Counsel in the applicant's field of practice.

Legal ability and practice

(a) sound intellectual ability and a thorough, comprehensive and up to date knowledge of law and procedures in the applicant's field of practice;
(b) a large and high quality practice based on demanding cases.

Professional qualities

(a) history of honesty, discretion and plain-dealing with professional colleagues, lay and professional clients and the courts; independence of mind and moral courage; and the trust and confidence of others;
(b) professional standing, having the respect of the Bench and of the profession in observing the advocate's duty to the court and to the administration of justice, while presenting their client's case; and being formidable, fair and honourable as an opponent;
(c) maturity of judgement and balance.'

Taken from *Judicial Appointments Annual Report 2001–02*, Lord Chancellor's Department

Questions

1. Who is eligible to become a Queen's Counsel?

2. How are Queen's Counsel appointed?
3. What is meant by 'advocacy'?
4. Briefly, in your own words, describe the qualities that a Queen's Counsel should have.
5. Which of these qualities do you think is the most important? Give reasons for your answer.

R RESEARCH

Find out more about Queen's Counsel. Try www.lcd.gov.uk.

EXERCISE 5 Statistics on women in the legal profession

This exercise and the next one are based on extracts from the same article on women in the legal profession. Read this part and answer the questions below; the answers can all be found in the extract.

'Not only are more women graduating with law degrees than men, but they also attain more firsts and upper seconds than their male counterparts. Women accounted for 51 per cent of those admitted to the roll of solicitors in 1997–98 and 46 per cent of those called to the Bar in 1998. The number of women entering the legal profession has been increasing significantly since the late 1970s.

However, such entry figures are in stark contrast to the numbers of women remaining in the profession over time and reaching high office. As of July 31, 1998, only 33.9 per cent of those on the solicitors' roll with practising certificates were women. Further, only 25 per cent of women solicitors in private practice were partners – the majority remaining at the level of assistant solicitor . . .

The situation is no better for women barristers. Men accounted for 75 per cent of barristers in independent practice in England and Wales and a staggering 93 per cent of Queen's Counsel, as on October 1, 1998. Yet, the number of women called to the Bar has been rising steadily since 1970 and during the last decade, women have, on average, made up more than 40 per cent of new entrants.

It doesn't take a statistician to work out that something must be happening to produce such a drastic disparity in the figures between women's entry into and subsequent progression within the legal profession. A brief delve into the past will help to set the scene and take us to the root of the problem.

"It may seem extraordinary," says Dr Eamonn Hail, but for most of mankind's history women were barred from entry to the legal profession. It was not until the enactment of the Sex Disqualification (Removal) Act 1919 that women could become members of the legal profession. It is indeed a startling fact which takes some time to digest.

1922 was a turning point in English legal history. It saw both the admission of the first woman solicitor and the calling to the Bar of Ivy Williams, the first woman barrister . . .

As late as 1913, the Court of Appeal in *Bebb v Law Society* held that women were not persons within the meaning of the Solicitors Act.

Given this background of historical prejudice against women entering the law, it is perhaps not surprising that all is not as it should be regarding women and the law today. Even after it was deemed illegal to prevent women from entering the legal profession, numbers actually rose very slowly until comparatively recently. Between 1923 and 1968 the number of female solicitors only increased marginally from two to nine per cent. The 70s saw the first significant rise in women entrants, reaching 26 per cent by 1978. Growth in the number of women barristers was even slower; they made up only eight per cent of those called to the Bar until 1970. And it wasn't until 1982 that they broke through the 30 per cent barrier for the first time.'

Taken from 'Equal in the Law? The case of the female lawyer', David Fisher, *New Law Journal*, 14 May 1999

Questions

1. Which Act allowed women to become lawyers?
2. Which year was the first woman admitted as a solicitor and the first woman called to the Bar?
3. What percentage of entrants to the solicitors profession were women in the following years?
   1923
   1968
   1978
   1997–98

4. In 1998, what percentage of practising solicitors were women?
5. In 1998, what percentage of partners in solicitors' firms were women?
6. What percentage of entrants to the Bar were women in the following years?
   1970
   1982
   1998
7. In 1998, what percentage of practising barristers were women?
8. In 1998, what percentage of Queen's Counsel were women?

RESEARCH

Find out the current figures for the percentage of:
(a) practising solicitors who are women
(b) practising barristers who are women
(c) Queen's Counsel who are women.

EXERCISE 6

Women in the legal profession – a glass ceiling?

This extract is a continuation of the article in the previous exercise. You will need to have background knowledge of the legal profession to answer the questions below.

'The law has spent most of its professional history in a male-dominated vacuum which has led to the creation of a culture that appears quite inimical to any other gender. So, what is happening to those women who now have membership of this, hitherto, men-only club?

Let us take a look first at salaries – are male and female lawyers equally well remunerated? On average female trainees were offered starting salaries which were 4.4 per cent below the average for males. The maximum differential observed between male and female trainees was 11.3 per cent in the Northern region. These figures are from the Law Society's own *Annual Statistical Survey* for 1998. This financial inequality is particularly worrying for two reasons: it is happening at the start of women's legal careers and, as we have seen, women are graduating with better law degrees than men.

The situation does not improve as women progress within the profession. Jessica Smerin has noted that Law Society research "revealed the median difference between male and female salaried partners' pay was £5,000, this rose to £15,000 for equity partners". Carole Willis of the Law Society, puts the case pretty plainly: "It is clear that whatever level women are at in the profession pay is not equal, allowing for experience."

We have seen that only a minority of women make it through to senior levels within the legal profession, so it would appear that career progression is as unequal as pay . . . [*See extract used in previous exercise*]

The glass ceiling seems to be still firmly in place, but its existence is viewed differently depending on whether you are male or female. A recent survey of 209 lawyers asked if there was a glass ceiling curtailing the promotion prospects of female lawyers, and the results were telling: 75 per cent of women lawyers believed there was a glass ceiling, but only 24 per cent of their male counterparts agreed with them. It is this very inability to see there is a problem on the part of some men – perhaps epitomised by a past president of the Law Society who is quoted as saying: ". . . it is a nonsense and a fiction to assert that there is any kind of prejudice against women" – which helps to sustain the unsatisfactory status quo.

Discrimination is a sad fact of life for many lawyers. A 1992 report *Without Prejudice*, commissioned by the Bar Council and the Lord Chancellor's Department, discovered that many women barristers believe work is unfairly distributed, with 38 per cent citing their clerk as the key source of discrimination. This fact is all the more disturbing when you consider that barrister, Ann Curnow has talked of her experience of this form of discrimination from "the older generation of barristers' clerks . . . the conduit through which work from solicitors is placed with individual barristers", when she was starting out in the profession in 1957. A 1997 survey commissioned by a legal recruitment consultancy, found evidence of sexual discrimination within many law firms, ranging from sexual harassment to unfair dismissal . . .

A lack of flexible working arrangements and adequate maternity leave policies within law firms, was highlighted by a 1989 survey of 275 solicitors in Liverpool and Manchester and a second survey of women solicitors in the region . . .

Several key issues are emerging from the above discussion. The legal profession, despite the influx of women over recent years, retains significant vestiges of its male-oriented past. In many instances female lawyers are paid less than men, have their progress through the ranks effectively blocked, and find themselves charged by society with the major responsibility for childcare without adequate organisational arrangements, such as flexible working, to enable them to carry on with their careers. It would seem logical to conclude, given the evidence, that many women are leaving the legal profession not through choice, but because of a lack of it.'

Taken from 'Equal in the Law? the case of the female lawyer', David Fisher, *New Law Journal*, 14 May 1999

Questions

1. What is the Law Society?
2. What evidence is there of discrimination against women in the levels of pay for solicitors?
3. Why does the article state that 'career progression is as unequal as pay'?
4. What is the Bar Council?
5. What key source of discrimination is identified as affecting women barristers?
6. What other factors are identified in the article as preventing women from being successful in the legal profession?

EXERCISE 7 Legal Services Ombudsman

Complaints about solicitors and barristers are dealt with by the complaints procedure set up by their professional bodies. Where a complainant is not satisfied with the way the complaint is handled, they may refer the matter to the Legal Services Ombudsman. Read the information in the following two sources and answer the questions below.

Source 1

Courts and Legal Services Act 1990

'21 (1) The Lord Chancellor shall appoint a person for the purpose of conducting investigations under this Act.

21 (2) The person appointed shall be known as "the Legal Services Ombudsman".

...

22 (1) Subject to the provisions of this Act, the Legal Services Ombudsman may investigate any complaint which is properly made to him and which relates to the manner in which a complaint made to a professional body with respect to–

(a) a person who is or was an authorised advocate, authorised litigator, licensed conveyancer ... or
(b) any employee of such a person,

has been dealt with by that professional body.'

Source 2

'The process available to consumers of legal services who wish to complain is an extended one ... A third of enquirers to the Office of the Legal Services Ombudsman (OLSO) reported that their cases had already been running for a year or more. All complainants have gone through earlier stages before the OLSO. Some may even have gone through four stages: solicitor, complaint partner in firm, Office for the Supervision of Solicitors (OSS) first instance decision, OSS decision on appeal ...

[Complainants] were asked to identify all the problems they had and then nominate their single main problem. The latter are set out in Figure 1. It was apparent from comments given, that many complainants were confused about the remit of the OLSO, expecting the Ombudsman to reopen the original case, rather than to review how the professional body had handled the complaint.'

Figure 1 Single main problem with lawyer and professional body[1]

	% of complainants
Did not agree with professional body's decision (wanted Ombudsman to overturn it)	20
Wrong/inadequate advice from lawyer	16
Lawyer disregarded my instructions	15
"Something else" to do with professional body	11
Breach of professional rules by lawyer	11
Documents lost/withheld	7
Delay	5
Other problem with lawyer	10
Other problem with professional body	5

[1]Professional body refers to the Office for the Supervision of Solicitors, The General Council of the Bar and the Council of Licensed Conveyancers

Taken from *Satisfaction in a super-escalated complaint environment*, A Report by the Customer Management Consultancy Ltd to the Office of the Legal Services Ombudsman

Questions

1. Who appoints the Legal Services Ombudsman?
2. Explain what a complaint has to relate to for the Legal Services Ombudsman to have authority to investigate it.
3. What are the three main reasons people complain to the Legal Services Ombudsman?
4. What difficulty does Source 2 identify about the process available to consumers?
5. What does Source 2 say that many complainants were confused over and expected the Ombudsman to do?

RESEARCH

Find out more about:

1. The Office for the Supervision of Solicitors (try www.lawsociety.org.uk)
2. The General Council of the Bar (try www.barcouncil.org.uk).

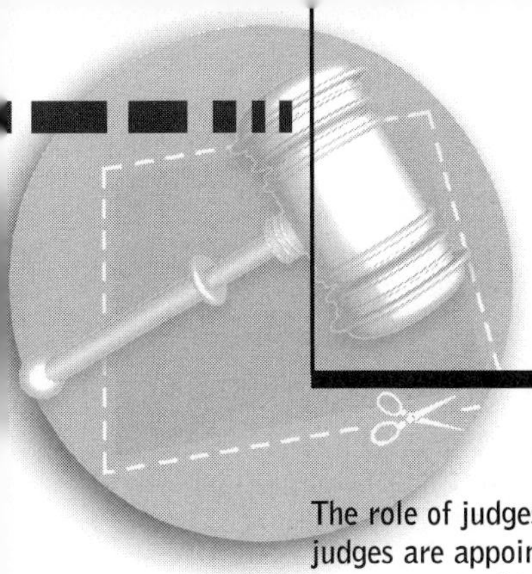

CHAPTER 13

THE JUDICIARY

The role of judges has become increasingly important; yet there are many criticisms about the way judges are appointed and trained. The independence of the judiciary is regarded as a safeguard of democracy and individual rights; yet the Lord Chancellor's role is a clear breach of the doctrine of the separation of powers.

All these points are dealt with in the sources in this section. There are exercises on:

- appointment of judges
- training of judges
- the background of judges
- the role of judges
- the independence of the judiciary
- women and ethnic minorities in the judiciary
- the role of the Lord Chancellor.

EXERCISE 1 Advertising for judges

The words below were used in the first advertisement for appointment of High Court judges (24 February 1998) Look at them and then answer the questions below.

'APPOINTMENTS TO THE OFFICE OF HIGH COURT JUDGE

The Lord Chancellor invites applications from suitably qualified practitioners and from serving Circuit Judges in England and Wales who wish to be considered for appointment to the office of High Court Judge to fill vacancies which may have arisen after 1 October 1998.

Circuit judges must have served in that office for at least two years as at 1 October 1998. *Other applicants* must have a 10 year High Court qualification (right of audience in all proceedings in the High Court) on the same date.

All eligible persons who make an application will be considered by the Lord Chancellor. It is not essential to make an application in this way and the Lord Chancellor reserves the right to recommend other candidates to the Queen for appointment. He will recommend those who appear to him to be the best qualified for appointment to this office regardless of ethnic origin, gender, marital status, sexual orientation, political affiliation, religion or (subject to the physical requirements of the office) disability.'

Questions

1. What qualifications are needed to become a High Court judge?
2. Is the advert for a specific post?
3. Is it possible to be appointed as a High Court judge without replying to an advert?
4. The main criticism of the previous system of appointment is that it was too secretive. Discuss whether this type of advert is likely to:
   (a) make the system more open
   (b) lead to a broader cross-section of people in the judiciary.

EXERCISE 2 Appointment of judges

Read this extract on the appointment of judges and answer the questions below.

'The first annual report of the new Commission for Judicial Appointments will make very uncomfortable reading for the Lord Chancellor. When the Commission, headed by Sir Colin Campbell, was set up by Lord Irvine last year, there was wide spread disappointment that Lord Irvine had not handed over his power to choose judges to a full appointing commission. Instead, the Commission was given two roles, one to hear complaints from unsuccessful candidates who believe that their application for Silk or judicial office has not been dealt with fairly and the other to scrutinise the system and make recommendations for change.

The report summarises the findings of six complaints on which the Commission has completed investigations within the period of the report. Three of these were upheld in full, one in part and two dismissed. From these investigations, and from the evidence it has heard from a range of interested parties, the Commission identified a number of areas of concern in the Silk and judicial appointments processes, including a lack of understanding of the system; a lack of a clear audit trial and undue delays.

The report recognises the importance of the consultation process which lies at the heart of the Silk and judicial appointments system. ... While it notes the potential value of the information obtained by consultation, the Commission expressed concern about the quality of the responses.

The Lord Chancellor's Department argues that this huge consultation exercise produces a vast amount of invaluable information about candidates. And indeed it does, for those who are known to the judges. But the majority of lawyers are unlikely to be able to name a single senior judge who knows their work and abilities. Senior judges come from a very small world. Almost all are former barristers from a limited number of elite chambers, The candidates they know best, and can speak for, are inevitably those from the same world with whom they have socialised before coming to the Bench.'

Adapted from 'Another nail in the coffin?', Dr Kate Malleson, *New Law Journal*, 18 October 2002

Questions

1. What are the two roles of the Commission for Judicial Appointments?
2. Who is the head of the Commission?
3. How many complaints had the Commission investigated?
4. What problems has the Commission identified with the judicial appointments system?
5. What problems with the consultation process does the article identify?

EXERCISE 3 Women and ethnic minorities in the judiciary

This extract comes from the same article as in Exercise 2. Read it and answer the questions which follow.

'It is not surprising that the people who are appointed to the Bench come from strikingly similar backgrounds to the judges who are consulted. The effects of the self-replication in terms of ethnicity and gender are well known. Women and minority lawyers are more likely to be found amongst those groups of lawyers outside the elite chambers. It is not surprising therefore that women still make up just under 14 per cent and minority lawyers two per cent of judges and eight per cent and three per cent of Silk respectively. The figures in relation to Silk are particularly important since this, in practice, remains the pool from which the senior judiciary is recruited, despite the fact that advocacy is not a selection criterion for judicial office. This lack of diversity is particularly marked at the top end of the judiciary. Since 1997 when Lord Irvine became Lord Chancellor, no minority lawyer has been appointed above the Circuit Bench, only three women have been appointed to the High Court and two to the Court of Appeal. We are still waiting for the first woman to be appointed to the Law Lords.

...

The Lord Chancellor's Department has approached the reluctance of lawyers from non-traditional backgrounds to apply as simply a perception problem. The solution according to Lord Irvine, is to increase confidence amongst those groups, hence his slogan "Don't be shy – apply".

This approach ignores the steady accumulating evidence about the difficulties which women, minority lawyers and others who are under-represented on the Bench experience in obtaining pupillage and training contracts in the elite firms and chambers, being promoted to partner and Silk and participating equally in the work and social networks which are still so crucial to success in the legal profession.'

Adapted from 'Another nail in the coffin?', Dr Kate Malleson, *New Law Journal*, 18 October 2002

Questions

1. What percentage of the judiciary are women?
2. What percentage of the judiciary are ethnic minority lawyers?
3. How many women have been appointed to high judicial office since 1997?
4. How many ethnic minority lawyers have been appointed to high judicial office since 1997?
5. What reasons are there for the small number of women and minority judges?
6. Discuss whether it is important for the judiciary to have more women and ethnic minorities.

RESEARCH

Look at the website for the Lord Chancellor's Department (www.lcd.gov.uk) and find the current figures on the number of women and ethnic minorities in the judiciary.

EXERCISE 4 Appointment of judges in Canada

This next article looks at how Canada appoints judges. Read it and do the work below.

'Most debates on reform of the current system have focused on the United States, where federal judges have to be approved by the Senate. It may, however, be more appropriate to look to Canada rather than the US for an example to adopt. The Canadian political system is almost identical to that of Britain, even having an unelected second chamber of Parliament. The courts system is similar, too. At the head is the Supreme Court of Canada, and each province has a Court of Appeal, a High Court (often called the Queen's Bench) and a Provincial Trials court, with both civil and criminal jurisdiction. At both levels, the Attorney-General is the Minister of Justice and combines functions which in England are spread among the Home Secretary, Attorney-General and Lord Chancellor.

In 1982 Canada incorporated into its Constitution a Charter of Rights and Fundamental Freedoms which copies the European Convention requirement for "an independent and impartial tribunal" . . .

Judges are appointed by the federal or provincial Attorney-General but only after they have been recommended for appointment by a Judicial Appointments Committee. There are a number of such committees across the country, comprising representatives of the legal profession, the judiciary and lay members. The criteria that committees follow allow them to consider not merely experience as an advocate but also "non-mainstream legal experience" and "politeness and tact".

After interview and assessment, candidates are graded as "recommended", "highly recommended" and "not recommended". Having been presented with the committee's recommendations, the minister is able to choose from it or may ask the committee to rethink things. There are no quotas for appointment of women or minorities to the judiciary, but 41 per cent of judges appointed in Ontario between 1989 and 1992 were women.'

Taken from 'How Canada can help choose judges' by Neil Addison, *The Times*, 30 March 1999

Questions

1. The article sets out the court system in Canada. What is the court system in England and Wales?
2. Explain how judges are chosen in Canada.
3. Explain how judges are chosen in England and Wales.
4. What is noticeable about women in the judiciary in Canada? Compare this to women in the judiciary in our system.

RESEARCH

The article mentions the Home Secretary and the Attorney-General. Find out more about the role of:

(1) the Home Secretary
(2) the Attorney-General.

EXERCISE 5 Training judges

The following information was taken from the website for the Judicial Studies Board (Lord Chancellor's Department). Read it and do the work below.

'The Judicial Studies Board (JSB) was set up in 1979, following the Bridge report which identified the most important objective of judicial training as being:

> *"To convey in a condensed form the lessons which experienced judges have acquired from their experience . . . ".*

This remains the essence of the JSB's role.

The JSB has five objectives:

Objective 1: To provide high quality training to full and part-time judges in the exercise of their jurisdiction in Civil, Criminal and Family Law.

Objective 2: To advise the Lord Chancellor on the policy for and content of training for lay magistrates, and on the efficiency and effectiveness with which Magistrates' Courts Committees deliver their training.

Objective 3: To advise the Lord Chancellor and Government Departments on the appropriate standards for, and content of, training for judicial officers in Tribunals.

Objective 4 To advise the Government on the training requirements of judges, magistrates, and judicial officers in Tribunals if proposed changes to the law, procedure and court organisation are to be effective, and to provide, and advise on the content of such training.

Objective 5 To promote closer international co-operation over judicial training.'

Questions

1. When was the Judicial Studies Board (JSB) set up?
2. Explain, in your own words, what that report saw as the most important objective of judicial training.
3. Where do the members of the JSB mainly come from?
4. Which Government department is responsible for the JSB?
5. Why is it important that the JSB is given a large degree of independence from that Government department?
6. The aims of the JSB mention 'full-time judges'. List as many types of full-time judge as you can.
7. Apart from judges in the main courts, what other areas of training does the JSB advise on?

RESEARCH

Use the Internet to go to the Judicial Studies Board's website on www.jsboard.co.uk and see what other information you can discover about the Board.

EXERCISE 6 The role of judges

This extract outlines the role of judges. Read it and answer the questions below.

'Judges are employed to decide disputes. Sometimes these disputes are between private individuals when neighbours disagree or one person is injured by another in an accident. Sometimes these disputes may be between large private organisations when companies argue about the terms of a commercial contract. But public bodies – government departments, local authorities, and others – are also legal persons and also become involved in disputes which lead to judicial activity. Most importantly, the courts may entertain applications for judicial review of administrative action.

Such disputes are dealt with by the civil law and in the civil courts. The judgment given will say where the rights and wrongs lie and the court may award damages to one party or even order a party to take certain positive steps or to refrain from certain criminal action.

In criminal law, the dispute is with the State. Over the years laws have been made and amended declaring certain kinds of action to be criminal and punishable with imprisonment or fine. This has been done because it is believed that the State has an interest in seeking to prevent those actions and to punish those who so act. So we have crimes called murder, manslaughter, rape, conspiracy, theft, fraud, assault and hundreds of others, some of them quite trivial. They are dealt with in the criminal courts.

If the judicial function were wholly automatic, not only would the making of decisions in the courts be of little interest but it would not be necessary to recruit highly trained and intellectually able men and women to serve as judges and to pay them handsome salaries.

It is the creative function of judges that makes their job important and makes worthwhile some assessment of the way they behave, especially in political cases. It must be remembered that in most cases for most of the time the function of the judge (with the help of the jury if there is one) is to ascertain the facts. But when questions of law do arise, their determination may be of the greatest importance because of the effect it will have on subsequent cases.'

Taken from *The Politics of the Judiciary* by JAG Griffith, 5th edition, Fontana Press (1997)

Questions

1. What does the extract say judges are employed to do?
2. Describe some of the civil cases that judges hear.
3. Describe some of the criminal cases that judges hear.
4. Who may help a judge decide the facts of a case? Give examples of cases in which this will occur.
5. In what way can a judge's function be described as 'creative'?
6. Why is a decision about a question of law important?

EXERCISE 7 Disciplining judges

This extract proposes reform of the way in which judges are disciplined. Read it and answer the questions below.

'[In Canada] judicial councils have been established at both federal and provincial level. These consist of the Chief Justice and other senior judges acting as a corporate body. Where a complaint is made against a judge, it may be referred to the appropriate judicial council for it to be investigated. The council may suspend the judge while the complaint is being investigated and may issue a reprimand or recommend dismissal. The accused judge is entitled to a proper hearing before any recommendation is made for his removal. Judicial councils lay down general guidelines on acceptable judicial behaviour.

Britain should establish a judicial council based on the Canadian model. Consisting of the Lord Chief Justice, Master of the Rolls, two circuit judges, two lay magistrates and three others appointed by the Lord Chancellor, it could take over the Lord Chancellor's disciplinary functions. The council would also be responsible for providing guidance to judges on such issues as conflict of interest.'

From 'How Canada can help choose judges' by Neil Addison, *The Times*, 30 March 1999

Questions

1. Explain the role of judicial councils in Canada.
2. What does the article suggest by way of change to the system in the English legal system?
3. The article mentions the following:
   (a) the Lord Chief Justice
   (b) the Master of the Rolls
   (c) circuit judges
   (d) lay magistrates.

   For each of them, explain which courts they sit in and their role.

EXERCISE 8 Judicial independence

The doctrine of the separation of powers states that judges should not be involved politically. This extract outlines some of the involvement of the Law Lords in political debate. Read it and answer the questions below.

'The source and strength of the convention that serving Law Lords do not become involved in political issues is obscure; and it is difficult to draw a clear line between what are and are not political issues, where law and politics intersect.

Recent practice includes well-known examples where serving Law Lords became involved in politically contentious issues in the context of measures affecting the administration of justice, penal policy and civil liberties . . . Lord Taylor of Gosforth, as Lord Chief Justice, supported a politically controversial Government measure which encroached upon the right of the accused to remain silent. On the other hand, he opposed the introduction of mandatory custodial sentences. Lord Browne-Wilkinson was strongly critical of a Government measure empowering the police to carry out electronic surveillance without a warrant . . . The present Master of the Rolls, Lord Woolf, opposed the provision in the *Criminal Justice Bill 1997* for mandatory sentences. The present Lord Chief Justice, Lord Bingham, supported the *Access to Justice Bill 1998*, but opposed the provisions in the *Youth Justice and Criminal Evidence Bill 1998* abolishing the right of someone accused of rape personally to cross-examine his alleged victim, and limiting the admissibility of evidence of the alleged victim's sexual history . . .

The merits of these politically controversial issues are irrelevant. What matters is that serving Law Lords have become involved as legislators in debating such matters, some of which have become, and may in the future become, matters to be decided by the senior judges in their judicial capacity.'

Questions

1. What three arms of State were identified by Montesquieu in the doctrine of the separation of powers?
2. In which two of these arms of State does the extract show that the judges in the House of Lords are involved?
3. Give one example of a judge supporting a Government Bill and one example of a judge opposing a Government Bill.
4. What does the article say matters about the fact that judges take part in political debates?
5. How important is it that judges should be independent?

R *RESEARCH*

Three different Bills are mentioned in the extract.

1. Select one of them and discover when it became an Act of Parliament.
2. Use the Internet to look at that Act of Parliament www.hmso.gov.uk/acts.htm

EXERCISE 9 The Lord Chancellor

The following extract shows just how wide ranging the Lord Chancellor's role is. Read the extract and answer the questions below.

'As regards the Lord Chancellor 's present judicial functions, he is the head of the judiciary of England and Wales, but not of the Scottish judiciary, nor of the Northern Ireland judiciary. He is president of the Supreme Court of England and Wales, and ex officio judge of the Court of Appeal, and President of the Chancery Division. He is entitled to sit judicially in the House of Lords and in the Judicial Committee of the Privy Council. When he sits, he takes the chair as the presiding judge. The Lord Chancellor is ultimately responsible for arranging the judicial business in the House of Lords and the Privy Council, and makes procedural rules for the Supreme and Crown Courts. He delegates to the senior Law Lord the selection of Law Lords to sit as members of an appellate or Appeal Committee in particular cases; but he can override the senior Law Lord as his delegate and can sit whenever he chooses.

The Lord Chancellor presides in the House of Lords. He is also a senior member of the Cabinet, and is subject to collective ministerial responsibility for Government policy. He is responsible to Parliament for a large spending department, employing some 11,000 civil servants. Criminal justice remains the responsibility of the Home Secretary, but the Lord Chancellor has a wide range of responsibilities for the administration of justice, including supervision of Magistrates' Courts. Apart from some matters which remain the responsibility of the Home Secretary and the Attorney-General, the Lord Chancellor's Department has grown into a Department of Justice for England and Wales. The present Lord Chancellor performs a wider pivotal role in implementing the Government's programme of constitutional reform, chairing several Cabinet Committees dealing with various elements of the programme. The Lord Chancellor is not, however, the Government's principal adviser on points of law. That function is performed by the Law Officers of the Crown.'

Exercises 8 and 9: *The Judicial Functions of the House of Lords*, JUSTICE written evidence to the Royal Commission on the Reform of the House of Lords, JUSTICE (May 1999)

Questions

1. What are the Lord Chancellor's judicial functions?
2. In which courts can the Lord Chancellor sit as a judge?
3. What political roles does the Lord Chancellor have?
4. What is the Lord Chancellor's Department responsible for?
5. Who has responsibility for criminal justice?
6. Who is responsible for advising the Government on points of law?
7. Discuss whether the Lord Chancellor's role conflicts with the doctrine of the separation of powers.

CHAPTER 14

LAY PEOPLE IN THE LEGAL SYSTEM

Lay people play an important part in the English legal system. The two main areas in which they are used are as lay magistrates and as jurors. There are also lay people in tribunals and as lay assessors in the Admiralty Court in the High Court. The use of lay magistrates and jurors are the areas which have been the subject of the most criticism.

This section includes exercises on:

- appointment of lay magistrates
- the view of a lay magistrate
- jury qualifications
- juries in criminal cases
- juries in civil cases
- awards of damages by juries in civil cases.

EXERCISE 1 Appointment of lay magistrates (1)

The Lord Chancellor has set out directions to Advisory Committees on the appointment of new lay magistrates. The directions include a list of six key qualities that candidates should have. These qualities are:

- good character
- understanding and communication
- social awareness
- maturity and sound temperament
- sound judgment
- commitment and reliability.

R *RESEARCH*

Find out what types of cases lay magistrates hear.

DISCUSS

In the light of the work that lay magistrates do:

1. are there any other qualities which you think a lay magistrate should have?
2. which of the qualities in the above list do you think is the most important?

EXERCISE 2 Appointment of lay magistrates (2)

The following is an extract from a consultation paper *Political Balance in the Lay Magistracy* issued in October 1998 by the Lord Chancellor's Department. Read it and answer the questions below.

'All candidates recommended to the Lord Chancellor for appointment will have undergone a two-stage interview process. These interviews will determine whether a candidate is personally suitable for appointment i.e. whether he or she possesses the six key qualities. The first interview is used to discover more about a candidate's personal attributes and to explore their attitudes on a number of criminal justice issues, such as juvenile crime or drink driving. The primary purpose of the second interview is to test potential judicial aptitude by discussion of at least two cases studies typical of those heard daily in a magistrates' court.

Once those candidates who are personally suitable have been identified, the Advisory Committee is then required to have regard to the need to ensure that the composition of the bench broadly reflects the community which it serves in terms of gender, ethnic origin, geographical spread, occupation and, at present, political affiliation. At this stage, it may be that a candidate who is personally suitable is not recommended for appointment because he or she would exacerbate a current imbalance on the bench e.g. he or she is in an occupation which is over-represented or has declared support for a political party which is already over-reflected. The Advisory Committee then makes its final recommendations on appointments to the Lord Chancellor on this basis . . .

Successive Lord Chancellors have accepted the requirement to balance benches in terms of politics, seeing it as a means of ensuring a social mix on the bench.

The requirement to achieve a political balance on benches is set out in the new Directions to Advisory Committees, in the following terms:

The political views of a candidate are neither a qualification nor a disqualification for appointment. However, the Lord Chancellor requires, in the interests of balance, that the voting pattern for the areas as evidenced by the last two general elections, should be broadly reflected in the composition of the bench.

. . . Of all the balancing factors, it is the notion of political balance which has been least realised in practice and most frequently criticised as a desirable objective. There are a number of difficulties in trying to achieve a political balance on benches.

The political affiliation of many existing magistrates is that recorded on their application form or at interview, on the occasion of appointment, which may have been a number of years ago and which may subsequently have changed. Some Advisory Committees do conduct period surveys. They have found that many magistrates have declined to provide the information or classed themselves as "uncommitted" . . .

Candidates for appointment are sometimes reluctant to give this information on the application form or at interview, because they are of the view that it has no relevance to the duties they will be called upon to perform if appointed as magistrates. Insistence on this being provided would give rise to issues of human rights and, indeed, the confidentiality of the ballot box.'

Questions

1. What are the two interviews of candidates trying to discover?
2. These interviews are conducted by Advisory Committees. What type of person is likely to be on such a committee?
3. In which five ways should the composition of the bench reflect the local community? Do you agree that these five matters should be taken into consideration?
4. Why is the political view of a candidate considered? Do you agree that this should be taken into consideration?
5. Why is there difficulty in trying to achieve a political balance on the bench?

EXERCISE 3 The view of a lay magistrate

The following is taken from an article written by a lay magistrate. Read it and answer the questions below.

'The public image of the JP is still that of the middle-aged, middle-class do-gooder. The recent advertising drive by the Lord Chancellor, Lord Irvine of Lairg, to attract a broader cross-section of people into the magistracy echoes a similar campaign in 1985. Has nothing changed?

I applied to be a JP in the mid-Seventies and I was astounded when appointed. Not only was I a journalist but, according to friends, far too direct. I had visions of sitting among behatted ladies or blimpish colonels who had nothing better to do. "I have absolutely no desire to sit in judgment," I told the friend who had urged me to apply. So who are the 30,000 men and women who decide 90 per cent of the criminal cases in England and Wales each year? We are a mixed bag of people including factory and office workers, bus and taxi drivers and self-employed business people . . .

The Lord Chancellor's advisory committees which sift the applications, look at aspects such as age, sex and occupation to achieve a mix on the bench. Lord Irvine caused something of a stir when he arrived in office and said he wanted more Labour-voting JPs. Instead, he insists he wants a broader mix of backgrounds.

Magistrates were always asked their political affiliations, although one does not have to answer. The main difficulty is persuading employers to give people time off for this unpaid job. I was fortunate in that my newspaper editor said: "Carry on. Nobody ever learnt anything sitting on their backsides in a newspaper office."

So what does it take to be a magistrate? Here I quote from a remarkable man who was one of the best Chief Metropolitan Magistrates, the late Sir David Hopkin. "Patience is a prime requirement." he once told me. "You have to sit and listen. Then you have to have the ability to realise what facts are important and be able to sift them. And you have to be able to recognise and control your own prejudices. When it comes to sentencing, humanity is vital but you have to match that with the public interest. It's no good whacking someone for a large fine when he's on supplementary benefit."

Today more [District Judges] like Sir David are being used in the courts to speed up justice. Yet he was a lawyer who believed strongly in the lay system. "Lay people," he said, "bring their own knowledge and experience to the courts and, by being included in the judicial process, they understand how it works."

There are fewer complaints against the decisions of JPs than against those in the superior courts. Yes, we do get appealed against but I always remember another piece of advice – "Be robust, they can always appeal." Perhaps that should be added to the qualities necessary for a magistrate which, for me, are a just mind, a fair outlook, understanding and imagination.'

Taken from 'Why magistrates are a mixed bunch', Paula Davies, *The Times*, 13 April 1999

Questions

1. What is meant by 'JP'?
2. What does the article state is the public image of JPs?
3. What type of people does the author give as being JPs?
4. According to the article, what is the main difficulty in becoming a JP?
5. What qualities does the article identify as being important?
6. What advantages are there of using lay people in the Magistrates' Court?
7. What disadvantages are there of using lay people in the Magistrates' Court?

EXERCISE 4 Qualifications for jury service

This extract looks at the Government's proposals in the Criminal Justice Bill 2002 to amend the qualifications for jury service. Read it and do the work below.

'Schedule 22 – Jury Service

620. Schedule 22 amends the principal statute governing jury service, the Juries Act 1974, to abolish (except in the case of mentally disordered persons) the categories of ineligibility for, and excusal "as of right" from, jury service, currently set out in Parts a1 and 3 of Schedule 1 to that Act. This means that certain groups of people who currently must not, or need not, do jury service will, when these provisions are brought into force, be required to do so unless they can show good reason not to. Schedule 22 also makes amendments to the category of those disqualified from jury service, as set out in Part 2 of Schedule 1 to the Juries Act 1974, to reflect developments in sentencing legislation, including those made by the Bill itself.

Paragraphs 2, 3, 14 and 15

621. These provisions have the effect of removing the status of "ineligibility" for jury service, and entitlement to "excusal as of right" from jury service, from a number of people; they will, as a result, in the future be regarded in all cases as potential jurors. Under the Juries Act 1974, as it currently stands, the judiciary, others concerned with the administration of justice, and the clergy, are "ineligible" for jury service and therefore barred from serving as jurors. That bar will now be lifted. Others including people over 65, members of parliament, medical professionals and members of certain religious bodies, are currently entitled to refuse to serve as jurors. That entitlement will be removed. If any person affected by these changes does not wish to serve as a juror, he or she will now be required to apply for excusal or deferral under section 9 or 9A of the 1974 Act, showing "good reason" why he or she should not serve as summoned.'

Taken from the *Criminal Justice Bill Explanatory Notes*, referring to the Criminal Justice Bill as introduced in the House of Commons on 21st November 2002

Questions

1. Which Act sets out the qualifications for jury service?
2. What is meant by 'ineligibility'?
3. Give examples of people who were ineligible.
4. What is meant by 'excusal as of right'?
5. Give examples of people who were able to claim excusal as of right.
6. What changes does the Criminal Justice Bill 2002 propose to the categories of ineligibility and excusal as of right?
7. Explain whether you agree that these changes should be made.

RESEARCH

Check on the final version of the Criminal Justice Bill when it was enacted to see if these changes were actually made.
Try www.hmso.gov.uk/acts.htm

EXERCISE 5 Using juries to try criminal cases

This extract concentrates on the reasons for using juries at the Crown Court. Read it and answer the questions below.

'There are various justifications for jury trial. Lord Devlin, in his Hamlyn Lectures on the Jury System, regarded the "best blend of logic and common sense" as being in the verdict of 12 jurors. Many judges will accept the pooled experience of 12 men and women is a better instrument for arriving at a just verdict than the experience of one person.

The jury is surely the best instrument for deciding on a witness's credibility or reliability, and so for determining the primary facts of a case. It is easy for a single mind (or even the mind of two or three) to be fallible about whether a person is telling the truth. This decision often has to be judged from the witness's demeanour and his way of giving evidence. As Lord Devlin said:

> "The impression that a witness makes depends upon reception as well as transmission and may be affected by the idiosyncrasies of the receiving mind; the impression made upon a mind of 12 people is more reliable. A judge may fail to make enough allowance for the behaviour of the stupid because he regards so much as simple that for the ordinary man may be difficult. The jury hear the witness as one who is as ignorant as they are of lawyers' ways of thought."

The jury has four purposes:

First, and foremost, it does justice and decides whether the prosecution has proved its case against the defendant whom it is considering.

Secondly, it helps to ensure the independence and quality of the judges. That great eighteenth century jurist Sir William Blackstone regarded the jury as a safeguard against the violence and partiality of judges appointed by the Crown. We are a long way from those corrupt days, but who knows what the future may bring, and it is helpful to have a check on the possibility of biased judges being appointed by some future administration, perhaps long in the future.

Thirdly, it gives protection against laws which the ordinary man or woman may regard as oppressive. It was the refusal of juries to convict sheep-stealers of grand larceny (they found that the defendant had stolen the sheep but that the value of the sheep was less than 5 shillings (25 pence), and hence it was petty larceny) that led to the abolition of hanging for theft. There are indeed modern examples of acquittals in protest at what are perceived to be unfair laws.

Finally, the jury system helps to ensure the maintenance of proper behaviour by investigating officers. The great majority of police and customs officers behave impeccably. There are, however, a small number who behave with arrogance and unfairness, or who are just bullies (whether physical or verbal) to the defendants in their charge . . .

There is an important constitutional point regarding juries. Were a dictator to seize power, apart from cowing from Parliament, he would abolish or restrict trial by jury. This is because no dictator could afford to leave a person's freedom in the hands of his country men. It is for this reason that Lord Devlin described trial by jury as "the lamp that shows that freedom lives".'

Taken from 'Juries in fraud trials', Robert Rhodes QC, *New Law Journal*, 20 February 1998

Questions

1. Summarise, in your own words, the reasons the writer gives in support of using juries.
2. The writer uses the views of two other people in his article. Who are those other people and what particular reasons do they give for supporting jury trial?
3. The article mentions that there are 'modern examples of acquittals in protest at what are perceived to be unfair laws'. Give an example. (If you do not know one, you should be able to find this information in textbooks on the English legal system.)
4. What disadvantages are there in using juries in criminal cases?

EXERCISE 6 Trial by judge alone

This extract is taken from the Government's proposals to have some cases tried at the Crown Court by a judge alone. Read it and do the work below.

'Trial by judge alone

4.27 We propose to implement Sir Robin Auld's recommendation that defendants in the Crown Court should in future have the right to apply to the court for trial by a judge sitting alone. The judge will have discretion whether to grant the application and will have to give reasons for this decision. He or she will also have to give reasons for the verdict at the end of the trial. This arrangement will be similar to what already happens in some other countries, including Canada and the USA, and the introduction of a similar provision here was widely supported by those commenting on the Auld recommendation.

SERIOUS AND COMPLEX FRAUD TRIALS

4.28 A small number of serious and complex fraud trials, many lasting six months or more, have served to highlight the difficulties in trying these types of cases with a jury. Such cases place a huge strain on all concerned and the time commitment is a burden on jurors' personal and working lives. As a result it is not always possible to find a representative panel of jurors.

4.29 As well as this, the complexity and unfamiliarity of sophisticated business processes means prosecutions often pare down cases to try to make them more manageable and comprehensible to a jury. This means the full criminality of such a fraud is not always exposed and there are risks of a double standard between easy to prosecute "blue-collar" crime and difficult to prosecute "white-collar" crime.

4.30 We have concluded that there should be a more effective form of trial in such cases of serious fraud. The Auld Report recommended that the judge should have the power to direct such fraud trials without a jury, sitting with people experienced in complex financial issues or, where the defendant agrees, on their own. We recognise that the expertise of such people could help the trial proceed. However, identifying and recruiting suitable people raises considerable difficulties, not the least because this would represent a substantial commitment over a long period of time. For these reasons, we propose such cases are tried by a judge sitting alone. We do not expect there to be more than 15–20 such trials a year and we expect their length to reduce as a result.

Taken from *Justice for All* Cm 5563, 2002

Questions

1. What was the Auld Report?
2. In which countries do defendants have the right to opt for trial by a judge without a jury?
3. What are the problems of using juries in serious and complex fraud trials?
4. What did the Auld Report recommend as the method for trying serious and complex fraud cases?
5. What proposal is the Government making for such cases?
6. Why is it not adopting the method recommended by the Auld Report?
7. What advantages are there in using juries to try cases?

DISCUSS

Should juries be used in complex cases?

EXERCISE 7 Juries in civil cases

The use of juries in civil cases has become rare. The rules on when a jury can be used in a civil case in the High Court are now governed by s69 of the Supreme Court Act 1981. The key parts of this section are set out for you to study.

s69 (1) Where, on the application of any party to an action to be tried in the Queen's Bench Division, the court is satisfied that there is in issue–

(a) a charge of fraud against that party: or
(b) a claim in respect of libel, slander, malicious prosecution or false imprisonment . . .

the action shall be tried with a jury, unless the court is of the opinion that the trial requires any prolonged examination of documents or accounts or any scientific or local investigation which cannot conveniently be made with a jury.

(3) An action to be tried in the Queen's Bench Division which does not by virtue of subsection (1) fall to be tried with a jury shall be tried without a jury unless the court in its discretion orders it to be tried with a jury.

Questions

1. This section applies only to the Queen's Bench Division of the High Court: what two other divisions are there in the High Court? Are juries ever used in these?
2. Which types of civil case are normally tried by jury?
3. In these cases who may ask for jury trial? Does the court have to agree to jury trial?
4. How are other types of case in the Queen's Bench Division normally tried? Can a jury ever be used?

EXERCISE 8 Refusal of a jury in a personal injury case

Read the summary of the case of *H v Ministry of Defence* [1991] 2 QB 103 and answer the questions on it.

Facts

The defendants admitted medical negligence which led to H (a solider) having to have the major part of his penis amputated. H applied to have trial by jury to decide the amount of damages he should receive. A judge granted his application, but the defendants appealed against this decision to the Court of Appeal. The Court of Appeal allowed that appeal saying that the judge should not have used his discretion to make the order.

Law

The Court of Appeal said that the policy which should be followed was that in *Ward v James* (1966) which had held that trial by jury was normally inappropriate for any personal injury case because the assessment of damages to compensate for injuries must 'be based upon or have regard to conventional scales of damages'. The Court of Appeal also pointed out that 'the very fact that no jury trial of a claim for damages for personal injuries appears to have taken place for over 25 years affirms how exceptional the circumstances would have to be before it was appropriate to order such a trial'.

Questions

1. Under which part of which section of the Supreme Court Act 1981 (see previous exercise) would H have applied for trial by jury?
2. Why is a jury unsuitable for deciding the amount of damages to be awarded as compensation for personal injuries?
3. What other problems are there in using juries in civil cases?

CHAPTER 15

FUNDING OF CASES

For justice to be accessible it is important that people are able to get legal advice and representation. One of the biggest problems is the cost of cases. For poor people and even for those on moderate incomes, it is often too expensive for them to be able to afford to take a case to court. To help with this problem, government-funded legal aid was established in 1949. However, the increasing size of the legal aid bill meant that alternative ways of funding cases have been developed. The Access to Justice Act 1999 established the Community Legal Service to oversee government-funded help and representation. The Act also increased the types of cases which can use conditional fees as an alternative way of funding.

The exercises in this section include material on:

- Citizens Advice Bureaux
- the Community Legal Service
- access to justice
- conditional fees
- help and representation in criminal cases
- the use of public defence lawyers.

EXERCISE 1 Citizens Advice Bureau

This extract is taken from the website for the Citizens Advice Bureau. Read it and answer the questions below.

'The Citizens Advice Bureau Service offers free, confidential, impartial and independent advice. From its origins in 1939 as an emergency service during World War II, it has evolved into a professional national agency.

Every Citizens Advice Bureau is a registered charity reliant on volunteers. Citizens Advice Bureaux help solve nearly six million new problems every year which are central to people's lives, including debt and consumer issues, benefits, housing, legal matters, employment and immigration. Advisers can help fill out forms, write letters, negotiate with creditors and represent clients at court or tribunal.

Many bureaux provide specialist advice, often in partnership with other agencies such as solicitors and the probation service. The government-funded National Homelessness Advice Service is a joint project between Citizens Advice and Shelter which complements Citizens Advice services through the provision of specialist support on homelessness and housing issues to CAB advisers . . .

There are 2,000 CAB outlets in England, Wales and Northern Ireland. Each CAB is an independent charity, relying on funding from local authority and from local business, charitable trusts and individual donations.

There are now nearly 25,000 volunteers working the Citizens Advice Service. Seventy nine per cent are volunteers.'

Questions

1. When and why did the Citizens Advice Bureau Service start?
2. On what types of matters does it advise?
3. How can it provide specialist help?
4. From where does the service receive its funding?
5. Why are volunteers so important to the service?
6. Why is it important to have a service such as the CAB?

EXERCISE 2 The Community Legal Service

This extract is taken from a leaflet on funding by the Legal Services Commission. Read it and do the work below.

'The Legal Services Commission (LSC) runs two schemes – the Community Legal Service which provides advice and legal representation for people involved in civil cases, and the Criminal Defence Service which provides advice and legal representation for people facing criminal charges. This leaflet covers civil matters only. Please see separate leaflets "A Practical Guide to Criminal Defence Services" and "Criminal Defence Services at the police station and in court".

Under the Community Legal Service the LSC has an important role in co-ordinating and working in partnership with other funders of legal services, such as local authorities. The LSC also directly funds legal services for eligible clients.

Since 2 April 2001 only organisations with a contract with the LSC have been able to provide advice or representation funded by the LSC. For family cases and specialist areas like immigration and clinical negligence only specialist firms are funded to do the work.

Note that claims for personal injury other than clinical negligence are not usually funded by the LSC. Such cases can instead be pursued under "conditional fee agreements" between solicitors and clients . . .

1.2 The different levels of service

The LSC funds a range of legal services. The different levels of service in civil matters are:

- **Legal Help**
  Legal help provides initial advice and assistance with any legal problem. This level of service covers work previously carried out under the advice and assistance or "green form" scheme.
- **Help at Court**
  Help at Court allows for somebody (a solicitor or adviser) to speak on your behalf at certain court hearings, without formally acting for you in the whole proceedings.
- **Approved Family Help**
  Approved Family Help provides help in relation to a family dispute, including assistance in resolving that dispute through negotiation or otherwise . . .
- **Family Mediation**
  This level of service covers mediation for a family dispute, including finding out whether mediation appears suitable or not.
- **Legal Representation**
  This level of service provides legal representation – so that you can be represented in court if you are taking or defending court proceedings. This is the level of service previously called civil legal aid.
  It is available in two forms:
  Investigative Help: funding is limited to investigation of the strength of a claim.
  Full Representation: funding is provided to represent you in the legal proceedings.'

Taken from *A Practical Guide to Community Legal Service funding by the Legal Services Commission* (2000)

Questions

1. What two services does the Legal Services Commission run?
2. What other roles does the Legal Services Commission have?
3. (a) What types of claim cannot usually be funded by the Legal Services Commission?
   (b) How can people get representation in these types of cases?
4. The extract mentions that the LSC 'directly funds legal services for eligible clients'. What tests are there for deciding if a person is eligible?
5. What services does the Legal Services Commission fund for advice in civil cases?
6. What services does the Legal Services Commission fund for taking a case to court?
7. Why is it important to have government funding available for legal help and representation?

RESEARCH

The extract refers to separate leaflets for advice and legal representation for people facing criminal charges. Look at those leaflets on the Legal Services Commission's website (www.legalservices.gov.uk).

EXERCISE 3 Access to justice

This article appeared in the *New Law Journal* on 27 September 2002. Read it and do the work below.

'A legal aid crisis is looming which could deny thousands of people access to justice and prevent the Government fulfilling its obligations under the Access to Justice Act 1999, the Legal Services Commission have warned.

The LSC officially confirmed that nearly half the firms who undertake legal aid work are seriously considering dropping it, and that six per cent of Community Legal Services suppliers left between March and April 2002.

"We believe this overwhelmingly because of remuneration and profitability. Our studies show that at current legal aid rates many firms are at best marginally profitable," the LSC report said.

This finding was confirmed by The Law Society's survey: 60 per cent of respondents said if they stopped legal aid work it would be because it was too uneconomical. Many sole practitioners also thought it was too bureaucratic.

The Law Society survey also highlighted another worrying trend: the number of areas of legal aid work that law firms offer is set to dwindle. The report predicts a 49 per cent drop in firms providing legal aid in consumer problems in the next five years, and the number of firms dealing with publicly funded employment, housing, landlord and tenant, and welfare benefits cases might drop by around 30 per cent.'

Questions

1. What is the role of the Legal Services Commission?
2. What two services do they oversee?
3. What is happening with firms doing legal aid work and what is the main reason for this?
4. What did the Law Society's survey show?
5. What areas of legal aid work are most likely to be affected by these problems?
6. Why is it important that government-funded legal aid is available to the public?

EXERCISE 4 Conditional fees or contingency fees?

This extract considers the differences between conditional fees and contingency fees. Read it and answer the questions below.

'The introduction in the 1990s of the so-called "no win, no fee" conditional fees sparked enormous controversy. Now, several years on, it seems safe to assume that conditional fees are here to stay. Some believe that it would be sensible to go further by allowing lawyers to agree on contingency fees calculated as a percentage of damages recovered. Contingency fees in that sense have traditionally been regarded as completely beyond the (English) pale. The question addressed here is whether that view still stands.

The crucial preliminary point is that both conditional fees (CFAs) and contingency fees (CYFs) make the fee dependent on the outcome. So the classic objections to contingency fees apply to both. Public policy does not today condemn a lawyer who conducts a case on the basis that he will be paid if he wins but not if he loses. That is the very essence of CFAs under the Courts and Legal Services Act 1990, s58 and the Conditional Fee Agreements Regulations 2000. Objections to CYFs founded on this consideration are therefore now outmoded.

That applies in particular to the objections voiced repeatedly over the years to the general effect that contingency fees would be liable to promote unethical conduct by lawyers . . .

There is no evidence as to whether such assertions are well or ill-founded, but whatever may be the case, they apply equally to CFAs and to CYFs. Such arguments therefore cannot sensibly be deployed to oppose CYFs – other than on the basis that "we don't want another variation on the contingency theme".

The same is true of the argument that if the lawyer's fee is dependent on the outcome it will cloud his judgment or turn him into a business person or affect his independence. It is true equally of the argument that where the fee is dependent on the outcome of the case, the lawyer will tend not to take on cases where the prospects of success are doubtful.

The same is also true of the chief argument for CFAs – that they increase access to justice by providing for would-be litigants who would not otherwise be in a position to bring their cases.'

Taken from 'If conditional fees, why not contingency fees?', Professor Michael Zander QC, *New Law Journal*, 24 May 2002

Questions

1. Explain what is meant by 'no win, no fee' agreements?
2. Which Act allows conditional fee agreements to be used in the English legal system?
3. Which regulations govern the operation of conditional fee agreements?
4. What is the main argument in favour of conditional fee agreements?
5. What are contingency fees and how is the payment to the lawyer calculated?
6. What are the arguments against allowing contingency fees to be used in the English legal system?
7. Why does the author of this article think that contingency fees should be allowed?

EXERCISE 5 Conditional fees

The following are comments made about conditional fees from two different sources. Read them and answer the questions below.

Source 1

'Research by a team from Sheffield University has found that some of the poorest people with more complex personal injury claims could be forced to "shop around" from solicitor to solicitor under Government plans to replace legal aid cases with conditional fees. The solicitors interviewed said that the poorest clients would be unable to afford insurance premiums and disbursements or take out loans to cover them and those with more risky cases would have to shop around to find a solicitor from a shrinking number of firms.'

Source 1 based on research findings

Source 2

'Two arguments might be advanced in favour of conditional fees. The first is that, the solicitor's entitlement to payment, being conditional upon a successful outcome to the litigation, a major incentive is given to solicitors to do the very best job possible for their clients . . . The second argument is that conditional fees may provide access to justice for litigants who do not qualify for legal aid and who cannot afford the risks of an adverse costs order if they fund the case from their own resources.

Another limitation of conditional fees is the number of litigants to whom they do not readily apply. A defendant without a counterclaim has no obvious way of paying his lawyers' success fee. Neither have [claimants] seeking a remedy other than damages. for example, claims for an injunction, boundary disputes between neighbours. An ugly spectre presents itself in these cases – litigant loses and opponent takes his house, litigant wins and lawyer takes his house.'

Source 2 taken from 'Reforming the system', David Capper, *New Law Journal*, 2 October 1998

Questions

1. What problems might there be with using conditional fees?
2. Who is likely to have the greatest problems in using conditional fees?
3. What advantages could conditional fees bring?
4. Compare the advantages and disadvantages of conditional fees with the problems of funding cases without conditional fees.

EXERCISE 6 The Criminal Defence Service

This extract is taken from a leaflet about the Criminal Defence Service published by the Legal Services Commission. Read it and answer the questions below.

'The Criminal Defence Service (CDS), administered by the Legal Services Commission replaced the old system of criminal legal aid on 2 April 2001.

The purpose of the CDS is to ensure that people suspected or accused of a crime have access to advice, assistance and representation, as the interests of justice require.

Since 2 April 2001, private practice solicitors' offices must hold a General Criminal Contract to carry out criminal defence work funded by the Commission. Firms are audited against the Contract to ensure they continue to meet quality assurance standards.

Since May 2001 the Commission has also directly employed a number of criminal defence lawyers, known as public defenders. The Public Defender Service is able to provide any of the services outlined in this booklet in exactly the same way as lawyers in private practice . . .

2.1 What does Advice and Assistance cover?

Advice and Assistance covers help from a solicitor including giving general advice, writing letters, negotiating, getting a barrister's opinion and preparing a written case. It enables people of small or moderate means to get help from a solicitor.

It does not cover representation in court. If you have to go to court your solicitor may advise you to apply for Representation; or, in some cases, Advocacy Assistance . . .

2.9 Police Station Advice and Assistance

If the police question you about an offence – whether or not you have been arrested – you have a right to free legal advice from a contracted solicitor. There is no means test for such advice . . . In some circumstances the police can delay but not stop you seeing a solicitor. Ask the police to contact the duty solicitor (available 24 hours a day) or your own solicitor. Alternatively you can choose a solicitor from the list the police keep . . .

4.1 When would Representation be appropriate?

If you have been charged with a criminal offence you can apply for Representation.

4.2 What does Representation cover?

Representation covers the cost of a solicitor to prepare your defence before you go to court and to represent you there, including dealing with such issues as bail. If your case requires a barrister, particularly if it is to be heard in the Crown Court, that will also be covered. Representation can also cover advice on appeal against a verdict or sentence of the Magistrates' Court or the Crown Court (or a decision of the Court of Appeal) and preparing the notice of appeal itself. Representation is not available to bring a private prosecution – that is, bringing a criminal case against another person.'

Taken from *A Practical Guide to Criminal Defence Services* (2002)

Questions

1. When did the Criminal Defence Service come into operation and what is its role?
2. Under the Criminal Defence Service, who can provide advice, assistance or representation?
3. Explain the different types of help available under the Criminal Defence Service.
4. Which Act of Parliament provides that someone held at a police station has a right to consult a solicitor?
5. What does Representation cover and what is it not available for?
6. Why is it important that someone suspected or accused of a crime has access to legal help?
7. Are legal aid and advice provisions in criminal cases satisfactory?

EXERCISE 7 Public Defenders

This extract is taken from research into the Public Defence Solicitors' Office (PDSO) in Edinburgh. Although it is part of the Scottish system, this research is interesting as a system of Public Defenders has now also been set up in England and Wales. Read the extract and do the work below.

'The Public Defence Solicitors' Office (PDSO) was established in Edinburgh on 1 October 1998. The enabling legislation required that it be formally evaluated, and a report presented to Parliament within three years. Research was therefore commissioned to compare criminal defence services delivered through the PDSO with those delivered through private practice solicitors under the legal aid scheme . . .

Criminal justice professionals judge defence lawyers largely on the basis of their advocacy. Those interviewed had observed public defence solicitors in court and they thought that the PDSO's quality of advocacy was much the same as that of other solicitor firms ...

Stage of resolution

The interviews did not reveal substantive differences between private and public defence solicitors in the way that they approached advice on plea. However, they did show differences in tone and emphasis. When in doubt, private solicitors said they would advocate a not guilty plea: one that exercised the accused's right to put the prosecution to proof. PDSO solicitors stressed that they would never pressurise a reluctant client to plead guilty. However, they felt that they were more focused on "not messing around" and "not wasting time and money". Arguments can be put for and against both approaches . . .

Conviction rate

Among privately-represented accused, 83% received a conviction of some sort. This was usually through a plea of guilty. Of those convicted, 91% pled guilty, compared with 9% found guilty after trial . . .

PDSO cases were more likely to conclude with a conviction of some sort. The difference in conviction rate was small but statistically significant. When one controls for variation in case type, 88% of PDSO clients were convicted, compared with 83% of private, non-directed clients.

Client satisfaction

Criminal clients valued the right to choose their solicitor, and many resented being directed to use the PDSO. This clearly affected their views of the public defence solicitors. Although many clients accepted the PDSO in the light of their experience of using it, others did not. When asked whether they would use the firm again, only 46% of directed PDSO clients said that they would, compared with 83% of private practice solicitors' clients.

The levels of trust and satisfaction expressed by directed PDSO clients were consistently lower than those expressed by clients using private practitioners. Directed PDSO clients were less likely to say that their solicitor had done "a very good job" in listening to what they had to say; telling them what was happening; being there when they wanted them; or having enough time for them. They were also less likely to agree strongly that the solicitor had told the court their side of the story or treated them as though they mattered. Of particular concern was the fact that only 39% agreed strongly that their solicitor "had really stood up for their rights", compared with 71% of private solicitor clients.'

Taken from *The Public Defence Solicitors' Office in Edinburgh: An Independent Evaluation,* Scottish Executive (2001)

Questions

1. What is meant by 'public defence solicitors'?
2. In what area did the evaluation find that there were no real differences between the public defence solicitors and private solicitors?
3. What differences were found in respect to advising on plea?
4. What differences were there in the conviction rate?
5. Summarise, in your own words, the findings on client satisfaction.

R

RESEARCH

Look up the Criminal Defence Service on the Internet to discover how many public defence offices are operating in England and Wales. Try www.legalservices.gov.uk.

CHAPTER 16

THE CONCEPT OF LIABILITY

This section looks at the concepts of liability both in criminal law and in the law of tort. It covers areas required by AQA Module 3.

The exercises are based on:

- criminal liability for omissions
- continuing acts and criminal liability
- strict liability
- different levels of assault
- the duty of care in negligence
- the standard of care in negligence.

EXERCISE 1 Criminal liability for omissions

The following is an extract from the judgment in the case of *R v Miller* (1983). Read it and answer the questions below.

Facts

Miller was a squatter in a building. After having a few drinks, he went and laid down on a mattress in a back room of the house and lit a cigarette. He then fell asleep and woke up to find his mattress on fire. He did nothing to put the fire out, but went into the next room and went back to sleep. The fire spread and damaged the house.

Judgment

LORD DIPLOCK

'Leave to appeal to the House of Lords was granted by the Court of Appeal, which certified that the following question of law of general public importance was involved:

> "Whether the *actus reus* of the offence of arson is present when a defendant accidentally starts a fire and thereafter, intending to destroy or damage property belonging to another or being reckless as to whether such property would be destroyed or damaged, fails to take any steps to extinguish the fire or prevent damage to such property by that fire?"

The question speaks of '*actus reus*'. This expression is derived from . . . *actus non facit reum, nisi mens sit rea* . . . As long ago as 1889 in *R v Tolson* Stephen J when dealing with a statutory offence, as are your Lordships in the instant case, condemned the phrase as likely to mislead, though his criticism in that case was primarily directed to the use of the expression *mens rea*. In the instant case, as the argument before this House has in my view demonstrated, it is the use of the expression *actus reus* that is liable to mislead, since it suggests that some positive act on the part of the accused is needed to make him guilty of a crime and that a failure or omission to act is insufficient to give rise to criminal liability unless some express provision in the statute that creates the offence so provides.

My Lords, it would I think be conducive to clarity of analysis of the ingredients of a crime that is created by statute, as are the great majority of criminal offences today, if we were to avoid bad Latin and instead to think and speak . . . about the conduct of the accused and his state of mind at the time of that conduct, instead of speaking of *actus reus* and *mens rea*.'

Questions

1. What are the Latin phrases which express the two elements of an offence?
2. How can each of these be expressed in English?
3. Can a failure to act make a person liable for an offence?

4. What had Miller failed to do?
5. Give three other situations in which an omission can make a person criminally liable.

DISCUSS

Should a person be criminally liable for failing to do something?

EXERCISE 2 Continuing acts

The following extract is from the judgment in *Fagan v Metropolitan Police Commissioner* [1969] 1 QB 439. Read it and answer the questions below.

Facts

A police officer asked Fagan to park his car at the side of a road where the officer was standing. In parking, Fagan drove his car on to the officer's foot. The officer asked Fagan to move off his foot. Fagan at first refused and swore at the officer. After the police officer had asked him several times to move the car, Fagan eventually did so. He was found guilty of assaulting a police officer in the execution of his duty. Fagan appealed against the conviction on the basis that:

- driving the car on to the officer's foot was not intentional, so there was no *mens rea* for a battery at that point;
- leaving the car on the foot was a failure to act which could not be the *actus reus* for a battery as a positive act was required for a battery.

Judgment

JAMES J

'In our judgment, the justices at Willesden and quarter sessions were right in law. On the facts found, the action of the appellant may have been initially unintentional, but the time came when, knowing that the wheel was on the officer's foot, the appellant (i) remained seated in the car so that his body through the medium of the car was in contact with the officer, (ii) switched off the ignition of the car, (iii) maintained the wheel of the car on the foot, and (iv) used words indicating the intention of keeping the wheel in that position. For our part, we cannot regard such conduct as mere omission or inactivity. There was an act constituting a battery which at its inception was not criminal because there was no element of intention, but which became criminal from the moment the intention was formed to produce the apprehension which was flowing from the continuing act.'

Questions

1. Explain the difference between an assault and a battery.
2. What are the two elements of a battery?
3. In *Fagan*, what was the *actus reus* of the battery?
4. What is the required *mens rea* for a battery?
5. At what point in the case of Fagan did he form the necessary intention?
6. Why did Fagan argue that he had not committed the offence?
7. Why did the court say that he was guilty?

EXERCISE 3 Strict liability

The following extracts are statements from two different cases on strict liability. Read both and answer the questions below.

Alphacell Ltd v Woodward (1972)

'It is of the utmost public importance that rivers should not be polluted. The risk of pollution . . . is very great. The offences created by the [Rivers (Prevention of Pollution] Act of 1951 seem to me to be prototypes of offences which "are not criminal in any real sense, but are acts which in the public interest are prohibited under a penalty." . . . I can see no valid reason for reading the word "intentionally", "knowingly" or "negligently" into section 2(1)(a) . . . This may be regarded as a not unfair hazard of carrying on a business which may cause pollution on the banks of a river. If . . . it were held . . . that no conviction could be obtained . . . unless the prosecution could discharge the often impossible onus of proving that the pollution was caused intentionally or negligently, a great deal of pollution would go unpunished and undeterred.'

Lim Chin Aik (1963)

'It is not enough . . . merely to label the statute as one dealing with a grave social evil and from that to infer that strict liability was intended. It is pertinent also to inquire whether putting the defendant under strict liability will assist in the enforcement of the regulations. That means that there must be something he can do, directly or indirectly, by supervision or inspection, by improvements of his business methods or by exhorting those with whom he may be expected to influence or control, which will promote the observance of the regulations. Unless this is so, there is no reason in penalising him, and it cannot be inferred that the legislature imposed strict liability merely in order to find a luckless victim ...

Where it can be shown that the imposition of strict liability would result in the prosecution and conviction of a class of persons whose conduct could not in any way affect the observance of the law, their Lordships consider that, even where the statute is dealing with a grave social evil, strict liability is not likely to be inferred.'

Questions

1. What is meant by 'strict liability'?
2. Give an example of a case in which the courts held there was strict liability.
3. In the first extract, why did the court think strict liability was necessary?
4. In the second extract, when did the court think that there was no point in making an offence one of strict liability?
5. What are the advantages and disadvantages of having strict liability offences?

EXERCISE 4 Different types of assault

Decide which offence(s) has/have been committed in the following situations.

1. Caitlin is rushing down the corridor at college, in a hurry to get to her next class. She bumps into Amos. He is very cross when this happens and kicks out at her, cutting her knee.
2. Dwight sneaks up behind Elton and punches him the back. Elton falls forward and hits his head on the wall, knocking him unconscious.
3. Harry shouts through a window at Tom that he is going to beat Tom up. As the window can only be opened a small way, Harry cannot carry out his threat at that moment. However the next day, when Harry sees Tom in a local pub, he deliberately smashes his glass into Tom's face, causing very severe cuts.

EXERCISE 5 The duty of care

The following two extracts are taken from very important cases in the development of the tort of negligence. Read them and answer the questions below.

Donoghue v Stevenson (1932)

LORD ATKIN

'The rule that you are to love your neighbour becomes in law that you must not injure your neighbour; and the lawyer's question, Who then is my neighbour? receives a restricted reply. You must take reasonable care to avoid acts or omissions which you can reasonably foresee would be likely to injure your neighbour. Who then is my neighbour? The answer seems to be – persons who are so directly affected by my act that I ought reasonably to have them in contemplation as being so affected when I am directing my mind to the acts or omissions which are called in question.'

Caparo v Dickman (1990)

LORD BRIDGE

'What emerges is that, in addition to the foreseeability of damage, necessary ingredients in any situation giving rise to a duty of care are that there should exist between the party owing the duty and the party to whom it is owed a relationship characterised by the law as one of "proximity" or "neighbourhood" and that the situation should be one in which the court considers it fair, just and reasonable that the law should impose a duty of a given scope on the one party for the benefit of the other.'

Questions

1. Explain, in your own words, the test for the duty of care in negligence put forward by Lord Atkin in *Donoghue v Stevenson.*
2. Lord Atkin referred to 'my neighbour'. What word does Lord Bridge use for the same idea?
3. What extra tests does Lord Bridge give, in addition to the test of foreseeability of damage?
4. As well as a duty of care, what two other matters must be proved to establish a claim in negligence?
5. Name and explain another case in which the claimant was successful in getting damages for injury caused by negligence. (This cannot be one referred to in any of sources 5, 6 or 7 in this chapter.)

EXERCISE 6 Fair, just and reasonable?

Read this extract about the case of *Mulcahy v Ministry of Defence* (1996) 2 All ER 758 and answer the questions below.

Facts

A soldier's hearing was damaged when his gun commander ordered that a howitzer (type of gun) be fired when the soldier was in an unsafe position. The incident happened during the Gulf War in 1991.

Judgment

LORD JUSTICE NEILL

'. . . it has been well settled law that the elements of foreseeability and proximity as well as considerations of fairness, justice and reasonableness are relevant to all cases of alleged negligence whatever the nature of the harm sustained by the [claimant].

In the present case it is accepted on behalf of the defendants that two of these components of a duty of care, proximity and foreseeability, are present. The issue to be determined is whether it is fair, just and reasonable that a duty of care should be imposed on one soldier in his conduct towards another when engaging the enemy during hostilities . . .

It is plain from the decision of the House of Lords in the *Marc Rich* case that in order to decide whether it is fair, just and reasonable to impose a duty of care one must consider all the circumstances including the position and role of the alleged tortfeasor and any relevant policy consideration. In this context one should bear in mind the dictum of Lord Pearce in *Hedley Byrne & Co Ltd v Heller & Partners* (1963):

> "How wide the sphere of the duty of care in negligence is to be laid depends ultimately upon the courts' assessment of the demands of society for protection from the carelessness of others." . . .

The question then becomes: "Is a duty of care to be imposed in [battle] conditions so as to make one serviceman liable for his negligent act towards another?" In my opinion, there is no basis for extending the scope of the duty of care so far.'

Questions

1. What two elements of a duty of care did Lord Justice Neill say were present in this case?
2. What other element of a duty of care had to be proved?
3. What did the House of Lords in the case of *Marc Rich* say had to be considered?
4. Why was the fact that the injury had been caused in battle conditions important to the decision in the case of *Mulcahy*?

EXERCISE 7 The standard of care

The general standard of care in negligence is that of a reasonable man. Read these two extracts from different cases and answer the questions below.

Bolam v Friern Hospital Management Committee (1957)

'In the ordinary case which does not involve any special skill, negligence in law means this: Some failure to do some act which a reasonable man in the circumstances would do, or doing some act which a reasonable man in the circumstances would not do; and if that failure or doing of that act results in injury then there is a cause of action. How do you test whether this act or failure is negligent? In an ordinary case it is generally said that you judge that by the action of the man in the street. He is the ordinary man. In one case it has been said that you judge it by the conduct of the man on the top of a Clapham omnibus. He is the ordinary man.

But where you get a situation which involves the use of some special skill or competence, then the test whether there has been negligence or not is not the test of the man on the top of a Clapham omnibus, because he has not got this special skill. The test is the standard of the ordinary skilled man exercising and professing to have that special skill. A man need not possess the highest expert skill at the risk of being found negligent. It is well-established law that it is sufficient if he exercises the ordinary skill of an ordinary competent man exercising that particular art . . .

In the case of a medical man negligence means failure to act in accordance with the standards of reasonably competent medical men at the time.'

Nettleship v Weston (1971)

'The responsibility of the learner-driver towards persons on or near the highway

Mrs Weston is clearly liable for the damage to the lamp-post. In civil law if a driver goes off the road on to the pavement and injures a pedestrian, or damages property, he is [on the face of it] liable. Likewise if he goes on to the wrong side of the road. It is no answer for him to say: "I was a learner-driver under instruction. I was doing my best and could not help it." The civil law permits no such excuse. It requires of him the same standard of care as any other driver . . . The learner-driver may be doing his best, but his incompetent best is not good enough. He must drive in as good a manner as a driver of skill, experience and care, who is sound in mind and limb, who makes no errors of judgment, has good eyesight and hearing and is free from any infirmity . . .

Thus we are, in this branch of the law, moving away from the concept: "No liability without fault". We are beginning to apply the test: "On whom should the risk fall?" Morally the learner-driver is not at fault, but legally she is liable to be because she is insured and the risk should fall on her.'

Questions

1. What is the normal standard of care expected in an ordinary case?
2. By whose standards does the judgment in *Bolam* say that you judge actions in order to decide if there has been negligence?
3. When will a higher standard be expected?
4. What is the standard of care expected from a doctor?
5. In the second judgment, what standard of care is expected of a learner-driver?
6. Comment on whether you agree with the two judgments.

REVISION

This section is divided up into the same order as the sections in the first part of the book. Each part has different types of exercises to help you revise.

1 Rule of law

QUICK FACT CHECK

1. Give a definition of 'law'.
2. What factors are needed to create a legal system?
3. Give an example of a moral rule that is not a legal rule.
4. What is meant by 'natural law'?
5. What is the Hart–Devlin debate?
6. Name two courts which hear civil cases.
7. Name two courts which hear criminal cases.
8. What is the standard of proof in civil cases?
9. What is the standard of proof in criminal cases?
10. Give two other differences between civil law and criminal law.

2 Judicial precedent

QUICK FACT CHECK

What do each of the following terms mean?

1. *stare decisis*
2. *ratio decidendi*
3. *obiter dicta*
4. persuasive precedent
5. distinguishing.

MULTIPLE CHOICE

Which is the correct answer to the following questions?

1. The Practice Direction applies to:
   (a) the Court of Appeal
   (b) the House of Lords
   (c) the European Court of Justice.
2. The Practice Statement was made in:
   (a) 1996
   (b) 1986
   (c) 1966.
3. *Young's case* decided that:
   (a) the High Court must follow the House of Lords
   (b) the Court of Appeal must follow the House of Lords
   (c) the Court of Appeal must follow its own past decisions.
4. The case of *R v Shivpuri* (1986) is an example of:
   (a) the House of Lords using the Practice Statement
   (b) the House of Lords distinguishing a case
   (c) the Court of Appeal following a decision of the House of Lords.
5. The case of *Davis v Johnson* (1979) is an example of:
   (a) the Court of Appeal refusing to follow a decision of their own
   (b) the Court of Appeal refusing to follow a decision of the House of Lords
   (c) the House of Lords refusing to follow a decision of the European Court of Justice.

3 Legislation and statutory interpretation

QUICK FACT CHECK

1. Name the stages a Bill has to go through before it becomes an Act of Parliament.
2. Give three different types of delegated legislation.
3. Explain the difference between the literal approach and the purposive approach to statutory interpretation.
4. Give a case to illustrate the literal rule.
5. What is *Hansard* and why is it useful in statutory interpretation?

MULTIPLE CHOICE

Which is the correct answer to the following questions?

1. An enabling Act is also known as a:
   (a) mother Act
   (b) father Act
   (c) parent Act.
2. The Latin phrase for saying that delegated legislation is 'beyond its powers' is:
   (a) *ejusdem generis*
   (b) *ultra vires*
   (c) *ex parte*.
3. *Fisher v Bell* is an example of a case being decided by using the:
   (a) literal rule
   (b) golden rule
   (c) mischief rule.
4. The mischief rule considers:
   (a) the mischief that the defendant has done
   (b) the gap in the law that the Act was designed to cover
   (c) the difficulty of using *Hansard*.
5. Which of the following is an intrinsic aid?
   (a) a dictionary
   (b) a definition section
   (c) *Hansard*.

STATUTORY INTERPRETATION – MATCH THE PAIRS

Match each item in the first list with the appropriate one from the second list.

1. *Pepper v Hart*
2. interpretation section
3. European law approach
4. *Fisher v Bell*
5. *Adler v George*
6. singular includes plural
7. *Heydon's case*
8. a dictionary.

A mischief rule
B Interpretation Act 1978
C *Hansard*
D extrinsic aid
E purposive approach
F literal rule
G intrinsic aid
H golden rule.

DELEGATED LEGISLATION PUZZLE

Answer the clues to the puzzle and work out what word is formed, reading down from the arrow. Then explain what relevance this word has to delegated legislation.

▼ (above column 3)

1 R	E	S	O	L	U	T	I	O	N
		2 C	O	U	N	C	I	L	
3 P	A	R	E	N	T				
	4 M	U	S	H	R	O	O	M	
	5 S	T	A	T	U	T	O	R	Y
	6 V	I	R	E	S				
	7 E	N	A	B	L	I	N	G	
	8 B	Y	L	A	W	S			

1. Parliament can pass a negative or affirmative ______________
2. The Queen and Privy Council can make Orders in ______________
3. (and 7) An Act giving power to make delegated legislation is called a ____________ (3) or an ________________ (7)
4. The *Aylesbury* ________________ case
5. Ministers can make ________________ instruments
6. *Ultra* ____________
7. see 3
8. Local authorities can make ______________

SCRUTINY COMMITTEE

4 European law

QUICK FACT CHECK

1. What treaty is the main treaty governing the European Union?
2. Who sits on the Council of Ministers?
3. What is the role of the European Commission?
4. How is the European Parliament chosen?
5. Which Article allows member states to refer a preliminary point of law to the European Court of Justice?
6. Give a case which the English courts have referred to the European Court of Justice.
7. What is meant by 'directly applicable'?
8. What is meant by 'vertical direct effect'?
9. What principle did the case of *Francovich* decide?
10. What effect has European law had on statutory interpretation in English courts?

MULTIPLE CHOICE

Which is the correct answer to the following questions?

1. Which European Institution can take cases against a member state who has failed to fulfil its obligations?
   (a) the Council of Ministers
   (b) the European Commission
   (c) the European Parliament.
2. The case of *Marshall v Southampton and South West Hampshire Area Health Authority* was about:
   (a) the right to equal pay
   (b) discrimination over pension rights
   (c) discrimination over retirement ages.
3. 'Horizontal direct effect' means that:
   (a) an individual can rely on European law to claim against another individual
   (b) an individual can rely on European law to claim against the State
   (c) one State can rely on European law to claim against another State.
4. Regulations have:
   (a) only vertical direct effect
   (b) only horizontal direct effect
   (c) both vertical and horizontal direct effect.
5. Which Act says that the treaties are to be given legal effect in the United Kingdom?
   (a) European Communities Act 1957
   (b) European Communities Act 1972
   (c) European Union Act 1972.

5 Law reform

QUICK FACT CHECK (1)

1. What is an election manifesto?
2. What relevance has an election manifesto to law reform?
3. When the Government wishes to reform a law, what will it usually issue, setting out its proposals for reform?
4. What opportunities do ordinary Members of Parliament have for introducing law reform?
5. Name two pressure groups.
6. What role do pressure groups play in law reform?
7. What is meant by a Royal Commission? Give an example of one.

QUICK FACT CHECK (2)

1. Which Act set up the Law Commission?
2. Name two other law reform bodies.
3. What is the main role of the Law Commission?
4. What is meant by 'codifying the law'?
5. Has the Law Commission been successful in 'codifying the law'?
6. What role does Parliament play in implementing the Law Commission's reports?
7. Give an example of a law passed as a result of the Law Commission's recommendation.

Overview 1

TRUE OR FALSE?

Are the following statements true or false? Be careful, some of them are not as obvious as they seem.

1. The House of Lords binds the Court of Appeal TRUE / FALSE
2. The Practice Statement was used in *Pepper v Hart* TRUE / FALSE
3. *Young's case* gives the House of Lords three exceptions when the court need not follow its own previous decision TRUE / FALSE
4. A Green Paper is a consultative paper issued by the Government TRUE / FALSE
5. An Act of Parliament always comes into force when it is given the Royal Assent TRUE / FALSE
6. The golden rule is an extension of the mischief rule TRUE / FALSE
7. *Hansard* can only be consulted if the words of an Act are ambiguous or obscure or lead to an absurdity TRUE / FALSE
8. European law uses the literal approach to interpretation TRUE / FALSE
9. If a point of interpretation of European law is involved, the House of Lords must send the case to the European Court of Justice TRUE / FALSE
10. The Treaty of Rome is directly applicable in the English legal system TRUE / FALSE
11. *Van Duyn v The Home Office* was the first ever case to be decided by the European Court of Justice TRUE / FALSE

12 Directives have horizontal direct effect TRUE / FALSE.

CROSSWORD ON SOURCES OF LAW

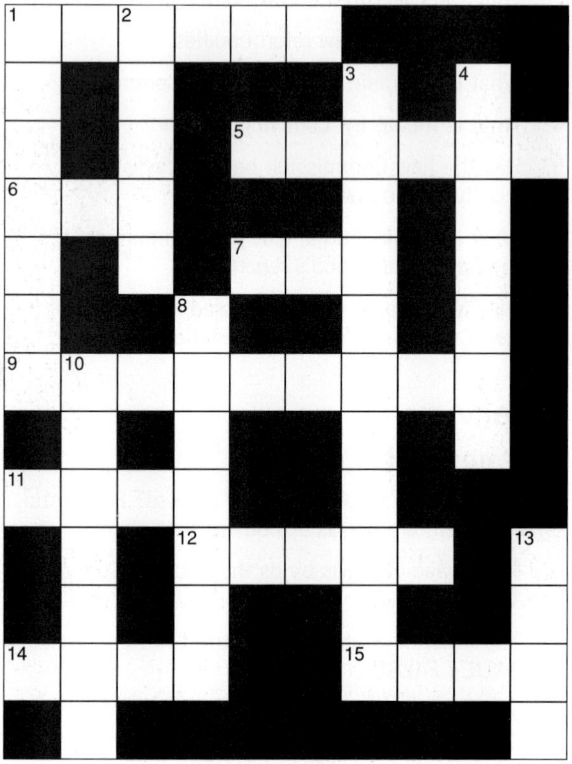

ACROSS

1. Early case which formulated the mischief rule
5. ...... *dicta*
6. In Re Sigsworth she was murdered by her ...
7. A law passed by Parliament
9. *See 12 across*
11. *See 8 down*
12. *and 9 across.* The Latin phrase for the binding part of a judgment
14. In *Fisher v ....* the court used 8 down 11 across
15. *Pepper v ....*

DOWN

1. The record of Parliamentary debates
2. In ..... *v Bristol Aeroplane Co* the Court of Appeal decided it was bound by its own past decisions
3. The method in judicial precedent where a judge refuses to follow a precedent because the facts in his case are materially different
4. *See 10 down*
8. *and 11 across.* This was used by the court in 14 across
10. *and 4 down.* A Latin phrase used in statutory interpretation meaning 'of the same kind'
13. Electors do this when they choose their MPs.

6 Civil courts

QUICK FACT CHECK

1. What is meant by a 'multi-track case'?
2. Describe two problems of bringing a civil case in the courts.
3. What type of judge normally sits to hear small claims?
4. Describe two advantages of small claims cases over cases tried in the main courts.
5. Which report led to major changes to the civil courts in 1999?
6. What is meant by 'damages' in a civil case?
7. What is meant by an injunction?
8. Name two methods of enforcing a judgment.
9. Where does an appeal from the decision in a fast-track case go?
10. What is a leap-frog appeal?

MULTIPLE CHOICE

Which is the correct answer to the following questions?

1. A small claims case is heard in:
   (a) a tribunal
   (b) the County Court
   (c) the Queen's Bench Division.
2. The person starting a civil case is called:
   (a) the applicant
   (b) the complainant
   (c) the claimant.
3. The Queen's Bench Division hears:
   (a) cases of claims for personal injury
   (b) divorce cases
   (c) cases for winding up companies.
4. 'Nominal damages' means:
   (a) an amount nominated by the person making the claim
   (b) a small award of damages where there has been no actual loss
   (c) damages which are not actually paid.
5. Specific performance is:
   (a) an equitable remedy
   (b) an order that one party hands over specific documents
   (c) an order that the losing party pays the costs of the other party.

7 Alternative methods of dispute resolution

QUICK FACT CHECK

1. Describe the way in which mediation usually works.
2. What other methods of ADR are there?
3. Name one body that promotes ADR.
4. Which Act governs arbitration?
5. Give three advantages of arbitration.
6. Give two different types of cases which will be dealt with at a tribunal.
7. Who usually sits to hear cases in a tribunal?
8. Which Council supervises and reports on the workings of tribunal?
9. Give two advantages of a hearing in a tribunal compared with a hearing in a court.
10. What problems are there with tribunal hearings?

MULTIPLE CHOICE

Which is the correct answer to the following questions?

1. ADR stands for:
   (a) Arbitration and Dispute Resolution
   (b) Alternative Dispute Resolution
   (c) Advantages and Disadvantages of Reform.
2. The object of arbitration is:
   (a) to obtain the fair resolution of disputes by an impartial person without unnecessary expense or delay
   (b) to have a preliminary decision before taking the case to court
   (c) to take a case to a tribunal.
3. A *Scott v Avery* clause is:
   (a) an agreement to go to arbitration
   (b) an agreement about paying costs
   (c) an agreement to settle a case.
4. An arbitrator is chosen by:
   (a) a trade union
   (b) the person making the claim
   (c) both parties jointly.
5. A dispute over unfair dismissal from work can be heard in:
   (a) a tribunal
   (b) the small claims court
   (c) the County Court.

PUZZLE ON CIVIL CASES AND ADR

Fill in the answers to the clues and find out what word reads downwards from the arrow

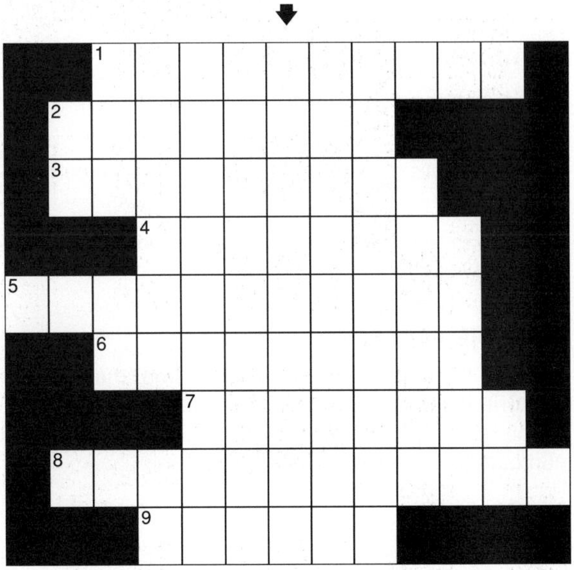

1. Type of case in which a civil jury can be used (10)
2. The three divisions of the High Court are Queen's Bench, Family and .... (8)
3. The legal term for the person against whom a claim is brought (9)
4. The legal term for the person starting a civil case (8)
5. Method of resolving a case without going to court in which a third person makes a binding decision (11)
6. Claims of £5,000 to £15,000 are dealt with in court by this method (4, 5)
7. The place where unfair dismissal claims are heard is called an employment .... (7)
8. Final court of appeal in England and Wales (5, 2, 5)
9. The courts which hear civil cases are the High Court and the .... Court (6)

8 Crime and police investigation

QUICK FACT CHECK

1. Which Royal Commission led to the passing of the Police and Criminal Evidence Act 1984?
2. What is meant by 'Codes of Practice under PACE'?
3. For what reasons may a police officer stop and search someone in the street?
4. What rights of arrest have private citizens?

5. For how long may a suspect be detained for a serious arrestable offence?
6. When can the police delay a suspect's right to consult a solicitor?
7. Which Act limited the right to silence?
8. In what ways is a suspect protected while detained by the police?
9. What types of search of a suspect may be carried out?
10. Who investigates complaints about police behaviour?

FIND THE PARTNERS

The first list of is of section numbers from the Police and Criminal Evidence Act 1984. The second list is of police powers or detainees' rights. Match the section numbers to the relevant power or right.

1. Section 24
2. Section 56
3. Section 1
4. Section 25
5. Section 8
6. Section 34
7. Section 61

A Power to enter and search premises with a warrant

B Power to stop and search

C Power to detain for 24 hours

D Power to arrest where an arrestable offence has been committed

E Power to take fingerprints

F Right of detainee to have someone informed of his detention

G Power to arrest to protect a child or other vulnerable person

9 Pre-trial procedure in criminal cases

QUICK FACT CHECK

1. Which Act gives the right to bail?
2. When can bail be refused?
3. What is meant by a 'summary offence'?
4. What is meant by an offence 'triable either way'?
5. Who is the head of the Crown Prosecution Service?

MULTIPLE CHOICE

Which is the correct answer to the following questions?

1. Manslaughter is:
   (a) a summary offence
   (b) an indictable offence
   (c) an offence triable either way.
2. Conditional bail means:
   (a) the defendant has to pay a sum of money to the court before he gets out
   (b) the police will not give bail but will ask the magistrates to decide
   (c) the magistrates give bail but ask the defendant to do something such as hand in his passport to the court.
3. The Crown Prosecution Service was set up by:
   (a) the Prosecution of Offences Act 1985
   (b) the Crown Prosecution Act 1985
   (c) the Criminal Justice Act 1988.
4. The Crown Prosecution Service decide whether a case should continue by applying two tests. One is the evidential test. The second test is:
   (a) the private interest test
   (b) the public interest test
   (c) the interests of justice test.
5. In 1999 a report was issued criticising the Crown Prosecution Service. Was this report called:
   (a) the Runciman Report?
   (b) the Glidewell Report?
   (c) the Woolf Report?

10 Criminal courts

QUICK FACT CHECK

1. Who sits to hear cases in Magistrates' Courts?
2. What is the role of the clerk to the magistrates?
3. In what types of criminal cases are juries used?
4. At which court do juries sit in criminal cases?
5. What age of offenders are dealt with by the youth court?
6. To which courts can a defendant appeal after being found guilty at the Magistrates' Court?
7. To which courts can a defendant appeal after being found guilty in the Crown Court?
8. What rights of appeal have the prosecution got?
9. What conditions must be satisfied before an appeal can be made to the House of Lords?
10. Which body has been set up to investigate miscarriages of justice?

MULTIPLE CHOICE

Which is the correct answer to the following questions?

1. The maximum sentence that can be normally be imposed at a Magistrates' Court is:
   (a) £1,000
   (b) £5,000
   (c) £10,000.
2. Magistrates' Courts can try:
   (a) summary cases
   (b) indictable cases
   (c) divorce cases.
3. Defendants prefer to be tried at the Crown Court because:
   (a) they will get a lighter sentence
   (b) they will be tried by a jury
   (c) it is cheaper than the Magistrates' Court.
4. A case stated appeal is made from:
   (a) the Court of Appeal to the House of Lords
   (b) the Magistrates' Court to the Crown Court
   (c) the Magistrates' Court to the Queen's Bench Divisional Court.
5. The Criminal Cases Review Commission took over reviewing cases from:
   (a) the Home Secretary
   (b) the Lord Chancellor
   (c) the Attorney-General.

11 Sentencing

QUICK FACT CHECK

1. What two types of deterrence are used as sentencing aims?
2. Explain what is meant by 'denunciation' in sentencing.
3. What is meant by 'individualised sentences'?
4. What is 'reparation'?
5. At what age can offenders be sent to an adult prison?
6. What custodial sentences are available for young offenders?
7. Name two types of community sentence.
8. What is electronic tagging used for?
9. What is a mandatory sentence?
10. In what ways can a mentally ill offender be sentenced?

MULTIPLE CHOICE

Which is the correct answer to the following questions?

1. 'Rehabilitation' means:
   (a) sending an offender to prison
   (b) trying to reform an offender
   (c) ordering an offender to pay compensation to the victim.
2. 'Retribution' means
   (a) making the punishment fit the crime
   (b) giving a severe sentence to make an example of the offender
   (c) making the offender pay compensation to the victim.
3. A conditional discharge is:
   (a) an order only used for young offenders
   (b) an order under which the defendant has to pay a sum of money if he re-offends
   (c) an order which means that the defendant may be re-sentenced for the offence if he commits another offence within a set period of time.
4. An action plan order can be made for offenders aged:
   (a) 10–17
   (b) 10–14
   (c) 14–17.
5. A minimum sentence can be given for:
   (a) a second burglary
   (b) a second serious crime of violence
   (c) a second offence of theft.

Overview 2

TRUE OR FALSE?

1. Lawyers are not allowed in small claims cases TRUE / FALSE
2. Personal injury cases can be heard in either the County Court or the High Court TRUE / FALSE
3. An agreement reached through mediation is binding on the parties TRUE / FALSE
4. An agreement reached through arbitration is binding on the parties TRUE / FALSE
5. A police officer cannot make an arrest unless an arrestable offence has been committed TRUE / FALSE
6. The police cannot detain a suspect for longer than 48 hours TRUE / FALSE
7. The police cannot grant bail TRUE / FALSE
8. Bail will only be granted by the magistrates if someone pays bail money TRUE / FALSE
9. A case stated appeal can only be made on a point of law TRUE / FALSE
10. The prosecution cannot appeal to the House of Lords TRUE / FALSE
11. An absolute discharge is given when a defendant is found not guilty TRUE / FALSE
12. The Court of Appeal sets guidelines for sentencing TRUE / FALSE

PUZZLE

Fill in the answers to the clues and find out what word reads downwards from the arrow

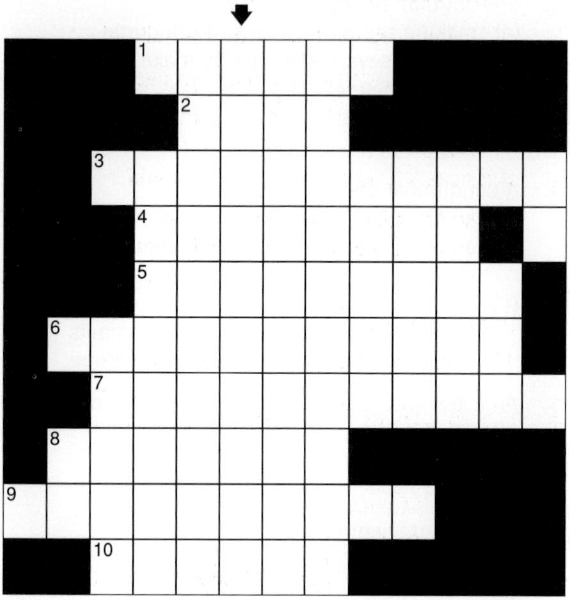

1. The High Court has three divisions: Queen's Bench, Chancery and .... (6)
2. If a defendant is allowed to be free while awaiting trial, he said to be on .... (4)
3. The police can do this under s61 of PACE (11)
4. Employment disputes are heard here (8)
5. These civil cases are between £5,000 and £15,000 and are intended to be heard in less than 30 weeks (4,5)
6. An method of dispute resolution where someone other than a judge makes the decision (11)
7. An aim of sentencing where the offender has his 'just deserts' (11)
8. These offences can only be tried at the Magistrates' Court. (7)
9. These offences can only be tried at the Crown Court (10)
10. The police have the power to do this under s24 of PACE (6)

12 The legal profession

QUICK FACT CHECK

1. What is the Law Society?
2. Explain the training of solicitors.
3. What is the Bar Council?
4. What are the Inns of Court?
5. Explain the differences between the work of solicitors and the work of barristers.

MULTIPLE CHOICE

Which is the correct answer to the questions?

1. 'Advocacy' means:
   (a) speaking to a client
   (b) representing a client in court
   (c) negotiating on behalf of a client.
2. 'Conveyancing' means:
   (a) going to court
   (b) drawing up a contract
   (c) dealing with the legal side of buying a house.
3. A Queen's Counsel is:
   (a) a judge
   (b) a senior barrister or solicitor
   (c) a magistrate.
4. Pupillage is
   (a) an educational stage a barrister must complete
   (b) an educational stage a solicitor must complete
   (c) an educational stage a judge must complete.
5. Complaints against the legal profession can be investigated by:
   (a) the Home Secretary
   (b) the Lord Chancellor
   (c) the Legal Services Ombudsman.

PUZZLE

Answer the clues and find the phrase going down from the arrow.

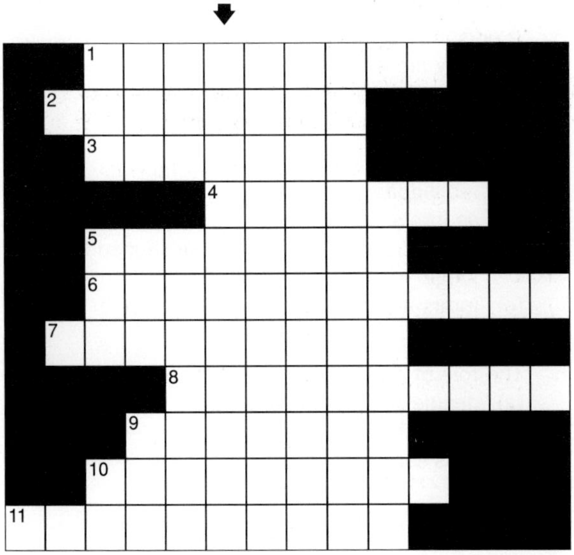

Questions

1. What is the 'on the job' training of a barrister called? (9)
2. Solicitors have to complete a two-year ___________ contract (8)
3. The governing body of barristers is the Bar ________ (7)
4. The governing body of solicitors is the Law ________ (7)
5. What is putting a case in court called? (8)
6. If you do not have a law degree you must pass the Common __________________ Examination (12)
7. This lawyer can be a partner in a firm (9)
8. To become a barrister you must pass the Bar ________________ Course (10)
9. A senior barrister is a Queen's ___________ (7)
10. This lawyer is self-employed and works in chambers (9)
11. There are also Legal __________________ who work in solicitors' firms (10)

13 The judiciary

QUICK FACT CHECK

1. Which judges sit in the House of Lords?
2. What role does the Master of the Rolls play?
3. What qualifications are needed to become a High Court judge?
4. What criticisms can be made of the appointment of judges sitting in the High Court and above?
5. Which Act means that judges sitting in the High Court and above cannot be easily dismissed?

MULTIPLE CHOICE

Which is the correct answer to the questions?

1. The doctrine of the separation of powers was put forward by:
   (a) Montpellier
   (b) Montesquieu
   (c) Monsarrat.
2. The doctrine of the separation of powers means that:
   (a) Parliament has power to appoint judges
   (b) the Lord Chancellor cannot appoint judges
   (c) the three arms of the State should be kept separate.
3. A circuit judge can be appointed from:
   (a) any barrister or solicitor with 10 years' experience
   (b) any barrister or solicitor with the relevant certificate of advocacy
   (c) only from barristers.
4. A recorder is
   (a) a part-time judge sitting usually in the Crown Court
   (b) a full-time judge sitting usually in the Crown Court
   (c) a full-time judge sitting usually in the Magistrates' Court.
5. The Lord Chancellor is appointed by:
   (a) the House of Lords
   (b) the Prime Minister
   (c) the Home Secretary.

MATCHING PAIRS

Match the judge to the court he/she could sit in. Be careful, as some can sit in more than one court.

1. Lord Justice of Appeal
2. Recorder (criminal case)
3. Law Lord
4. District Judge (criminal case)
5. Master of the Rolls
6. High Court Judge (criminal case)
7. Circuit Judge (civil case)
8. District Judge (civil case)
9. Lord Chief Justice.

A County Court
B County Court
C Court of Appeal
D Court of Appeal (Civil division)
E Court of Appeal (Criminal division)
F Crown Court
G Crown Court
H House of Lords
I Magistrates' Court.

14 Lay people in the legal system

QUICK FACT CHECK

1. What is the minimum number of times a lay magistrate must sit in court per year?
2. What qualities should a lay magistrate have?
3. At what age do magistrates have to retire?
4. Give two advantages of using lay magistrates.
5. Give two disadvantages of using lay magistrates.
6. What are the age limits for jurors?
7. Who is disqualified from sitting on a jury?
8. When can a juror be challenged?
9. Give three advantages and three disadvantages of using juries to decide cases.
10. What civil cases may juries be used in?

MULTIPLE CHOICE

Which is the correct answer to the questions?

1. A bench of lay magistrates must have:
   (a) between two and seven magistrates sitting
   (b) two or three magistrates sitting
   (c) three or five magistrates sitting.
2. Lay magistrates are appointed by:
   (a) an Advisory Committee
   (b) the Lord Chancellor
   (c) the Queen.
3. A person is disqualified from jury service if:
   (a) they are a lawyer
   (b) they are a doctor
   (c) they have a previous conviction.
4. 'Jury vetting' means that:
   (a) individual jurors are asked if they wish to sit as jurors
   (b) the decision of the jury is questioned by the judge
   (c) jurors are checked to see if they are disqualified from sitting.
5. The role of a jury in a criminal case is to:
   (a) decide the facts of the case
   (b) decide the law in the case
   (c) pass sentence on the defendant.

15 Funding legal cases

QUICK FACT CHECK

1. In what situations are duty solicitors used?
2. Which 1999 Act of Parliament has provision to set up the Community Legal Service?
3. What is the service for publicly funded civil cases called?
4. What are conditional fees?
5. What is considered in the 'interests of justice' test used in criminal legal aid cases?

MULTIPLE CHOICE

Which is the correct answer to the questions?

1. The body controlling publicly funded help is:
   (a) the Law Society
   (b) the Legal Services Commission
   (c) the Community Law Service.
2. 'Conditional fee' means:
   (a) the solicitor is paid a percentage of the damages
   (b) the solicitor is paid an uplift on the agreed fee if he wins the case
   (c) insurance against being sued.
3. 'CAB' stands for:
   (a) County Advice Bureau
   (b) Citizens Arbitration Bureau
   (c) Citizens Advice Bureau.
4. A merits test in civil cases means that the claimant must show that:
   (a) they cannot afford to take their case to court
   (b) they have the necessary determination to take the case all the way to court
   (c) the case is likely to be successful.

5. Publicly funded representation is available for:
   (a) small claims
   (b) employment tribunals
   (c) family cases.

F blood transfusion needed
G silent phone calls
H tracheotomy (tube in throat)
I baby thrown at pram
J started fire accidentally

16 Concepts of liability

QUICK FACT CHECK (CRIMINAL LAW)

1. Give three situations in which an omission can create criminal liability.
2. In causation, what is meant by an 'intervening act' and why is it important in criminal liability?
3. Which case decided that switching off a life-support machine did not break the chain of causation?
4. What is meant by 'foresight of consequences'?
5. What is 'subjective recklessness'?
6. Which case decided that 'maliciously' in a statute meant intending or being subjectively reckless?
7. Using a case or an example, explain the concept of transferred malice.
8. Explain the *actus reus* of an assault.
9. Explain the *actus reus* of a battery.
10. In which two sections of the Offences Against the Person Act 1861 is it necessary to wound or cause/inflict grievous bodily harm?

MATCH THE CASES (CRIMINAL LAW)

Match the cases in the first list with the appropriate point in the second list.

1. *Roberts*
2. *Woollin*
3. *Ireland*
4. *Miller*
5. *White*
6. *JCC v Eisenhower*
7. *Blaue*
8. *Cunningham* (1957)
9 *Sweet v Parsley*
10. *Cheshire*

A cyanide
B smoking cannabis
C eye hit by shotgun pellet
D jumped from car
E gas meter

QUICK FACT CHECK (TORT)

1. What are the three elements of negligence which must be proved for a case to succeed?
2. Which case in 1932 set down the initial tests for negligence?
3. What extra tests did the case of *Caparo v Dickman* (1991) add to the duty of care?
4. Using a case, explain the concept of 'reasonably foreseeable'.
5. What is meant by 'proximity'?
6. Explain the idea of 'fair, just and reasonable', with cases.
7. Briefly explain the standard of care in negligence.
8. What is meant by 'things speak for themselves' and why is it important in some negligence cases?
9. What is the 'thin skull' rule?
10. Explain the case of *The Wagon Mound* (1961).

MATCH THE CASES (NEGLIGENCE)

Match the cases in the first list with the appropriate point in the second list.

1. *Donoghue v Stevenson*
2. *Nettleship v Watson*
3. *Jolley v Sutton London Borough Council*
4. *Roe v Minister of Health*
5. *Scott v London and St Katherine Docks Co.*
6. *Paris v Stepney Borough Council*
7. *Caparo v Dickman*
8. *Barnett v Chelsea and Kensington Hospitals*

A repairing boat
B arsenic poisoning
C 'fair, just and reasonable' test
D snail
E anaesthetic ampoule
F bags of sugar
G learner driver
H blind in one eye

THE KEY SKILL OF COMMUNICATION

The Key Skill of commmunication can be practised while studying your law course. When you are ready you may well be able to use a law assignment to produce evidence for your Key Skills portfolio. This chapter gives suggestions on the type of things that can be covered.

There are different levels of Key Skills. For anyone who is studying law for A Level, the one which is generally most appropriate is Level 3. However, Level 2 is also covered in the following suggestions as this may be more suitable to those studying at AS Level. In addition, Level 2 provides a good basis before going on to Level 3.

Communication Level 2

C2.1A: CONTRIBUTE TO A DISCUSSION ABOUT A STRAIGHTFORWARD SUBJECT

Law is an ideal subject for discussion as there are many controversial points involved. For this level, a straightforward subject is the requirement. A suitable discussion could be on whether cannabis should be legalised. There is an article on this point in Chapter 1, Exercise 7.

Other straightforward topics which could be used are:

- Should lay people be used as decision-makers in the legal system? A discussion on this could focus on either lay magistrates or juries. (See Chapter 14, Exercise 5 for a good starting point on juries.)
- What type of punishment should be given to burglars? (See Chapter 11, Exercise 2.)

Before you start a discussion, think about the points you want to make. It is sensible to have evidence to back up the arguments you want to put forward. So, reading about a topic is good preparation. The more information you have and the greater the understanding of the topic under discussion, the better you will be able to contribute to that discussion.

During the discussion, listen to what others want to say. Don't interrupt, but be ready to put your point of view, whether you agree with the previous speaker or not. When you do contribute to the discussion, make sure that what you say is relevant to the points then being discussed. Don't go off at a tangent, on to something that is completely different. However, there may come a point when it is right to bring in other ideas. Perhaps you feel that one point has been discussed for long enough and there are plenty of other things which need to be considered. In this case, a good skill is to summarise what has already been said and then say something along the lines of 'Well, I think we will have to disagree about that point, but have you thought about . . . ?'

C2.1B: GIVE A SHORT TALK ABOUT A STRAIGHTFORWARD SUBJECT, USING AN IMAGE

As with C2.1a, there are many subjects in law which can be used for this. It is possible to give a talk about a specific topic in law such as the work of the Magistrates' Court or the process a Bill has to go through to become an Act of Parliament. This could also be based on something more practical, for example, a talk describing a visit to court. Alternatively, it could be a talk describing different careers available in law.

Preparation is important. Once you have decided on the topic, you need to make sure of your information. If you are talking about something like the Magistrates' Court, then you must read up on the work it does. (This preparation can also form part of the evidence needed for C2.3 – see next section.) If it is about a career in the law, then brochures and other information can be obtained from the Law Society, the Bar Council and the Institute of Legal Executives. If the topic is an area of law which is controversial, then there may well be newspaper articles on it or there may be information available from a relevant pressure group.

For the speech, you need to have notes ready to refer to. Do not write out the whole speech and just read it out. Instead, have headings written down and use these to base your talk on. By listing headings, it will help you to make sure that your talk has a structure, as well as reminding you about what you are going to say.

During the course of the talk, you must use an image to illustrate your main points clearly. Again, this needs preparation. Depending on what your chosen subject is, there are many different types of image you can use. For example, if you are talking about a visit to court, you could draw a sketch plan of the layout of the courtroom. You can then use it in the talk to show where the different people involved in the trial sat. If you are using a drawing, remember to make it large enough so that those at the back of the room can see it! Another way of using images is on an overhead projector. If you choose this method, you can draw a diagram, either by hand or by printing one off from a computer. As with everything else, practise using the OHP before your talk. It is also possible to create computer-generated graphics to support your talk. Other images such as pictures or posters can also be used. It is up to you to decide what suits you and the subject you are talking about the best.

C2.2: READ AND SUMMARISE INFORMATION FROM TWO EXTENDED DOCUMENTS ABOUT A STRAIGHTFORWARD SUBJECT. ONE OF THE DOCUMENTS SHOULD CONTAIN AT LEAST ONE IMAGE

For this, it is necessary to use at least two different sources to obtain relevant information. So the first point is to decide what you want to get information on. What do you want the information for? Possibly this could be for researching the background for the talk you intend to give under C2.2. Or maybe you need to read up on a topic in order to write an essay.

Once you have decided the topic, then you need to select sources with relevant information. In law, the most obvious type of extended document suitable for this purpose is a textbook. But there are other extended documents which can be used. These include articles more than three pages long in a legal journal. Check your school or college library to see what magazines and journals they have. Another source is research reports. In particular, Home Office Research Studies are useful (and can be obtained free – tell your librarian – or look up the Home Office on the Internet). If you look at Chapter 8, Exercise 5 in this book, you will see an extract from Home Office Research Study 174. This sets out information in a reasonably clear way, often using sub-headings and bullet points. Home Office Research Studies are also useful because many of them contain graphs or bar charts or pie charts, so that this covers the requirement that one of the documents should contain at least one image. Law textbooks do not always have images in them but some do.

Another source is Government Consultation Papers which are produced for most areas when the Government is considering changing the law. They usually set out the existing law and then set out possible changes, giving the arguments for such a change.

C2.3: WRITE TWO DIFFERENT TYPES OF DOCUMENT ABOUT STRAIGHTFORWARD SUBJECTS. ONE PIECE OF WRITING SHOULD BE AN EXTENDED DOCUMENT AND INCLUDE AT LEAST ONE IMAGE

An 'extended document' means one of more than three pages. One such document could be an essay on a legal topic. This could be the topic you have researched in C2.2. Suggested essay titles are:

- Explain who can sit on a jury and what the role of the jury is. Discuss the advantages and disadvantages of using a jury in Crown Court trials.
- Describe the different types of delegated legislation. Explain what control there is over delegated legislation.
- Describe the different types of sentences available for adult offenders. What factors are taken into account when an offender is sentenced?

These are just a few suggestions. Your tutor/teacher will be able to give you many more essay titles which could be used to produce evidence for this Key Skill.

To cover the requirement that one piece of writing should contain an image, it is possible to scan in pictures of a barrister (with wig and gown) or a judge in his robes, if you have the relevant computer equipment. Other options for including images are a chart of the court structure or bar charts of statistics or even a sketch.

The second document has to be of a different type. This could be a set of notes on a legal topic. Another suggestion is a letter applying for work experience in the legal field, possibly to a local solicitors' firm. The main point with the second different document is to write in a way that is suitable to the type of document chosen.

Don't forget to check spelling and grammar!

Communication Level 3

C3.1A: CONTRIBUTE TO A GROUP DISCUSSION ABOUT A COMPLEX SUBJECT

If you have taken part in a discussion for Level 2, then this gives a good basis to the requirements in Level 3. The first matter you now need to consider is that the subject is more complex (and more challenging) than the topic used in Level 2. The types of topics that could be used for a discussion at this level include:

- the conflicting rights of a pregnant woman and the foetus she is carrying (Chapter 1, Exercise 5)
- whether the literal approach or the purposive approach should be used in statutory interpretation (Chapter 3, Exercises 3 and 7)
- the balance of interests between giving the police powers to investigate crime and the rights of individuals (Chapter 8, Exercises 2 and 3).

Preparation is essential. You should be presenting fairly complicated lines of reasoning or argument, so you must make sure that you have a good understanding of the subject which is going to be the focus of the discussion. Read around the subject and consider different aspects of it.

In the discussion, you need to be aware of others in the group. Part A of Key Skill C3.1a says that you must know how to listen and respond sensitively. People may have strong feelings about the topic being discussed. There may be cultural or gender issues involved. Be aware of this. You should also make openings for others to put their points. For example, ask a question about a point made by another person, so that they can develop their own argument.

C3.1B: MAKE A PRESENTATION ABOUT A COMPLEX SUBJECT, USING AT LEAST ONE IMAGE TO ILLUSTRATE COMPLEX POINTS

Many subjects in a law course will be suitable for this. In fact, you can investigate virtually any legal point and present your findings. Below are a few suggestions for topics that you could give a presentation on:

- the way in which the doctrine of judicial precedent works in the House of Lords (see Chapter 2, Exercises 2 and 7)
- how European law has affected one aspect of our law (possibly employment law – see Chapter 4, Exercises 7 and 8)
- the different ways of resolving a civil dispute (Chapter 7, Exercises 1, 2, 3 and 4).

The references to the exercises in this book will give a starting point for ideas, but you need to do your own research as well.

A presentation needs to be more polished than a talk. Make sure that it has a good structure, with the points following on in a logical order. You should give examples to explain the more complicated points. Make notes to use in the presentation, but do not simply read your written notes out. They should normally only be 'memory-joggers' for your benefit. However, there may be some points where you want to quote from a source and reading from notes for this purpose can be useful and vary the effect and pace of your presentation.

Another good way of practising this Key Skill is to take part in debates. These are more formal than a classroom discussion and you need to learn about the format they take. There are debating competitions for school and college teams to take part in.

You need to use at least one image in making the presentation. In fact, a good presentation will probably make use of more than one image. As already pointed out under C2.1b, there are many different types of image you can use. Diagrams or charts are particularly useful in presenting legal topics. But you may be able to use a wider range, depending on the topic you have chosen. How you present the image is equally important. Are you going to use a flip chart? Or an overhead projector? Or computer-generated graphics? You might even be able to incorporate a short video clip.

C3.2: READ AND SYNTHESISE FROM TWO EXTENDED DOCUMENTS ABOUT A COMPLEX SUBJECT. ONE OF THESE DOCUMENTS SHOULD CONTAIN AT LEAST ONE IMAGE

It is necessary to know how to skim read in order to be able to identify relevant material. You must use at least two different sources to obtain information. Decide what subject you wish to find information on. Possibly you may be given an assignment by your tutor which identifies an area of law to be researched, or you may be interested in a particular aspect and want to research it more deeply. Perhaps this could involve research for your presentation in C3.1b.

Once you have decided the topic then you need to select extended documents which contain relevant information. The obvious starting point is one or more textbooks. However, you must also use at least one other type of extended document such as articles from legal journals, research reports or Government reports or Government consultation papers. As well as your local library, the Internet can also be a useful tool in helping to track down suitable sources. There is skill in identifying suitable sources and you should try to find articles which have a different slant on the topic.

Don't forget that one of the extended documents must contain at least one image. As already pointed out in C2.2, Home Office Research Studies are useful in this respect because many of them contain graphs or bar charts or pie charts. Also, reports by the Government, for example *Judicial Statistics*, or annual reports by bodies such as the Crown Prosecution Service, the Legal Services Commission or the Law Commission often contain different types of chart.

When you have all the information you require, you must bring it together in a coherent form. You could then use it in a presentation or to write an essay or report.

C3.3: WRITE TWO DIFFERENT TYPES OF DOCUMENTS ABOUT COMPLEX SUBJECTS. ONE PIECE OF WRITING SHOULD BE AN EXTENDED DOCUMENT AND INCLUDE AT LEAST ONE IMAGE

As there is a requirement for two different documents, one will almost certainly be an extended essay on a legal topic. This could be the topic you have researched in C3.2. Your tutor/teacher will be able to give you suitable essay titles which could be used to produce evidence for this Key Skill, but here are a few suggestions:

- Critically discuss the role of the Lord Chancellor
- Discuss the problems of bringing cases in the civil courts and explain what alternative methods of dispute resolution could be used
- Explain and comment on the role of the European Court of Justice
- Evaluate the role of the Criminal Cases Review Commission.

If you are studying a substantive area of law, such criminal law or the law of contract, then an essay explaining the way the law has developed in one area and/or considering possible reform of the law would be suitable.

The second document has to be of a different type. This could be a set of notes on a legal topic or a letter. You must select and use a form and style that are appropriate to the type of document chosen and also to the subject matter.

Don't forget that one piece of writing should contain an image (see C2.3 for suggestions on images) and don't forget to check spelling and grammar!

INDEX

Access to Justice [Woolf Report 1999] 41–3
actus reus 111
Allocation Questionnaires 43–4
Alternative Dispute Resolution [ADR] 47, 49–50, 79
  arbitration 50, 79
  mediation 47–9, 79
  online 51
  tribunals 51–2
appeals
  after acquittal 68
  hierarchy of courts 8–9
  Magistrates' Courts 67
  prosecution 67–8
arbitration 50, 79
  online 51
arbitrators 50
arrests
  conditions of 56
  Crown Prosecution Service 59
  detention 57, 59
  police powers 56
  summary 55–6
  women 82

bail
  applications 59
  decisions 59, 60–1
barristers
  complaints against 88
  pupilages 84–5
  role 84
  women 87–8
blind-bidding 51
British Crime Survey [BCS] 53
burglary, sentences 74–5

Canada
  judicial appointments 93
  judicial complaints 95
cannabis, medical uses 6
children
  criminal liability 37–8, 39
  welfare of 3–4
Citizens Advice Bureau Service 105
civil courts
  judges 94
  juries 103–4
civil law 1
codification, criminal law 34, 35
common law 32
  evolution 11, 13
Community Legal Service 106–8
community sentences 77
conditional fees [CFA] 107–8
contingency fees [CYF] 107
Court of Appeal
  and House of Lords 8–9
  per incurium decisions 9–10
  precedents 9, 10, 11–12, 37–8
court judgements, enforcement 43, 44–5
courts
  barristers 84
  delays 44
  Fast Track 42–3
  hierarchy 7, 8–9, 23, 38
  small claims 44
  solicitors 84
Crime and Disorder Act 1998 16
crime statistics
  'justice gap' 80
  recording 53, 54
Criminal Cases Review Commission [CCRC]
  evaluation of 71
  operation 70
  role 69
criminal courts, judges 94–5
Criminal Defence Service [CDS] 106, 108–10
  Advice and Assistance 109
  Representation 109
criminal law 1
  actus reus 111
  codification 34, 35
  mens rea 34–5, 111
Crown Courts
  cases heard 65–6
  young defendants 68–9
Crown Prosecution Service [CPS] 59, 62
custodial sentences 77–8

death, definitions 2–3
definitions
  aids to interpretation 19
  Hansard derived 18
delegated legislation 15, 16
detention
  following arrest 57, 59
  legal advice 57
  right to silence 58
Directives [EU], Working Time 27–9
Director of Public Prosecutions, role of 62
district judges 43
doli incapax 37–8, 39

double jeopardy 33
drug testing, offenders 78
duty of care 113, 114

employment, definition 20
enforcement, court judgements 43, 44–5
ethnic minorities
  judges 92–3
  police bias 81
European Communities Act 1972 23, 40
European Court of Justice
  and English system 25–6
  sexual discrimination 27
  supremacy 23–5
European Union [EU]
  medical treatment rights 5
  and statute law 25, 40
  Working Time Directive 27–9
euthanasia 2–3
evidence, disclosure 59, 61
export restrictions 26

Fast Track 42–3
fraud trials 103

Hansard
  definitions from 18
  statutory interpretation 17–18
High Court
  appeals after acquittal 68
  judicial appointments 91
House of Lords
  and Court of Appeal 8–9
  precedent 7–8
human rights
  conception 5
  pregnant women 4–5

imprisonment 73
injustices, and precedent 8

judges
  appointment of 91–2, 93
  civil courts 94
  complaints against 95
  criminal courts 94–5
  district 43
  ethnic minorities 92–3
  independence 95–6
  as interpreters 40, 95
  Lord Chancellor 96
  training 94
  trials 103
  women 92–3
judicial law-making, guidelines 39
judicial precedent 7
jury service 101
jury trials
  civil courts 103–4
  election for 61
  personal injury cases 104
  reasons for 102
justice, and law 5–6
juvenile crime, arrests 57

law
  and European law 25–6
  judicial development 13
  and justice 5–6
  and morality 1, 2–5, 37
  and social values 11–12
Law Commission
  criminal law 34
  effectiveness 33
  legislation promoted 32, 33–4
  reform brief 32
law reform
  politically motivated 31
  pressure groups 31
  private members' bills 31
  socially desirable 11–12, 31
  statutory bodies 31
legal advice
  Citizens Advice Bureau 105
  on detention 57, 106
  police questioning 57–8
Legal Services Commission [LSC]
  Community Legal Service 106–8
  Criminal Defence Service 106, 108–10
Legal Services Ombudsman 88
legislation
  delegated 15, 16
  statutory 15–16
liability
  duty of care 113, 114
  foreseeability 114
  omissions 111
  positive acts absent 112
  proximity 113, 114
  standards of care 114–15
  strict 112–13
life, artificially sustained 2–3
literal rule, the 17
Lord Chancellor 96

magistrates
  appointment of 99–101
  politics 100
  qualities 99, 100–1
Magistrates' Courts
  appeals from 67
  bail applications 59
  cases heard 65–6
  restrictions 65–6
  sentencing consistency 66
  youth courts 68–9

mediation
online 51
pilot scheme 48–9, 79
process 47–8
mediators 49
medical treatment
advances 1–5
refusal 4–5
Members of Parliament, private bills 31
mens rea 34–5, 111
Mental Health Act, medical treatment 4–5
miscarriages of justice 61, 69–71
mischief rule 19
mobile phone muggers, sentences 75
morality
and law 1, 2–5, 37
sexual 11–12

negligence 114

Offences Against the Person Act 1861, need for reform 34
online dispute resolution
arbitration 51
blind-bidding 51
mediation 51

Parliament
private members' bills 31
statute law 15–18, 37
persistent vegetative state [P.V.S.] 2–3
personal injury cases 104
police
arrests 56
crime statistics 53
detection rates 80
racial bias 81
stop and search 54–5
police questioning, legal advice during 57–8, 109
politics
and judges 95–6
and magistrates 100
Practice Statement [1966], precedent 8
precedents
and binding nature 37–8
Court of Appeal 9, 10, 11–12, 37–8
hierarchy of courts 38
House of Lords 7–8
and injustices 8
judicial 7
judicial law-making 39
mechanics of 7
overruling 12–14
Practice Statement 8
pressure groups 31
prosecutions
appeals 67–8
private 63
public 59, 62
proximity 113, 114
Public Defence Solicitors' Office [Scotland] 109–10
purposive approach, the 20

Queen's Bench Division
delays 44
work of 43–4
Queen's Counsels 85, 86

race
harassment 20
police bias 81
reconviction rates 73, 74
referral orders 75–6
remands, decisions 60–1
retrospective overruling 12–14
right to silence 58

sentences
aims of 73
burglary 74–5
community 77
custodial 77–8
drug testing 78
guidelines 74–5
Magistrates' Courts 66
mobile phone muggers 75
women 82
sexual discrimination 27, 87–8
sexual morality, change of social values 11
small claims courts, delays 44
social values, and law 11–12, 31
solicitors
complaints against 88
conditional fees 107–8
contingency fees 107
court representation 84
Criminal Defence Service 108–9
Legal Services Commission 107
Public Defence Office 109–10
role of 84
training 83
women 86–8
standards of care 114–15
statute law
amendments to 15–16
criticisms 15
and European law 40
Parliamentary process 17–18, 32
statutory interpretation
ambiguities 19
Hansard 17–18
the literal rule 17
mischief rule 19
the purposive approach 20
stop and search, police powers 54–5
strict liability 112–13

Treaty of Rome 1957 23, 26
triable either way offences 59
trials
  by judges 103
  by jury 61, 102
  fraud 103
tribunals 51–2
twins, conjoined 3–4

women
  arrests 82
  barristers 87–8
  judges 92–3
  rights of conception 5
  rights of pregnant 4–5
  sentences 82
  solicitors 86–8
Woolf Report 1999 [*Access to Justice*] 41–3
Working Time Directive 27–9

young defendants
  Crown Courts 68–9
  welfare issues 81
young offenders
  contracts 76
  referral orders 75–6
  sentences 81
  sentencing reviews 76–7
youth courts 68–9, 80–1